UNDER THE NEEM TREE

UNDER THE NEEM TREE

Susan Lowerre

University of Washington Press

Seattle and London

Dedicated to Sekou Dabo

Library of Congress Cataloging-in-Publication Data
    Under the neem tree / by Susan Lowerre.
    p.   cm.
    Originally published: Sag Harbor, N.Y. : Permanent Press, 1991.
    ISBN 0–295–97273–4 (alk. paper)
    1. Walli Jalla (Senegal)—Social life and customs.   2. Peace Corps (U.S.)—
Senegal—Walli Jalla.   3. Fula (African people)—Senegal—Walli Jalla—Social
life and customs.   4. Walli Jalla (Senegal)—Description and travel.   5. Lowerre,
Susan, 1962–   .   6. Fish-culture—Senegal—Walli Jalla.   I. Title
DT549.9.W33L68   1993   92–43188
966.3—dc20   CIP

The paper used in this publication meets the minimum requirements of American National Standard for Information Sciences—Permanence of Paper for Printed Library Materials, ANSI Z39.48–1984. ∞

Title page illustration: The neem tree decorated for Christmas. One of the boys climbed high to hang the star.

Acknowledgments

Without family this book never would have been written—my Senegalese family who cared and helped me through the experiences this book is about, and my American family who gave me the courage—not only to experience new worlds, but to write about them. I thank my mother for her proof-reading and sense of dreams—Mom, the ability to dream is one of the most precious things you have ever given me; and my father for the computer and his practicality. I knew Dad, if *you* thought I could write a book it was not just a pipe dream. Jim, Julie, and Juliette, thank you for your patience and belief in me, and Ned—I will never be able to thank you enough for keeping the Jeep running.

Karen Brandecker, Pat Malone, and Susan Holliday, thank you for helping me keep sane and for understanding when I was somewhat borderline. I must also thank "the fish"—Jon Bell, Dirk Bryant, Cindi Horton, Kevin Turner, Kevin Nelson, and Linda Figgins—we had something special. Susan Burke, Jamie Koehler, and Al Filreis, thank you for your advice and excitement. Kevin Lynch, thank you for your porch and those long summer talks, and Lula Barbieri for your warmth.

Lastly, I would like to thank those without whom these experiences would not have happened: Peace Corps, for giving me the opportunity to live in Senegal; Doctor Webb and Doctor Parker for making it possible for me to live there as long as I did; and more than anyone, the Senegalese people—for caring, and teaching, and showing me the beauty of their country.

Contents

CHAPTER ONE

Home

The Doué, a tributary of the Senegal River, flows inside its red-tan banks past a small village of clay houses with thatched roofs. This is Walli Jalla: a Pulaar village with neem trees and acacias, goats and donkeys and chickens, and the steady rhythm of women pounding millet in the mornings. In the evenings, when the light is soft, fishermen float on the river in dugout canoes, setting their nets against the setting sun. It is always the same, sunset after sunset, the men dipping their wooden paddles into the green water, cutting across the pink evening sky.

I used to like to sit and watch the fishermen, and think that someone might have sat on the bank a hundred or two hundred years before me, watching fishermen in their dugout canoes floating on the passing green water, their gill nets held just for a second like spider webs against the sun before being plunged down into the river—the magical river which flowed between desert banks.

I would sit and watch until the sun was almost gone, and the bats had come out to swoop down over the glass-smooth water, and the mosquitoes woke up from their day's rest. Then I would stand and rewrap my *pagne*—a piece of cloth which Senegalese women traditionally wear wrapped around their waists like a skirt—and walk the little path past the *boutique*, where they sold tea, sugar, and oil, winding between compound walls—the Aan's and the Si's, and the family who I never really got to know, but who invited me to drink tea with them one time when they were celebrating their daughter's wedding. I would follow the path and it would lead me back home.

My compound was fancy with two clay houses covered over

1

with plaster and whitewash, roofed with corrugated tin. It must have been something when it was first built, shining so white, like a diamond in the center of the brown village. I am not sure who it was built for, but it was owned by the *marabout*, a Moslem religious man, who lived in the village of Guia and owned a TV which he tried to run off a car battery. Maybe it had been his house, but now it was crumbling with time and the rains, and the plaster was chipped. One whole wall of the main house was bowed out, as though it was trying to lean over the compound wall to see what was on the other side. In places the red clay had broken through the plaster and run down the whitewash leaving behind stains that looked like tears of blood, and the green-painted doors had turned almost gray from age and neglect.

There had been Peace Corps volunteers before me who had lived in this house. Supposedly, no one else would rent it because they all believed it was haunted. I never saw the ghost, although there was a huge rat who lived in the locked-up house I did not use who made an awful lot of noise at night. Dirk named him Julius Caesar. The main house was haunted by five small bats who lived in the storage room, and a mouse, who had frequent visitors and I think later a whole family, and there were uncountable insects, but I never did see the ghost.

The inside wall of my compound was shared by the Diengs, my next-door neighbors. They would pop their heads over to see how I was doing, to greet me, or to tell me something was going on. I would pop my head over to see who was passing siesta in their compound, whether anyone was making tea, and to ask what was for dinner—*gosi* or *lacciri*. *Gosi* is like cold rice pudding, only sometimes made with corn, and *lacciri* is steamed millet, which we usually ate with leaf sauce. I hated *gosi*. We ate it when the Diengs could not afford millet.

The Diengs adopted me. At first, I only knew them as the family of Aisata, the girl I paid to wash my clothes in the river and to bring me a bucket of the cool passing water each morning, which I kept in my house as a treasure against the heat of the day. I poured it into my *loonde*, a sphere made of clay which breathed, keeping the river water cool even when the air danced with the heat.

Aisata had taken the job because Fatu, who originally brought my water and also cooked my food, told me she had too many other things to do. Aisata was a teenager and wanted to know all about America and clothes and fashions and American men. Her body was just becoming a woman's and she liked to prance at the river's edge in her *pagne*, making me smile and think of when I had been sixteen. Sometimes Mbinté or Fatiim and their children would come visit my compound with Aisata and they would hold my hands and exchange soft Pulaar greetings, or they would ask me to drink tea, or try to teach me new Pulaar words. Slowly the Diengs seeped into my life this way, a little at a time, an afternoon, a few words, a reflected smile.

I did not begin to know Samba, who became my village father, until one day after I had lived in Walli Jalla for half a year. That afternoon the village children taunted me beyond what I could endure and I decided to catch one and beat him. Aisata heard my anger and came to see what was wrong. She said I must speak to Samba, the old man of her compound.

I did not want to speak with anyone. I had been walking across the makeshift soccer field with Dirk's dog Sahné, when the children collected into little clumps and ran after us chanting "Sahné, Sahné," and threw sticks and stones at her, staying just out of reach, and poor Sahné shook with fear.

It was too much. Taunting the white woman was great fun. Sometimes the children threw stones at my house. It was the most entertaining of village games. If you could catch one of the children, then you could hit him, supposedly teaching him respect, and the rest would let you alone. I could never catch one.

Aisata must have seen in my face that this time I meant to catch one. She tugged on my arm and said again I must come to her compound; Samba would help me. I had never spoken to Samba before. I could just barely picture him as the elderly man with white hair who sat on his mat in the evenings working his prayer beads and listening to the Pulaar station on his transistor radio. Aisata would not stop until I said I would come.

We walked inside the Diengs' compound walls, and Samba was sitting where he always seemed to sit, on his mat in front of the house he shared with his wife. His face was softly wrinkled, the color of warm earth touched by the evening sun. His hair was very white. I wondered how old he was, and how I could not have noticed him before. He seemed a living history, as though he had been given secrets to hold over time, like an old church, its wood shining from generations of hands.

He shook my hand and told me to sit and asked what bothered me. My Pulaar was not very good, but I spit out the words I knew with hatred and frustration, thinking of how the children had made Sahné, who would not hurt a thing, shake with fear and roll her soft brown eyes.

Samba watched me as I spoke. He was like the river, flowing, always flowing for so many years, surviving this world of dust and heat and disease the way the river survived its desert banks. He had seen so much. Any one point in time seemed small set before the patience in Samba's eyes. He soaked up my frustration and anger the way the river pulled away the heat of my body at the end of each day. He nodded his head at my words, saying quietly that the children were bad, he would talk to the elders of the village. He said I was a guest of his family in the village and he would not let anyone mistreat me.

That was the first time I spoke to Samba, and he never broke his word. He took me in as one of his family. After that, he would call to me every evening over the compound wall, using my Senegalese name. He would call, "Mariyata, Mariyata," in the soft evening light, as he stood on the other side of the wall leaning on his cane, waiting to greet his white-woman daughter. He would greet me, holding my hand in his dry, softly-old hand asking after my health, my tiredness, and my work. Always he told me I worked too hard, I should take better care of myself. Now and then he would tell me I needed a husband. It worried him that I did not have one, and he would ask me when I was planning on getting one— even though he knew how much his question annoyed me, and that I would only answer I did not need one: I had come here to work.

Once Samba gave me medicine when I was especially sick. He had bought little yellow pills from someone who walked from village to village selling "white-people" medicine. They were very precious to him, and he handled them as gingerly as though they were age-old eggshells that might crumble to dust with his touch. He took them from their plastic bag and put them into my palm, telling me I must get well.

Someone was always sick. I gave my family aspirin for everything, because I had nothing else to give. One time I made Tiijon Instant Lipton Chicken Noodle Soup. My Mom had sent me the little silver packages in the mail and I thought Tiijon would get a kick out of being treated like a sick American—only I think he had malaria, so no one would have made him soup. He would have been put in a hospital.

Sometimes, I would wake up in the middle of the night, out under the neem tree where I slept, and hear Samba on the other side of the compound wall worrying that the village children did not show me enough respect, saying something must be done. I could always hear the Diengs on the other side of our wall. Sometimes, it was just a lulling blur of Pulaar that I did not bother to dissect into words. Other times I would hear the laughter of Mariam and Mbinté and Fatiim and Aisata, and it would float over into my compound and make me smile. One time there were wails.

It was a *fête* that day, and at first I thought the noise had something to do with the holiday. But the noise was pain. I had been sitting on my front step writing in my journal; it was still in my hand as I looked over the wall. Miamoun, Fatiim, and Mbinté were crying. In a year, I had never seen adult tears. Pulaars did not show emotion once they had passed puberty. They would laugh, but they did not cry. It was horrible to see them in tears. Someone must have died. I thought it was Samba. I could not imagine Walli Jalla without Samba, without his calling "Mariyata" into the evening's darkness, without the sound of his footsteps and his cane as he came to my compound to greet me, without the wrinkles we brought to the corners of each other's eyes when we sat on the millet stalk mat under the thatched awning of his house in the afternoon. There would be nothing left of my world, nothing but the hot blowing dust, which never seemed to end. There would be nothing left of me, nothing left inside. If Samba had died, the wind would blow straight through me, drying my bones with its heat, and leaving nothing behind but pockets of the fine reddish sand to slowly fill me.

I stood to go to the Diengs' compound to learn who in my family had died. I walked out of my compound toward the point where my wall turned into the Diengs' wall, past where Oumar's horse ate, past the acacia tree, across from Fatu's compound, and was about to enter the Diengs' when I saw Fatu across the way, listening to the pain. I asked her who had died, and she told me it was Penda.

Penda! I was not even sure who Penda was. I tried not to feel happy it was Penda. She must be the old, old woman with opaque eyes, who had come to visit and was mad because I had no gift for her from America. I had not seen her for a long time. I thought she had left, and now I had to think of her lying sick and dying inside clay walls, inside my family's compound, without my having known it.

Just inside the compound wall, Mbinté sat in the dust, her mouth open with pain and tears streaming down her face. She was wringing the edge of her *pagne* as though it were wet, twisting and twisting it as she wailed. Her two little girls, Huley and Maimoun clung to her—one on either side. There was fear and confusion on their little-girl faces, as their high-pitched screams mingled with their mother's. Mbinté paid them no attention. She seemed unaware that they were there. I had never seen such anguish.

So many people had died in the last month. Demba, one of the men I worked with, had taught me that in Pulaar you must say *"Yeromoba yafaam"* when someone dies. What help was that to my family? I sat down next to Mbinté. I couldn't stand it and tried to hug her. She was wailing stone. She looked at me as though she had never seen me before. What was a white woman doing in her compound? What did a white woman know of pain and death? I should not have touched her. I didn't know what Pulaars did to show they cared. I did not belong. Mbinté got up to do something, and I got up and left. Someone had died in my family and I had been unable to do anything to help.

I went back to my place and sat in the dusk. The bats were beginning to come out and flitted through my doorway. I tried to write in my journal again, but that seemed wrong. I could hear Samba's voice. I wanted so much to do something to help.

Later, Oumar called to me over the wall and I got up to speak to him. He explained that his mother had died, only the words he used were that she was very sick. He asked if I could drive them to the graveyard in the project truck. I didn't want to understand all he had asked; I was so glad they had asked me to do something.

Oumar told me to back the truck up to the end wall of the compound and then to turn it off; they still had things to do. It was very dark. They were going to put the body in the back of the truck. I had seen a dead body once at a wake, but it had lain in a satin-lined coffin and was fixed up to look as though it was not really dead at all, only sleeping. I would be driving a hearse. Four men carried the body out on a stretcher made of branches. It was completely covered with a blanket.

I drove the men and the body to the village burial ground in Guia. After it had been lifted down, an old man came to the driver's window and told me to go away. Women were not allowed to attend the burial ceremony. I drove to the edge of the road, climbed out, and sat down in the desert night hugging my knees and thinking of death.

I did not think of scary American death, of hospital rooms and white sheets, ambulances, or funeral parlors. Death made sense in this world of dust and heat and flies and disease. It was large and incomprehensible like the stars, the baobab trees, or the ocean, and somehow comforting. In America it is so bad to die, as though someone cheated. In Senegal it is much easier.

But I am not in Senegal anymore. Now I live in Arlington, Va. I have been back for a year. I ride the metro with men in blue suits and silk ties, men who have gray faces, read the newspaper, and never seem to smile. I watch them and the women who ride the metro with them. They seem so poised, like Barbie dolls, with perfect hair and nails and plastic expressions, and no one ever seems to talk.

So often I am in a hurry. I forget to look at the shadows of the wire fence which look like fish scales, making me smile. I buy a sixty-seven-dollar pair of boots. I want a job title that when people ask me at a party, "What do you do?" I can answer in a sentence or two they will understand—the type of job your aunt can tell her neighbors about. Sometimes, at a party, someone will still ask me about Africa and I will tell them how we went camping by the pool with the lone hippo and the little red monkeys who came down to drink at the water's edge across from us, and they will nod their heads. I do not tell of Samba or Penda because I can no longer bear their looks of boredom. And then I am scared.

One night I walk the beach. It's late and the waves are lapping quietly at the sand, like a cat drinking milk. It is clear and the stars are out, but this is Virginia Beach, so they must compete with the city's lights. Highrises stand silhouetted against the unnatural glow, and I walk with my head turned toward the grayness of the ocean.

This same ocean laps against the beaches of Virginia and Senegal. That seems impossible to me and makes me wonder if there is some place out there in the middle of the Atlantic where waves decide to go to the east or to the west, split down the middle as though parted with a comb. There is no such place, I tell myself, but I cannot stop picturing it. I like the idea of a place in the middle of the ocean where east-going waves split from west-going waves, and I feel if there is anywhere left in the world where I truly belong, it is at that spot.

CHAPTER TWO

The Kitten

We had been in Senegal for four days before we went to The Corniche bar. Those first days are faded by time, turned to pastels and grays, hazy images that waver in my mind—but not The Corniche.

The outside of the bar was painted purple. It had a corrugated tin roof, and over the door opening someone had painted "The Corniche" in dripping red letters. There was no actual door, just brightly-colored strips of plastic you pushed through to enter. The front room ran the width of the building, with a bar to the left, and it was crowded with black men in African clothes and one woman. She stood by the bar, wearing her *pagne* and a bright red rayon camisole without a bra. She had a nice face and smiled at us when we walked in, while the drunken men leered.

Everything was covered with a thick layer of crawling flies. They darkened the walls and floor, table tops, the bar, open beer bottles, the ceiling, the people, the air itself. In the back courtyard, large shiny black men sat drinking warm beer from the bottle, rolling their white eyes and grinning with loose lips. They wore *boubous*—pieces of cloth the size of single sheets sewn at the shoulders and at the side seams starting at the waist, left free to fall to the floor, with matching draw-string pants underneath.

The courtyard reeked of spilled beer, urine, and too many sweating bodies packed closely together. In the middle of the cement floor a pair of filthy white cats lay panting—as though they would die of the heat. Each breath seemed to exhaust them, and you couldn't imagine how they would have the strength to take another. They were ugly—nothing but ribs moving up and down in dirty fur. A tiny kitten cried a few

9

feet away from the cats, its eyes closed with mucus. The adults had energy for nothing but their own labored breathing—and the kitten continued to cry.

Dirk, who would be our technical trainer for the next week and who was a veteran volunteer of one year, had led us through the front room and into the back courtyard with the panting cats. We sat huddled together in the one-hundred-degree heat watching the cats breathe and the kitten cry. I thought of the painted turtle my brothers and I had brought home and kept in the bathtub, feeding it sliced hot dogs. Dirk explained that the woman in the other room was a whore and that the cheapest beer was Gazelle—three hundred francs for a twenty-ounce bottle. He didn't even glance at the cats.

The Corniche was a favorite bar of Peace Corps volunteers in the city of St. Louis. It sold cheap, warm beer and was directly across the street from the Peace Corps *maison du passage*. St. Louis was a big enough city that you could find white people bars—*tubab* bars—with stuffed lion, antelope, and boars' heads, fancy padded chairs, a man to keep out beggars, and faded photographs of an earlier Africa decorating the walls. Peace Corps volunteers couldn't afford those bars. Only real *tubabs* could afford to pay five hundred francs for a twelve-ounce bottle of beer.

I sat with Cindi, Cynthia, Kevin, and K.T. We were the new fisheries volunteers, and had just arrived. For some reason we got to Senegal two weeks ahead of the other trainees. They were not ready for us at the language training center in Thiès, and so we were being shipped up to the Fleuve region to spend a week at the fish station in Nianga, to see a little of the region we would be living in, and to learn about fisheries in Senegal.

The Fleuve is the northernmost region in Senegal, just south of Mauritania, the border being the Senegal River. Its people are predominately Pulaar, the second-largest tribe in Senegal, Wolof being the largest. Their language is difficult and few white people speak it. Wolof is easier to learn and almost universally understood.

The land along the river has become part of the Sahel—

the region in sub-Saharan Africa which is slowly being taken over by the desert—and we were warned of its desolation. No one could believe the Peace Corps was sending trainees, just off the plane, up to the Fleuve. The older volunteers thought we would be overwhelmed, panic, and decide to terminate early when we saw where we would live for the next two years. It was too soon after America. They made it sound as though the Fleuve was the worst of horrors, and we were being sent to miserable, sand-filled deaths.

The one hundred and fifty miles between Thies and St. Louis did nothing to contradict them. The road was a narrow black strip, with potholes and asphalt waves which catapulted cars off their crests. It played connect-a-dot with dark brown thatched-hut villages, cutting through them and changing them forever. We had sweated a lot, and goats, sheep, and donkeys had run out into the road, making us careen around them. We had driven for three hours and the scenery never changed. It was as though photographs were pasted to the inside of the car windows.

Senegal was nothing but shades of brown. Camel-colored sand was everywhere. Now and then huge, hulking brown baobab trees or dusty brown acacias writhed against the horizon. The earthen huts were one shade of brown, their weather-beaten thatched roofs a little darker. The sky was blue, but blue that was trying to survive under a layer of brown. The people were very deep brown, black.

We had been told the Fleuve was terrible but that the St. Louis house almost made up for it. Supposedly, it was one of the best houses in the country. It was a hovel. In front of the broken wrought-iron gates goats and sheep picked at trash and a leper with no hands sat begging in the dust.

Inside the gates was worse—it was recognizable. It would exist in American slums. Shutters hung awkwardly from one hinge, doors were left open with no screens, a poster of St. Louis, Missouri, was peeling off one of the walls. Something was wrong with each piece of furniture: chair seats had worn through to the springs, tables were missing one leg, a couch sagged to the floor. An inch of fine sand-like dust turned everything reddish-tan, and the whole house smelled of the toilet—the water was turned on only at irregular hours. A small separate building was used as a kitchen. Its floor was covered with empty green beer bottles surrounding a broken-down gas stove, and a refrigerator that did not work.

Looking at the house, I remembered my friend George's comment when he heard I had joined the Peace Corps. He had said I would learn to be poor. At the time, I thought it an odd thing to say.

Dirk showed us around the house, explaining about regional *maisons du passage*. Volunteers were posted in different regions and almost every region had at least one house in a town with running water and electricity. No volunteers lived in them permanently. They were places to come to from your village for recuperation and pampering: to cook food which wasn't of millet or rice, to drink beer—not necessarily cold— and to speak to other Americans.

Dirk came back to our table with his hands full of Gazelle beers, doled them out like medicine, and sat down. He was the skinniest man I had ever seen. He wore dusty Levi corduroys he repeatedly pulled up around his waist and work boots that made his feet look three sizes too big for his frame. His hair was brown and hung down into his eyes until he flicked it back with a jerk of his head. A cigarette was always between his lips and he wanted to know what the latest American movies were. He was not wonderful.

We worked at pleasant conversation. Dirk asked each of us why we had joined the Peace Corps, where we were from, and where we had gone to school. Cynthia asked Dirk if the fisheries program had any chance of success, what he ate, if he had a village counterpart, and what the other posts were like.

Sweat glistened on our white skin; it rolled in drops into our eyes, and made Cindi's and Kevin's glasses slip off their noses. It wrapped around us like a blanket, making it hard to breathe, to move, to think. Taped Senegalese music played in the background—a band called Toure Kunda was playing *Toubab Bi*. A high-pitched male voice sang foreign words to a grating non-American beat. The flies landed and buzzed, landed and buzzed. They tickled as they crawled on our bare skin. Frantically we waved them away, but they always came back, patiently. The heat and the flies clung to us like the softest of prisons—movable and inescapable.

It was terrible to know that the sweat, the smell, and the insects would cling to me not for two weeks, or two months, but for two years. There was no escape. Time became a dead weight. Before, there had never been enough time, never enough time to sit on the porch drinking daiquiris, to play soccer, to study for the next genetics exam. It had flown past while I tried to grab it, to slow it down, always trying to spend it one hundred different ways; and now it just sat. The thought of those two years became heavier and heavier and heavier. I was being buried alive, slowly suffocating. I wanted to scream.

I looked around The Corniche, at the fat drunken African men now and then pushing the edges of their *boubous* up onto their shoulders only to free their hands to reach for a bottle of beer, not to flap at the flies—which crawled on their arms, in their hair, and over their lips. Their loose laughter mingled with the sound of the taped African music and the buzz of the flies, and underneath was the stench—spilled beer warm with the heat and sweat and urine. I hated it all.

We sat talking. I stared at the cats. Someone asked Dirk if there was any wildlife on the Fleuve. He spoke matter-of-factly, telling us that the last of the wildlife had migrated, died from the drought, or been hunted down over the past ten years. However, there were a lot of rats he said, tons of them, because their natural predators were gone, except for some snakes, and there were birds—hawks and egrets and once he had seen a marabou stork, which was exciting.

It would be all right. Everything could not be like The Corniche and Dirk. Everything could not be filthy and smell. We had not yet met our second technical trainer. He was meeting us later that afternoon. His name was Keith and he would be wonderful; the station would be well-organized and functional. There had to be something on the Fleuve besides dust and rats. This could not be it; I couldn't live like this. No one did, not even people in the slums of America. It would be all right.

Keith joined us almost an hour later. He looked dirty, wore a slave top: two pieces of cloth sewn at the shoulders with

three strips on each side of his ribs holding the pieces together. His pants were baggy, barely held up under his
stomach with a drawstring. The pants and top didn't match;
the top was brown with black spiral designs on it, and the
pants were blue with red fish jumping across them. He wore
rubber flip-flops, had an unkempt beard and mustache, and
smelled.

Keith was an *ancien* volunteer. Technically, anyone who
had been in Senegal for more than a year was an *ancien*, but
Keith had almost finished two years and truly deserved the
title. He spoke very slowly. Often he didn't speak at all, not
because he was otherwise occupied or because he felt awkward and could think of nothing to say. He simply chose not
to speak at times. He would sit there silently, not speaking,
not listening, just sitting. He tapped his foot to the music,
and drank his warm beer greedily. Once he broke into conversation in Wolof with one of the men next to us. We didn't
understand a word, and he didn't bother to translate.

A fat man in a blue *boubou* kept staring at our white faces.
Finally, he came over and said something to Cynthia. She was
excited; it was the first African who had spoken to her. Her
face lit up and she giggled and said, "No *Français*". She
smiled to show the language barrier was hopeless, but that
she meant well. Keith said something to the man in Wolof,
ending the conversation. The man walked away muttering
and we waited for Keith to explain what had happened. He
just sat staring at a puddle of beer between his feet. After
about five minutes, he said, "You know you don't have to be
nice to everyone just because they're Senegalese. There are
assholes here too, just like anywhere else."

No one knew what to say. Keith was the asshole. I wanted to
tell him so; I wanted to tell him we had come to help these
people and had a responsibility other than living in filth. I
said nothing, quietly sweating, but I would never forgive
him. I did, within a month.

The cats were still panting, the men were still grinning;
some of the shadows had changed. The kitten continued to
mew, but its cries had become much softer. When we had
arrived at the bar, it had been barely wobbling on its legs,
now it no longer moved. I wanted to save it.

"Look at the kitten," I said. Everyone's head turned, and then they went back to their beers. Dirk asked what group was being played on pop radio in the U.S. For awhile we spoke about Cindy Lauper. I asked Dirk where the bathroom was and he pointed to a little hallway behind us. Cindi and I started to walk toward the door he had pointed out.

The door was rotting and opened onto a closet with a Turkish toilet, a pipe over a hole in a porcelain square set into the concrete. There were little raised places to put your feet, and a chain to pull that flushed water out of the pipe and down into the hole. There was no toilet paper. It was a feast for the flies.

We returned to our table; it was covered with empty beer bottles. No one had the energy for conversation. Even the kitten no longer cried. We continued to sit and ordered another round. Dirk or Keith got them, because none of us knew how to ask for five beers in French.

I tried not to watch the kitten, but couldn't keep my eyes off it. It was so tiny; its life almost gone. It tried to lift its head, which must have felt like it weighed a thousand pounds; it struggled and strained, raised it two inches, and then quickly, it fell back down.

"Can't we do anything about that kitten?" I blurted. The words proved how new I was, soft, although I wanted to be tough.

I ran over and picked it up. The kitten sat in my hand—a warm scrap of fur with perfect paws. I wondered what diseases you could catch from sick kittens in Africa.

Dirk said he needed a cat at the station to keep the rats down and asked the bartender if we could take it with us. The bartender was big, black, and looked at Dirk as though he had just asked if he could take home a handful of the flies. He nodded and we took the kitten across the street to the Peace Corps house. Cindi and I went to one of the *boutiques*— tiny Mauritanian-owned shops that lined the roads—to buy canned milk after Dirk explained how to get there, what the milk would look like, how much it cost, and exactly what words to use to ask for it.

We took the milk back to the house in triumph and watched the kitten drink; then played with it for the rest of the afternoon, not talking of what we had seen, the Corniche, the whore, the leper who sat in front of the house begging for coins in a bowl which he held up with stumps that had once been hands.

The next day we drove to the fish station and to Dirk's house in Walli Jalla. The kitten sat in my lap during the three-hour drive east into the desert, while the flat dusty land passed by the windows without a break. Dirk's house made us understand why St. Louis was considered luxury. It was nothing but crumbling walls, tin, dust, and unbearable heat. The flies were even worse than they had been at the Corniche. Dirk drank warm, muddy river water and had a roach-infested hole for a bathroom.

Kitty, as we called her, grew much stronger and began to play with people's shoelaces. She stayed in the house and greeted us when we returned from the station. She was frisky and liked to ambush unsuspecting passers-by. She was warm and alive while the world around us was dead. It had dried up and died, and all that was left was the dust and the hot blowing wind that felt as though it came from a furnace, blasting the dust up against our sweating skin. I liked to sit on the front step of Dirk's house and watch the kitten try to crawl up into the house. She would repeatedly topple over, tail over nose; then get up and try again. She made me laugh.

One night we came back to the dark house and Dirk opened the doors and went to light the kerosene lamp. We all trooped in to get our things for the night. There was a quiet mewing and I searched with my hands to find the kitten. I felt something warm and wet and then fur. I could feel her moving.

Dirk came with the lantern. The kitten was convulsing in its own blood. Someone had stepped on her.

Dirk told me to go outside. He took the kitten in back and pounded its head in with a rock so it wouldn't suffer any more.

I sat in the dark on the broken-down cane bed that Dirk usually slept on, sat there in the huge desert night, silent. I wanted to cry. I needed to cry very badly for a tiny kitten with perfect paws, but my eyes remained dry, the pain somewhere far away inside of me. I had not yet learned how to cry in Senegal.

CHAPTER THREE

Dabo

For once the dust had cleared and the sky was bright blue. The blue sky and brown earth met in a perfectly straight line at the horizon. Nothing crowded the sky out—no skyscrapers or radar towers or even tall trees. It filled half the world, and the dusty tan earth the other half. It was a jealous boundary. The river was the only exception, and it didn't look real. It seemed a part of the sky, as though the brown land had been able to capture one thin line of the sky's blue.

Dabo, Sahné and I sat in the late afternoon sun on the bank of the Doué river. We were fishing; and Sahné, Dirk's dog, was curled up in a black ball asleep under a thorn bush. Dabo and I each held long thin sticks with clear fish twine tied to their ends. The lines dangled over the bank and into the water, ending with hooks, sinkers, and hunks of village bread put on the hooks for bait.

Everything was covered by warm yellow light, as the sun began to lose its glare and to once again make shadows. The water passed by, pulling at our lines, as we sat quietly.

It was not a peaceful silence. I was on my last live-in—a week during which each trainee goes to his or her assigned post to set up living arrangements. The fish station was my post. I had asked for it. I had come to Senegal to gain aquaculture experience and the fish station was where I would get it. This first year might be unbearable—Dirk and I disliked each other, and Dabo was good friends with Dirk; but I would live through it. In a year I would be coordinator of the fish program—by then I hoped to make a difference.

Dabo was manager of the fish station. He was of the Mandeng tribe from the south of Senegal. He had been there before Dirk, when a volunteer named Steve had come and

17

hired the workers to make a fish station out of a patch of dust. Dabo was short, for an American man, only a little taller than my five feet four inches, but well-built with taut muslces which slid under blue-black skin. He always wore Western clothes, shorts at the station, pants with a belt and a button-down shirt in Walli Jalla. He liked to listen to Cat Stevens, spoke French, and had gone with Dirk and Keith to the big Christmas party in Dakar the year before. Some of his draw-ings were published in "The Teranga"—a Senegalese Peace Corps magazine that came out every three months. Keith had shown them to us. They were good.

I met Dabo for the first time when we all came to the station to see what fisheries in Senegal consisted of—one new fish station and two village posts with stocked ponds after five years of volunteers. Keith and Dabo were great friends; they joked a lot as we worked. I remembr Dabo planing wooden slats, which would be used as part of the monk drains, telling Keith a story about how he had sex with a woman until she vomited. Someone translated this for us, Keith and Dabo laughed, and then they continued speaking Wolof.

Kevin Turner and I came to Walli Jalla this time; only K.T. was going on to Cas Cas, another three hours to the north-west. Dirk said he would take him. Dirk had lived in Cas Cas until Steve went to the States and never came back. Then Dirk had been asked to take over the station.

On final live-ins an *ancien* volunteer is sent with each trainee to help with the language, to introduce the trainee to people, find a good family for them to live with, and to keep the rent and price of food reasonable. At the end of the week the trainee is usually left alone at the post for a day or two. Dirk said I was welcome to come with them to Cas Cas, and then that I could not stay in Walli Jalla unless Dabo did, and Dabo was thinking of traveling to Richard Toll for the holi-day of *Tabaski.*

Dirk had told me this the first night as we all sat out under the desert stars, and I had wanted to go to Cas Cas. It would be fun to go with two other Americans in the truck, to see a new village, an adventure. I was afraid to stay in Walli Jalla. There was a cholera epidemic on the Fleuve and the Thiès language training site was a fourteen-hour trip away on

public transport. I didn't know how to say, "help" in Pulaar.
All I knew was how to ask after a person's health and tiredness. Everyone was so black.

I knew I should spend my live-in at Walli Jalla. It was the
right thing to do, even though I was afraid. As it turned out,
Dabo stayed, so I could too. But I had already decided I
would.

Half the week was over when Dabo asked me to go fishing.
I thought it was a breakthrough. The first three days we had
barely spoken, only a few words as we sat across from each
other with the lunch bowl of lukewarm oily rice and one or
two finger-sized dried fish, which smelled as though they had
been rotting for years. The flies buzzed around us in a black,
crawling mass. We dripped with sweat while we lifted handfuls of the rice to our mouths and tried to think of something
appropriate to say to one another in French.

Dabo's French was good; it would wash over and around
me in a torrent, and I would pick up a few words, such as
blue, or people, or sometimes a verb, like walk or read. I
would take whatever words I caught and hold onto them like
a drowning person, asking any question which popped into
my head connected with those words until I thought I might
have an idea of what Dabo had said, and we both were
exhausted. I asked Dabo to speak more slowly, so I could
understand better. He never did.

Even on *Tabaski*—the Moslem holiday celebrating Abra-
ham's willingness to sacrifice his son and the biggest Senegalese holiday when everyone eats meat—Dabo and I went
our separate ways. He woke up early, dressed in Senegalese
clothes and walked out of the compound. Dirk had told me
Dabo would take me visiting that day and everyone would
have wonderful bowls of goat meat and rice. We could eat
and eat until we were stuffed. Dabo didn't come back until
the sun had almost set. I didn't mind too much. I had spent
the day sitting under the neem tree, listening to my Walkman
and drawing a picture of the house.

Now we sat on the bank, the water dragging at our lines,
and I kept thinking of how I had meant to win Dabo over,
and how half of my week was gone and I had not even
started. I looked sideways at him. I thought of him planing

those boards, his hands so deft, as though they had minds of their own, his arm muscles bunching up tight under his skin as though they might burst. He had showed us how to plane the slats and I had tried and tried, blistered my hands, and made a mess.

I wanted Dabo to respect me, but could think of no reasons why he should. At least I could fish. I loved to fish. In the first grade I wrote that I wanted to grow up to be a fisherwoman. I used to call my brother Ned's friends to go fishing with me when he couldn't go—but I liked it better when he could. We would get up and dig worms in the cold early light, packing them in a bucket, and then ride our bicycles to the Raquette River to spend the whole day watching our bobbins and maybe catching a bass and some sunfish. Nothing was better than feeling that first live tug on the line.

I tugged at my line now, but because it was snagged. At first I pulled only a little, hoping it would dislodge easily, but it did not. I pulled harder and harder finally giving it a great yank, and the line snapped. Where the line had been pulled taunt before, slicing through the air, it now danced gaily in little loose loops, down over the edge of the bank.

I pulled my line in silently, and then asked Dabo for more weights and another hook. I tied the hook on, and started to clamp the weights down. I don't remember why I couldn't get them on. I had put thousands of weights on, but now I kept fumbling with the line. I couldn't ask Dabo how to weight my fish line. There were so many things I didn't know and this was one of the things I did know. I could feel him watching me, the reasonable amount of time to weight a line slipping away. I kept hoping for a miracle. Then Dabo took the line from my hands and put the weights on in seconds.

I put another hunk of bread on the hook and returned it to the water. If I caught a very, very big fish, it would make up for the weights. I might. I was lucky.

The sun was sinking lower and lower, taking away my chance to show Dabo I could do something. I caught nothing while Dabo caught two *Clarius*; I remembered the name from my college ichthyology class. Dr. Bulger would have been proud of me. Dabo did not know genera existed.

It was getting late. I didn't want to stop fishing until I caught something, and thought guiltily about the promise I had made to the man in plaid polyester pants. I had vowed to visit his compound. The man had been stopping by Dirk's compound every morning and afternoon to greet me and to ask me why I did not return the honor and come to greet him and his family. The afternoon before, when he had asked me to visit, I had said I was too tired. He had asked if I had worked, looking very surprised.

I hadn't answered right away. How could I explain that his country tired me? I was tired of the insects and the heat, trying to wash correctly in the river wearing only a *pagne*, cocks crowing at all hours (Who made up the myth about dawn?), and amorous donkeys braying throughout the night. What a worthless word, the sound is nothing like a bray and goes on and on, starting low and ending in a high screech. It woke me up, whenever the cocks did not. I was tired of trying to speak two languages I did not understand, of the women pounding millet in the morning, of the dust that turned my skin brown, collecting in my mouth and nostrils, of eating those rotting fish.

I had looked at the village man, who even tired me with his eagerness and said no, I had not worked. He looked baffled. I had done nothing all day and yet felt tired. To get rid of that baffled expression, I had told him I would come *jango*, tomorrow, and then asked him where he lived. He vaguely waved his arm in the direction of everything behind Dirk's compound, so I decided to ask his name. "*Yetoode-ma?*", I asked and he answered, "Min." He continued speaking Pulaar, none of which I understood, so I stood there nodding my head, thinking I would not be happy if I ended up going to every compound behind Dirk's house asking, "Is this the house of Min?"

I told Dabo I had to stop fishing; I had told Min I would come visit this afternoon. We pulled in our lines, collected our gear, Sahné woke up, and we trudged back to the house in silence.

I wished Min would come by, I would make another excuse. I did not want to wander through village compounds, mumbling the five or six things I could say in Pulaar. I wanted to take a nap. I walked into the house and picked up my Pulaar notebook to take with me.

It was a short walk to the compound I thought Min might have pointed at. I tried to think of the Pulaar I knew. The only word in my head was *dogdude*. It was the verb "to run," and when it was conjugated it sounded like "dog-do." For the life of me, I couldn't think of any other words, only *dogdude* and the greetings.

I entered the break in the compound wall. There were three square clay buildings with thatched roofs, surrounded by a wall made of sticks stuck into the ground. One part of the wall had been extended to make a pen for goats, and they bleated and jumped at the fence as I walked past.

Two women sat on a straw mat under a thatched awning. One was very old, with leathery crinkled skin and grey corn rows. The other was young with a pretty face and a scarf tied around her head. They wore *pagnes* and *boubous* of bright cloth—one patterned with large yellow and black butterflies and the other with big, red telephones. Their earlobes drooped with heavy gold earrings which bobbed as they smiled at me. I smiled back. What was I doing here?

The woman with the grey corn rows disappeared into one of the buildings and came back with a small camp stool which they insisted I sit upon. She sat back on the mat and the two women stared up at me. Behind them stood a millet mortar with two pestles lying beside it. In the corner was a broken *loonde*—one of the round clay containers they use to hold river water. Chickens pecked delicately at the dust of the compound and the goats continued to bleat.

I started my greetings, "*Mbad-daa? Ada selli? Galle ma wadi? Alhumdillilah, Tabarikalla, Alhumdillilah.*" They asked me the same questions, using the same words, and we nodded our heads and smiled and went through them a second time. I was willing to do them a third, but the women were slowly trailing off into nothing but soft *Tabarikallas* and *Alhumdillilahs*. We were enveloped by silence. I had asked them about their health and their family and their tiredness. I tried to think of something else to ask them. The only other question I had prepared was, "Where is Min?"

"Holto woni Min?" I asked. The expressions on the women's faces deepened. They had been perplexed and surprised from the beginning, white women did not usually wander into their compound; but now they looked genuinely confused. They broke into a rush of Pulaar, and I stared at them very hard, not understanding a word of it. *"Mi famaani,"* I said. I do not understand, and now I was shaking my head and looking equally confused.

I asked the question again. I had looked it up before I left the compound. It was right; I was sure of it. Maybe I had just not pronounced it correctly—except it was only three words and one of them was a name, hopefully, of someone who lived in this compound. The women looked more and more confused. They were speaking volumes of Pulaar and I still understood none of it. They stopped, as I shook my head back and forth, and again there was silence, unbroken except by the goats.

The women sat so still, staring up at me, that I started riffling through my notebook. It took me forever to find where I had written down *"Holto woni,"* but I did find it and right next to it the definition, "where is?". This must not be his house. I looked up house. It was one of the greetings, *"Galle ma wadi?"* "How is your house?" but I had forgotten it, because I was sitting up on that damned stool, with two African women wearing telephones and butterflies patiently watching me.

I found *galle. "Galle* Min?" I asked.

They became very animated, bobbing their earrings, using their hands, looking concerned, and speaking Pulaar faster and faster. I went back to the pages of my notebook. It was written there, *"Galle*—house", *"Holto woni*—where is". I remembered the day we learned those words, Cindi, Adam, Chris, and I sitting in the little hut at the Thies training center, our professor drilling us over and over again.

This could not be me, sitting on an old camp stool, wearing jeans and a T-shirt, my blond hair in a pony tail and my white skin glaring, facing two Pulaar women on a millet-stalk mat, in *boubous* and cornrows with warm, dark, brown skin, their ears hung with thick gold hoops. Their Pulaar was becoming softer and softer as they realized I understood none of it.

Soon we would be back in silence. I tried to think of what I was going to do when that moment came.

It hit me suddenly and I grinned with excitement. I could tell them my name. "*Mbietami* Mariyata Cham," I said. We had all been given Senegalese names by the language professors. The women grinned back at me, equally excited. Something had been said which we all understood. Now the three of us were animatedly nodding our heads. Then silence returned.

I told them my name a second time, just because it had worked, and again we nodded our heads and smiled. Now, I had completely used up my Pulaar and there was nothing else I could say which they would understand, and nothing I would understand if they said it to me. I sat very still, overwhelmed by the realization.

I stood up to leave and the young woman stood up too. She walked me partway back to Dirk's house. They obviously thought I was stupid. Did she think I was lost as well? I asked the woman her name as we walked. I had already asked it once, but I kept wanting to call her Omo, which was the Pulaar pronoun for he/she, and I knew it could not possibly be her name.

We were about half-way between her compound and Dirk's when some men called to us. She directed me over to them. I looked at each of the men's faces. Could one of them be Min? I would not know him if he was not wearing his polyester plaid pants. That was all I noticed when I met someone Senegalese, their clothes and how dark their skin was. No one came forward to ask why it had taken me so long to visit and I decided he was not there.

I think one of them was "Omo's" father. He wanted to show me how he could write and wrote a Pulaar word on his plastic pointy-toed slipper with a Bic pen, then looked into my face to see if I was impressed. I nodded my head and smiled. I was tired of nodding my head. Next he asked if I would marry him, and I nodded my head sideways, and everyone laughed.

I said I must go now, and walked out and directly through Dirk's compound wall to the cane bed under the neem tree and lay down. Dabo poked his head out of the house, looked at my prostrate form and asked if I would like some of the fish he had caught and just cooked. "No," I said. I wanted nothing but silence, privacy, and above all, no more Pulaar or French. Dabo looked hurt. It was probably a Senegalese rule never to turn down *Clarius* in the afternoon. I didn't care. I was working at becoming completely inert, a part of the cane bed, when Min walked into the compound and greeted me cheerfully. He was wearing his plaid pants.

I might not have worked, but this time I could say I had tried to visit. As soon as our greetings were over, he asked me to his house, the way he did each day. I felt a little triumphant as I told him I had already been there. He didn't understand and became as perplexed as the women. The words were right. What was wrong? I pointed at him and said, "Min". Min was shaking his head back and forth looking concerned. He said, "*Miin ko* Ya Ya Dieng."

Oh my God, "*miin*" was the Pulaar word for "me." It was one of the first words we had learned. I had walked through the village asking, "Where am I" and "Is this my house?" I had been asking two grown women, "Where is me?"

I decided to set up my outdoor bed and go to sleep. There was still a lot of light and the dinner bowl had not yet arrived. Dabo would think I was deranged. I walked into the house and dragged out a mattress, mosquito net, and my sheets. Dabo came and stood on the front doorstep watching me tie my net to the branches of the tree, and announced to no one in particular that I had not eaten dinner. He had his "white-women-are-crazy" expression on his face. It was becoming familiar. I said I wasn't hungry and laid down.

When I woke up, the night was pitch black, the wind purposefully whipping me—as though I had angered the sky gods and they wanted to teach me a lesson. The neem tree's branches and my net were thrown one way and then the other, and the air was thick with a million pinpricks of dust. I lay as flat as I could, the world tearing itself apart around me. The night was enraged.

I couldn't believe it might be going to rain. This was the desert. Maybe it would go away. I rolled myself tighter in the sheets; then felt guilty for not wanting the rain.

Dabo came again to the front step, only this time with a
flashlight, which he shone toward my bed. I didn't want to
move. Fast, heavy raindrops began to pelt me. I tore at my
net, folding everything in half, and ran for the house. Dabo
frowned as I dragged it all inside, dripping.

He helped me set the bed back up in a corner of the room
which was called the kitchen. He was speaking very quickly in
French, all of which was lost in the pounding of rain on a tin
roof. When the bed was set up, he walked back to his bedroom. I sat cross-legged in the open doorway, held by the
violence of the storm.

The rain crashed down in opaque walls of water which
came too fast for the hard-baked earth to drink in. It was like
no rain I had ever seen, more as though something were
breaking—water that had been held back for day after day,
months, finally tearing free to throw itself fiercely against the
earth. There was nothing soft in this land—vengeful sun,
vengeful rain. The neem tree danced in agony, as though the
water scalded it, and everything man-made seemed very
small. I wondered if the house could withstand the power of
the storm, and wished Dabo had stayed to meet it with me.

I became drenched after a few minutes, the wind throwing
the rain in all directions, and decided to lie down. The roof
leaked over my face, and fat water drops broke onto my
cheeks and nose and forehead. I reversed my head and feet.
The roof leaked there as well; it leaked almost everywhere. I
tried the next room.

There was a pile of old rubber mattresses thrown on the
floor of Dirk's room, and I took my sheet and lay on them. It
was Sahné's bed. She woke to find me there and wanted to
play. She took the corner of my sheet in her teeth and would
not stop tugging. By the time she finished, the flies had
begun. It was dawn and they came with the light. They
landed on, crawled on, and tickled every piece of my exposed
flesh. I couldn't get up, not yet. I wrapped myself completely
in my sheet—leaving only a tiny flap for my nose, then
sweated horribly and had a lot of nasty, weird dreams.

There was no hope. I lay on the mound of mattresses,
accepting that the day must begin. There was something else
wrong. I was wet, but not from rain or sweat. I had gotten my

period during the night. I couldn't discuss menstrual cycles with Dabo. I lay silent, unmoving, while the mess became worse, listening for him. The minutes passed and there was no sound. I decided it was safe and ran for the latrine with some water and my *pagne*. I took my pants to the river, praying no children would want to help me with my laundry, washed them and myself and returned to the house. Sahné and I sat on the front step, while I scratched her behind the ears.

Dabo entered the compound and joined us, telling me I would not have spent such a horrible night if I had listened to him and slept in his room—the only place, he said, where the roof did not leak. It took half an hour before I understood what he was trying to say. I explained I had not heard him above the noise of the rain. He did not believe me.

We gave up trying to become friends after that. I didn't like Dabo. He hadn't taken me anywhere for *Tabaski*; he had introduced me to no one, spoken too fast, explained nothing, looked annoyed when I asked questions. We went our own ways, Dabo still doing God knows what, and me counting the days until Dirk's return.

Dabo and I, by chance, were sitting next to one another on the doorstep, when the headlights of the truck shredded the darkness of the village night. It stopped in front of us, bringing Dirk—finally an American—and failure.

The week was over, and Dabo and I were not friends. Those headlights somehow changed everything. Everyone thought Dabo was wonderful but I hadn't been able to get along with him. I was too uptight, tried too hard to prove I should become his boss. I should have been honest, told him I had a lot to learn. Everything was so confusing now; I was new, but it would pass.

Dirk greeted us and went to wash in the river. Dabo and I were back on the doorstep in the Walli Jalla night. I had been given a second chance.

"Dabo," I said, "I am sorry about this week. I would like us to be friends."

We spoke, as though for the first time. We were getting somewhere when Dirk returned from the river. Dabo suggested we go for a walk and finish our conversation. That was good. This was between us; we could work it out.

We went up the path to the big concrete pumping station that brought the river water from the Doué to the Nianga perimeter and sat on the metal railings bordering the main canal. I had never known a desert sky. The stars were so bright, so many. A soft breeze blew, cooling the land with so few living things to hold either heat or cold.

Dabo was speaking and I tried to clear my head of thoughts about African nights and to fill it instead with translations of his French words. It was hard to catch them, but for once I didn't want to break the conversation into pieces with my questions. I would understand what I could, and then speak slowly when it was my turn, so I could be sure he understood me.

He was speaking about friendship. That was good. I watched his lips and face very closely, as though I might somehow see the words I could not grasp. There were so many words, spilling from his mouth, faster and faster, too fast for me to hold them, too many to understand. I had learned if I looked as though I was listening hard, people would think I understood. I understood almost nothing, as I sat up on the railing looking intent. Slowly my insides went tight, and I lost my sense of the African night and whispering wind, replaced with a feeling Dabo was talking about sex. I did not know any of the words for it, or even why I thought that. It was just a reaction in the pit of my stomach I couldn't explain.

I continued to watch him, but no longer tried to follow his words. It made no sense that he would be talking about sex. It didn't fit into this night, our quiet conversation, our finally becoming friends. His speech was melting into a blur of foreign syllables.

I didn't know what to trust—my mind or my insides. There were no words I had understood, to say to myself, "he said this, he must have meant that." He had been talking about friendship. Maybe he had said something about another volunteer coming to visit. I could tell him it would not be a problem, but what if he had not been talking about sex? I had no reason to believe he had been, except for my instincts. It would be terrible if he had been speaking of friendship and work and I asked about sex. It was safer to keep still, and when it was my turn, tell him how serious I was about fish.

Dabo's speech ended. This was my chance to explain that I was nervous, everything was new and difficult, but I was strong and hard and would work. I had so much to learn, but I didn't give up. I had come here to try to grow fish in a desert and I believed it could be done. I was willing to do whatever it took to make it come true. Dabo had seen me as a young girl. I wanted him to see my determination. I told him we could turn the fish program around—he, Dirk, and I. I would work like a man. He would see.

I stopped, and the breeze blew past us quiet and soft in the silence as we smiled. The tension was gone and I felt happy. We turned to walk back to the compound, along the baked earth, hard like rock, with no signs of life. As we walked side by side, Dabo took my hand. Senegalese men do not hold women's hands. They hold each other's, in friendship and respect. My hand felt strange in his; mine so soft and white and his black and hard, calloused. Dabo of the Mandengs walked holding my hand lightly, and I was proud.

Two days later I sat across from Dirk in The Corniche bar. It had already become a good place to be, sitting on a bench speaking Engish and drinking a beer. I could not wait to tell Dirk all the things I had been through and overcome. There were days of conversation bottled up in me, just waiting to pour out into someone's American ears. I half-wanted to tell Dirk about Dabo. It meant so much to me, but I decided it was between the two of us, too important to take out and share with someone else.

When I looked up at Dirk the stories died in my throat. He looked terribly embarrassed and fidgety. He obviously had something to say to me and didn't know how to start. It had to be bad or he wouldn't look like that.

Finally, he spoke all in a rush.

"I probably should not tell you this, since it was told to me in confidence, and it's really your own business, but . . . do you really think you can have an affair with Dabo and work with him too?"

CHAPTER FOUR

The Dinner Party

It was another brown day. The ponds were brown dips with darker brown water. The station building was a lump of brown with a tin roof. The canal ran brown between weeds covered in a layer of brown dust. The air itself was brown, a wall of dust. It clogged my nostrils and collected in crescents under my fingernails. It even turned sweat brown, and little trickles of perspiration dripped off my chin, arms, and legs, leaving behind streaks of white.

The fish station was only a year old. It was a square cement building with wooden doors and shutters at the end of a short driveway. There were eight ponds—three big and five small. The land was completely flat in all directions, making the station look small and lonely—more desolate than if the wasteland had been left unbroken. Nothing broke the wind. It would blow and blow leaving dust everywhere; on our shelf of tattered aquaculture books, clogging the keys to our manual typewriter, obscuring the numbers of the feeding and growth sample schedules tacked to one wall.

Dabo, Abdoulaye, and Demba worked at the station. But more often than not Abdoulaye and Demba worked as night watchmen, to guard against theft, and Dabo was the only one who always worked during the day. The project could not afford to hire any others. Heavy work was usually scheduled on Thursdays or Fridays, when Abdoulaye or Demba would be there to help. This Friday we were to do a growth sample of one of the big 33-are (one-third of a hectare) ponds, but Demba was sick and Dirk was in Matam delivering furniture, so it was only Dabo and me.

The net had been brought from the storage room and dumped on the pond bank. The brails—long pieces of wood the float and lead lines would be tied to—had been carried out and set next to the net. Buckets, for carrying the fish from the net to the office, were lined up along the bank, while another set of buckets had been filled with water, weighed, and sat under the scales in the office. Fish would be counted into these and the buckets weighed a second time.

The pond we were to sample was a little less than an acre, and almost impossible to seine with only two people. Our net was not big enough to cover the width, and usually we had someone walk along splashing the fish away from the bank the net did not reach, scaring them into the center of the pond and the path of the seine. Without a third person, the fish sensed the movement of the net, many of them escaping around its free edge. We were a week behind in sampling. It would be a long day.

Dabo and I each took an end of the net and started tying it to the brail. Dabo had shown me how to do this when I first came to the station, but the lines I fastened had a tendency to loosen with the water and came undone after a couple of pulls. I hated that. I wanted to do it right. I took one end of the net and wetted the mud-encrusted lines in the pond, then twisted them tightly around the wooden pole, pulling them hard with a jerk, and tying them at each loop. Dabo watched me tying my end as he tied his. He seemed always to watch me, waiting for me to make a mistake, so he could correct me. He loved to correct me, his whole body, voice, face would tingle with it—another chance to tell me I was wrong. Each time I asked Dabo to do something, it was as though I had slapped him. Dabo wanted to sleep with a white woman, not have her as a boss.

After the brails were tied, I went to the office to change. My pond clothes lay over the window sill, stiff, as though they had once been alive and now had rigor mortis. I took them and stood in the corner where no one could see me, pulling on my huge drawstring pants with big red fish, which the tailor had sewn upside down, and my gray T-shirt with the arms cut out, a pattern of tiny holes just beginning to appear across the back as the material deteriorated with sweat and heat and rough washing.

The fabric crackled as I put the clothes on, and little flakes of dried mud came off and fell to the floor. My pond clothes smelled like the station—perspiration and mud with too high a level of hydrogen sulfide. I didn't like putting them on while I was still clean and dry. It was better after I was wet.

Dabo and I filled the buckets: standing knee-deep, dipping the edge of the black buckets under the brown surface of the water, skimming off the donkey dung, returning it to the pond—it fertilized the water—then lugging the full buckets up the bank one by one. My bare feet made funny squishy noises and looked glaringly white, like grubs, as the dark mud oozed between my toes. I set the last bucket down, and looked up to see a small silver car pulling into the station's driveway.

A short white man, with grey hair that caught in the wind, climbed out of his car and started walking quickly toward us. My pants were wet and muddy, clinging tightly to my legs from the thighs down. White people came to the station for tours, facts and figures, a history of the fish project—all to be delivered in French. My French was bad.

The little silver car in the station's driveway ruined the one aspect of the day I had looked forward to—to be alone at the station, forced to make a few of my own decisions, to learn I could organize a day's work without creating a disaster. I was *la petite patronne*—a glorified assistant, rather than my own person. It was not Dirk who made me this, it was time. Dirk knew everything better than I did—the culture, French, the workings of the station. For my entire first year he would know better. Whenever we were together, he would be the boss.

This white man would ask a lot of questions: how long has the station been in production, what stocking rates did we use, what were our feeding percentages, water costs, growth rates, and kilos per hectare produced? I knew the questions, but not the French answers. I was not the coordinator of the program, Dirk was.

The man virtually ran up to us, thrust his hand out, and introduced himself as Tallyrand. He seemed to do everything very fast and his eyes were bright and bird-like, darting from Dabo to me. He was French. I liked to think how much easier it would be if I was. For a moment I stepped outside the rituals of the station—seining ponds, fixing dikes, harvesting fish, and saw myself as this man must see me. My shirt was rotting, my pants dirty and wet and five sizes too big. There was mud on my hands and in my hair. Occasionally I was a technical advisor, more often a menial laborer. I was a child barely out of college, who could not speak French.

I tried to remember how to say 2.75 ares—the size of the brood ponds—in French and what production and stocking rates Dirk had told the last group of people touring the station. Tallyrand asked if I would join him and his friends for dinner that Saturday. He explained: he had seen me running in the mornings, was having only a small get together, and hoped I would come. I had just figured out that 2.75 was *deux virgule soixante quinze*. He had seen me running?

It had started as a bet with Kevin, another fisheries volunteer. I would run four times a week and Kevin would stop smoking. Whoever lost had to take the other out to dinner in Dakar. I wanted that dinner. Four days out of five I ran the six kilometers to the station, just as the sun began to come up, and the rice fields looked unbelievably green—as though they were on color TV and the TV needed to be tuned. My running had started as a bet, but it turned into a necessity. I could do it independently of everyone else. It was something to have accomplished four times a week.

Tallyrand was still speaking. He said he lived in Nianga Cité, the government base. I knew where that was; I ran by it on my way to the station. They had electricity, running water, refrigerators, and TVs. It was a tiny modern outpost in the middle of nowhere. There was a rumor that someone living there owned a VCR. Tallyrand was saying he had invited a Dutch irrigation specialist, two Italian expatriates, me, and of course he would be there to make five. I must have looked skeptical. He added the others were all his age, as though to reassure me.

Tallyrand wore tan pants with a leather belt and a white shirt that was still white, looking as though it had been ironed, and grey suede lace-up shoes. He lived in another world. I thought of my muddy days dipnetting fish, cutting weeds with a machete, using a pickaxe and hammer and shovel, and then of my house in Walli Jalla, the crumbling walls, corrugated tin roof, a hole for the latrine, bathing in the river.

I could not imagine myself at Tallyrand's party. It was not a part of my life. I felt as though an astronaut had come to ask if I would like to fly to the moon. I explained how tired I was by the end of the week, hoping Tallyrand would accept that and leave. He did not. He said that was no reason not to meet the European community and share in a good meal. He told me he was an excellent chef. I said the other volunteer was out of town with the project truck, leaving me with no means of transportation. He would come pick me up, he said, just tell him where. I said the pumping station; he said 7 p.m. Saturday, and it was decided. I would attend a Nianga dinner party.

Tallyrand drove off in a cloud of dust, and Dabo and I entered the pond and started the growth sample.

Dabo took his brail and waded to the other side of the pond. The water was up to his chest. When the net was stretched tight, and I had my side up close to the other bank, we both passed the brails over our heads so we could push our chests up against them, the float lines pointed out toward the banks and the lead lines in toward the middle of the pond. The weight of the water, the sucking clay pond bottom, and the seine all pulled at us. We leaned into the brails and dragged the seine forward. When we reached the other bank, we walked in toward each other and lay the brails close together in the mud, making the net into a bag. Dabo sat down in the shallow water and pulled the lead lines together, while I held the float line up, keeping the fish from jumping over its edge. Dabo pulled the lines in closer and closer until there was only a small section of the net left filled with fish. We dipnetted them out and into the buckets, to be hauled to the office for weighing.

The fish jumped and flopped, wiggled like animate grease in our hands, trying to spine us with their dorsals. They had to be counted one by one into the water-filled preweighed buckets sitting on the floor of the office. There was a hook on the scales, to hang the buckets for weighing, and a rough table was penciled on a piece of paper for the number of fish, weight of water with fish, and weight of water without fish which someone would later use to figure out average weights and growth rates. We needed a twenty-percent sample. There were 6,600 fish in the pond and we had just caught seventy-three.

As we walked back to the seine, Dabo asked me if I was really planning to go to Tallyrand's dinner. He passed one of the brails up the bank to me, and then we stood on either side of the net pulling the soaked float and lead lines up into a pile, topping it off with the second brail. The net was heavy and slippery with water and mud. We each stood on one side and encircled an end of the mess with our arms trying to keep more of the net up off the ground than under our feet, as we slogged back to the other end of the pond. I said yes, I was going to Tallyrand's dinner, and a strange look came over Dabo's face.

Dabo resented me as his boss, but would have liked to have me as his girlfriend. He wanted Western clothes, Western music, a Western woman. They were all signs of prosperity. He was very disappointed when I explained I only wanted to work at the fish station. He did not believe for a minute I would last in Senegal without a man. Someone would snatch me up, take what he had wanted and been unable to obtain. He watched closely to see who it would be. White men always got the things Dabo wanted.

We continued to seine. We pulled the net seven times, until the brown of the air had turned to pale cream, touched by the sinking sun, and we ached, with no energy left over to pull the seine even one more time. My arms burned from pulling in the lead line and holding the brail. My legs ached from fighting the pond's clay bottom, and my eyes hurt from squinting against the sun. My hands were cut with a million tiny slashes each marked by an angry red line. Still the day was not over until the net was hung—so it would not rot or be eaten by the rats that lived in the warehouse.

It took two people to hang the seine. There were three metal hooks hanging from the rafters of the warehouse ceiling. One person had to stand on an old gas barrel and the other on the broken unused transport box to reach them. The net was weighted with mud, water, and weeds, alive with inch-long water bugs that resembled roaches and had long, nasty pincers. There was always a point at the middle hook, just as the bag was reached, when the net was at its heaviest. You would hold it out at arm's length to reach that hook and your arm would start to shake from the weight. There would be only a quarter-inch to go to slide the lead line over the metal curve and your body would strain, your face twitch from the effort. You would almost fall from the barrel as you gave it one last heave and the line finally caught. Somehow, Dabo always managed it so I had to catch the middle hook.

This day was no different. My arm quivered, the skin of my face pulled tight as I reached for the middle hook and Dabo stood loose-limbed, at ease, a slight smirk on his lips, waiting for me to fall or ask for help. I would not.

The net was hung, the buckets put away, the night watchman had shown up, and we had rinsed ourselves off in the canal and changed out of our pond clothes. We both had to walk to the Cité, Dabo to get a ride—he had moved to Podor when I moved to Walli Jalla—and I because it was on the way home. I asked Dabo if he was coming with me and he said no, he would stay and talk to Abdoulaye for awhile. I left alone.

I liked the walk home. It gave me time to think and look around. Sometimes I would bring Pulaar words to memorize; usually I fumed about Dabo. This afternoon I wondered how I had ended up telling a Frenchman I would come to dinner, fantasizing about the meat he might serve, and thinking I probably would not get home until after dark when the mosquitoes were out—which meant washing in the river while they ate me alive.

Before Tallyrand's party I spent the afternoon at Fatu's. Fatu brought us water from the river. She carried it on her head in a huge purple plastic bucket. She would stand just inside my door, next to my water containers, the heavy bucket sitting perfectly still on the crown of her head, and I would take a handle and she would take a handle and we would let it down slowly, sloshing water on the cement floor because it was so heavy. Fatu cooked our meals and did our laundry. We paid her at the end of each month, and she was always asking if "the month had died yet?"

Fatu was big. She had heavy lips, wide hips, and a rear-end that jutted out. Her eyes were large and round and she rolled them when she laughed. She wore fifteen gold hoops in each ear that jingled if she shook her head. She always put her hands on her hips and shook her head when she was mad. She was a terror when angry, and few people dared cross her.

She and Dirk did not like each other much, but I liked her. She was happy there was a woman in Dirk's compound and would stay after bringing us something, to joke and laugh. She loved to tease. She would tease me about my Pulaar, my ignorance, my inability to cook Senegalese food, the fact that I was not sleeping with Dirk. She teased me about everything, but it was never mean. I would tease her back, the best I could, and we would hold each other's hands and laugh.

She was the first person in the village I really got to know. I wanted her to teach me Pulaar, so I decided to go to her compound. I knew it must be just around the corner, because at night I could hear her voice as she laughed or gossipped with her neighbors.

It was easy to find Fatu's compound. It was directly across from the Diengs', my next-door neighbors. I walked inside the wall, holding my Pulaar notebook, to find Fatu and her mother sitting on a mat preparing *haako*. Their *boubous* made two bright spots on the mat, their arms and faces showing dark brown against the colors. They were surrounded by leaves, which they were cleaning, stripping, and putting into a big bowl to set over the fire that night to make leaf sauce. *Lacciri e haako*, millet and leaf sauce, was one of four traditional village dinners, my favorite.

Fatu stood when she saw me, ran to the entrance, grabbed my hands, and greeted me, her eyes rolling with excitement. Giggling, she did not let go of my hands until she had me sitting in a chair next to their mat.

I sat, looking around. Fatu's mother was very old, with gray hair. She had a small brown house to herself. Fatu, her husband, and their three children lived in another tiny square house, and Bautch, Fatu's brother-in-law who worked at Nianga Cité, had a big fancy house which made an uneven "u" of the buildings and took up most of the compound. I watched Fatu's and Habi's hands deftly working the *haako*, flicking here and there quickly, while Fatu continued to chatter with me and Habi smiled an old woman's quiet smile.

I told Fatu I did not want to sit in the chair, but she didn't understand me, so I left it and sat with them on the mat, causing an uproar that took a little time to die down. Fatu had stopped cleaning the leaves to watch me expectantly. I opened my notebook and announced that I wanted her to teach me Pulaar. Fatu started pointing to things, telling me their names. She told me the word for big leaves, little leaves, their veins, what they were called after they were prepared, the place where they grew them, the name for the partially cooked sauce, the pot, the fire, and the spoon.

Her Pulaar was too fast, too detailed. Her words rushed over themselves like a gurgling waterfall. To try to slow her down, I pointed first to the chair, then the roof, and later the sky—asking very slowly how to say each in Pulaar. Fatu had such energy; I wondered sometimes how she stood the slow pace of village life. She loved any little drama that might break the boredom of her days. The white woman coming to her compound was drama, and Fatu's excitement was contagious. Soon we were both laughing and rolling our eyes. Other women heard the hullabaloo and began to trickle into the compound, pointing to things, telling me more and more words, until I was surrounded by village women and not understanding anyone.

We moved the mat as the sun moved the shadows. It felt good to be a woman among village women. I looked at the female faces and had no names to put with them. I was engulfed by a village kaleidoscope: brightly patterned *boubous* or *pagnes*, intricately woven corn rows, little magic leather pouches hung around waists or arms that showed as someone leaned forward or pointed, wide white smiles standing out against black faces. For the first time in my life I felt very white and looked at my arms and hands. They seemed ugly and pale.

I pointed to one woman's braids and asked the name for them. *"Moorde"*, they said. I wondered what I would look like with my hair done like theirs. *"Ada yiddi?"*, "You like?" they asked. I nodded my head and one of the women, Mbinté I think, took strands of my long straight hair into her hands and tried to braid it. She had never felt white people's hair. It was too slippery and she couldn't get it to stay where it should, as she reached for other strands to work into the braid. She laughed self-consciously and gave up.

One of the other women tried, but failed too. Mbinté suggested something and came back to sit behind me. She was taking much bigger handfuls now and making large braids all over my head. She would braid the hair all the way to the very end and then take two little pieces and wind them around the remaining hair, tying them into knots. When she finished, I had eight braids, and all the women were giggling.

Fatu stood before me with her hands on her hips, shaking her head back and forth, laughing, and saying *"moyyaani,"* "bad, bad." She ran into one of the little clay buildings and came out with a piece of mirror which she presented to me.

I looked hideous. There were braids sprouting from the top of my head, the sides, and in back. It looked as though there had been an explosion. I had seen some of the little girls with their hair like this, but it had looked nice on them. It didn't on me. I laughed and they asked me if I wanted to keep the braids. Fatu absolutely forbade me to do so. She said they were not good for a white person, only for a village girl and she loosened my hair, undoing the braids, combing it back straight with her fingers.

It was time for me to leave and I stood to go. The women said I should stay, pointed to the *haako* and told me to have dinner with them. I had never eaten dinner in one of the village compounds. It would be fun, but I said I had to eat dinner with a white man in Nianga Cité. I tried to explain how that made me feel—out of place, a little scared—and that I would rather stay with them.

I washed quickly in the river. I was late and couldn't decide what to wear. I was sure I didn't have anything appropriate. Why had I done this? I asked our dog and our two kittens and none of them had an answer. I finally decided on a blue tie-dye dress with alligators swimming around its bottom. I had bought it in Dakar. I had hairy legs and didn't have a razor. Anyway, I could hardly shave at the river. I tied my leather sandals on instead of my plastic flip flops, locked the animals into the house, and walked up to the pumping station, where Tallyrand was supposed to meet me.

I tried to imagine the night. I pictured myself with four fifty-year-old men, having a polite conversation about different types of development careers. Worse yet, it would be in a language I could barely understand or speak. I decided to think of food instead, remembering the last Western meal I had eaten in St. Louis, the richness, variety, both vegetables and meat, a huge price tag. This would be free. Dirk would be jealous.

Tallyrand was there in his silver car exactly at seven. He jumped out to open my door and I climbed into the coolness I normally had only at night time or while dunking myself in the river. We drove to his house in the Cité, a real house with glass windows, screens, tiled floors, and an inner courtyard where he had planted flowers. He had a modern oven and refrigerator, running water, a toilet, sofas, chairs, and a dining-room table. He offered me my choice of sodas or orange juice, to be mixed with bourbon or gin or vodka.

I sat on the edge of the sofa as though I was quite accustomed to it, while inside my head thoughts rushed around in a whirl. How could I decide what I wanted to drink? The choices were too good, too many. The sodas and orange juice sat in a cooler on the table in front of me; the bottles buried under ice—ice! I thought of my clay *loonde* letting a little of the river water seep through and evaporate to keep it lukewarm while the rest of the world was sweltering. I couldn't make a serious decision and said the first thing that came to mind—vodka and orange juice. I had thought I would not drink orange juice for two years.

Tallyrand made my drink and introduced me to his guests, whose names I immediately forgot. The Dutch irrigation specialist I had met before. I had already nicknamed him Mr. Reverse. It seemed whenever I saw him he was furiously backing up his car—going way too fast—lost in a cloud of dust on one of the perimeter's dirt roads.

He had come by the station a couple of times; I am not

sure why. He came once during our technical training and, while he was talking with Dirk, I pickaxed my toe. He offered to take me back to his house at the Cité for first aid. Dirk had said I should go.

His house was completely barren. There was not one thing that was not a necessity. The walls, floors, and kitchen all shone as though they had been sterilized for a hospital. I had been in the canal and left a little muddy puddle everywhere I stepped. He had me wash my foot in the bathroom shower and gave me peroxide and a bandaid. I kept apologizing for the mess and he kept saying it was nothing. He offered me a soda from his refrigerator, and I felt it was a bribe. He seemed starved for conversation, or rather for someone to hear his problems.

He wasn't happy and hated Senegal. Everything was fouled up here, the whole country was fouled up. No one did what you asked them to, or if they did they did it months later. They were all lazy, these Senegalese, just looking for handouts. They asked for technical advisors and then did not listen to them. He had had it and couldn't wait to leave. They couldn't pay him enough to stay in a hell hole like Nianga Cité.

I had listened to him politely and was happy when my soda was finished.

Now Tallyrand introduced us and I shook his skinny hand, smiling in recognition and wondering what tales of doom I would hear this night. Mr. Reverse sat to my left in a straight-back chair and the two Italians shared the couch with me. Their names were very long. In my head I called them the fat Italian and the dead Italian.

The fat Italian had pale skin and red hair. There was a fringe of red going round his head, with only a couple of long strands left to comb from one side to the other. He had a big bushy moustache, as though to make up for the bald-ness of his scalp, and his stomach hung over his belt. He kept trying to get me to talk about American politics, telling me repeatedly all the things wrong with U.S. foreign policy.

The dead Italian was quiet. He wore a white shirt the same color as his skin, making it difficult to tell where the shirt ended and his flesh began. His hair was also white, but his eyes were bright blue. I liked him best. Later, at another of Tallyrand's parties, he saved me from the fat Italian's politics by dancing with me around the courtyard.

Tallyrand darted about trying to be everywhere and do everything at once. He wanted to make sure his Senegalese cook was preparing things successfully, that his guests were happy, and that the table was appropriately set. At one point he alighted on the couch and told me he painted. The painting hanging on the wall to my left was one he had done. It was good. He asked if I drew and I said I did, but not very well. We would have to paint together sometime, he announced. I didn't say anything because his houseboy had begun to set out the food.

Tallyrand told us who was to sit where, and I was seated next to Mr. Reverse and across from the fat Italian. I tried not to let my eyes widen but there was roast beef, green beans, a tossed salad, real French bread and a whole stick of butter sitting on the table. I couldn't buy a meal like this. We passed the platters around and served ourselves. I ate more than the fat Italian.

By dinner I had drunk two orange juices and vodkas, and felt as though all this was meant to be—sitting in air conditioning, eating like an American, talking and joking with four fifty-year-old men of different nationalities as though they were my friends. I tried not to let the fat Italian down, and began adamantly denying everything he said. "Ce n'est pas vrai," I said over and over, until he finally seemed satisfied with my spunk, or was going to scream if I said, "Ce n'est pas vrai," one more time. He said we should talk politics again, sometime after I had been here a little longer, and he had less of a language advantage.

The dishes were cleared and Tallyrand came out of the kitchen carefully holding a tray, which he set down on the table with a flourish. On the tray were a dozen small porcelain cups filled with chocolate mousse. He apologized; the mousse had not set correctly, was runny. I didn't notice and ate two. I would have eaten three, if anyone had offered.

Conversation wound down. We each had another drink and everyone politely said we would have to get together again soon. Mr. Reverse offered me a ride home so Tallyrand could stay and clean up, and I accepted. We didn't talk much during the ride. My French had been stretched to its utmost during dinner and I no longer could think of things to say.

Mr. Reverse pulled the car all the way into my compound, almost up onto the front step. I climbed out, thanking him for the ride, and went to unlock the door while he sat in the car, his lights glaring at me. I fumbled with the key. The lights were so bright. I felt trapped like a runaway in a searchlight and couldn't get the door unlocked. Mr. Reverse was not going to leave until I was safely inside and I would burst if I had to speak French for even one more minute.

I knew the window shutter was unlocked. I jimmied it open, pulled myself up onto the window ledge and scrambled over, into the house. I was inside the familiar warm darkness and all I wanted was for Mr. Reverse to go away. I unlocked the front doors from inside, and waved my hand. Finally, he backed up too fast, screeched his brakes, and left.

I went to find Sahné and the kittens. They were in my room and I sat down on the dusty floor to pet them. Sahné stuck her wet nose under my hand and the kittens climbed into my lap. I told them about my night in the white people's world, and they purred and Sahné wagged her tail. I told them I liked our world better, and was surprised by how much I meant it.

Leaving my room to sit on the front step, I watched the stars. Sahné came to join me. The sky was so huge. It wasn't a patch of blue, like in Tallyrand's courtyard. There were no artificial lights stealing from the stars, no deadening whir of the air conditioner muting the night. I could hear Fatu laughing. A donkey brayed somewhere off in the village. I set my bed up under the neem tree, and climbed under the mosquito net. It felt good to be home.

CHAPTER FIVE

The Deserted Village

There is a short cut from the fish station to the paved road.
It follows one of the perimeter's dirt roads for a ways—past a
clump of thatched huts, up a ramp and over a bridge, and
then out into the *waalo*. The *waalo* is open land—flat, dusty
open land that seems to go on forever. The openness swal-
lows the road until there is nothing left but tire tracks, and
the tire tracks are only there until the wind comes and sweeps
them away. The sole landmark is a broken-down electric
line—brown pole after brown pole that seemingly lead to
nowhere.

But if you followed the poles they would take you past
occasional huts, through a dead forest, and into little dips of
hard-baked clay deeply cracked by the heat of the dry season.
During the rainy season these shallow ditches collect water
and people plant them with sorghum or millet, in a race
against the sun. Sometimes along the short cut, another car
would pass. Quite often there would be people walking, or
someone herding goats or sheep, but no villages. There is
only one village along the short cut—the deserted village that
sits up on the hill.

It sits there against the horizon—crumbling earthen walls
melting back into the earth. Near the bottom of the hill are
broken semicircles which were once huts. Toward the top,
they give way to rectangular walls, some still holding the
shape of cut-out windows. In the middle of the rectangles
and the semicircles is a peak, higher than the other walls.
This peak is where two walls came together to make a corner,
but now the walls are broken and their edges trail off, form-
ing triangles with the ground. Once this building was taller
than any of the others, and its walls were layered with mortar

44

and whitewash. But time has worn it away, leaving only one peak to mark the remains of the village mosque.

The first time I saw these ruins, when Dirk was driving us to the station for our technical training, I had thought they spoke of nothing but death and desolation. Three months had passed since then and I had come to think the walls whispered of secrets, life they had seen, ghosts they knew. Each time we passed, Dirk and I would say we wanted to come back, to stop, to feel the deserted village, but we always needed to get to the station to work or to a meeting. This night we would stop at the deserted village. We were going to spend Halloween with the ghosts who lived in the lonely walls.

We went to the big *marché* in Podor to look for squashes that could be made into jack-o'-lanterns. The *marché* was in a large courtyard, surrounded on three sides by rows of Mauritanian boutiques called Nar shops, and on the fourth side by the taxi *gare*. There was a large cement platform under a thatched roof, where women sat in brightly colored *boubous* with little piles of tomatoes, okra, eggs, lemons, *jaya-jii*—my favorite squash—pounded millet, little pats of tomato paste, cabbage, eggplants, hot peppers, goat's milk, or dried fish sitting before them. The women would call to us to look at their wares, to come see how fresh their eggs were, to tell us how cheaply they would sell them to us. They would all be yelling as we walked by—if we glanced at them they would begin to bargain.

As the women tried to get our attention, streams of children wound in and out between them, calling us names, playing tricks, or running errands for the grown-ups. Goats bleated, chickens clucked, the taxis honked, and occasionally blared African music, and the butcher's knife made a hard thwack as it hit bone. There was an old man who sat surrounded by plastic beads and cheap plastic watches who would let us know he had just gotten some new bracelets, and another young man selling Chinese T-shirts and potatoes and onions who knew just the thing we wanted. Friends would greet us and tell us to buy from them or from their friends. Children would chant, "*tubab*", attaching themselves to us and not letting go until we left the *marché*. The air smelled of curdling milk, reeking fish, and fresh cow's blood. Fat, black flies crawled over everything, flying up when we moved and then settling, never leaving the open piles of food baking in the desert heat.

We pushed our way through the crowd, fought off the attacking children, greeted the bread man, and went to ask Si, the bead lady, if she knew of any round squashes. She did and sent us off amongst the piles to a friend who had a cantaloupe and a watermelon. We looked around at the other piles but found nothing better to make faces and so began to bargain. It took fifteen minutes before she stopped giving us the *tubab*, or white person's price, and came down to the Pulaar price. We bought the melons for a hundred francs each and escaped to the truck.

When we got back to Walli Jalla we sat on the front step with a bowl between us for the sweet insides of our melons and our Swiss army knives ready to carve jack-o'-lantern faces. I wanted mine to be happy and Dirk wanted his to be fierce. Dirk said the whole idea of Halloween was to be scary and scared. What was the sense in carving a happy face? If I was going to create something, I wanted it to be happy. We had a slight argument over pumpkin faces and then went ahead and carved the melons the way we had each wanted to in the first place.

Our friend Ya Ya, alias Min, came by the compound to greet us. He stopped by every night to say hello and ask of our tiredness and health, but he had never yet found us doing something as strange as making heads out of melons. Today he stood before us going through the greetings and staring down at our bizarre creations.

He wanted to know what we were doing, but I didn't have the Pulaar words to explain and he wouldn't have understood anyway. How could Ya Ya understand children dressing up as skeletons and monsters, going trick-or-treating door-to-door for Snickers and Milky Ways and M & M's? He wouldn't understand Americans deliberately scaring themselves. The only ghosts and goblins Ya Ya knew were real.

I told him it was an American *fête*, and that on this day we bought squashes and made them into heads, setting candles inside them, and letting them look out into the night. He stood watching us, with an expression of confusion and incredulity that he seemed to reserve especially for his American village friends, and then he left abruptly.

We finished the jack-o'-lanterns—one scowling and one grinning and started loading up the truck. We had planned our Halloween for weeks. We were taking a mattress to sleep on in the truck bed, the fruit cocktail from our "pumpkins", slices of goat meat that we had bought at the *marché* and were cooking as a treat, the little coal grill, a kerosene lamp, and our teapot and tea.

We had bought a brown paper cone of the strong Chinese tea the Senegalese are forever drinking, heating their bright blue fat-bellied pots over the coals, steeping the tea and then pouring it into what look like shot glasses. They pour the steaming tea from one glass to another, back and forth, back and forth, until there is a layer of white foam sitting at the bottom of each glass. The tea is poured back into the pot, sugar added—cubes and cubes of sugar—and the pot is held up high over each glass and tipped forward with tea streaming forth in a thin brown line that makes the glasses smoky as it fills them.

If we were to spend the night in a haunted Senegalese village, it was only appropriate we make Senegalese tea. It was one of the most common rituals, with a grace and beauty all its own. Once you learned how to make it—it took a lot of practice—you could not get the feel of it out of your hands. There is a rhythm, a deftness, an inherent patience telling of many, long-past, dust-filled, unbearably hot afternoons spent making tea. We thought we would make tea for ourselves and also for the spirits, so brought three glasses.

We were almost finished packing the truck, when Ya Ya walked back into the compound grinning from ear to ear. He was holding a perfectly round watermelon. He gave it to us, saying it was his gift for our American festival and that we must make a grand head of his melon. He had grown it himself in his garden and was very proud of it. He pointed out how nicely round it was, comparing it to his own head, and we all laughed. I don't remember if he stayed to see what

type of head it would become or not. I have forgotten its face.
Maybe Dirk and I compromised and made a grinning,
frowning schizophrenic jack-o'-lantern out of Ya Ya's gift.

By the time the truck was packed and Ya Ya had left, night
had fallen. There were no lights along the short cut except
for the truck's headlights and the stars' pinpricks. Birds,
which had been resting in the tire tracks, flew up into the
high beams' glare and dust clouds billowed before us, coming
to life and then floating away into the night, like the spirits
we had talked of. It was all so empty. Anything could happen.

It took fifteen minutes to get to the village, but they were
very long minutes, and by the time we saw the walls caught in
our headlights I felt far away from all I knew. I was afraid I
would act embarrassingly frightened. We turned the engine
off and were immediately wrapped around with black silence
as we climbed from the truck and started to set up camp. We
took out the grill, our melons, the food, the candles, the
kerosene lamp. People had lived and died here. We were
going to eat fruit cocktail and tell ghost stories. The walls
seemed to look down at us in scorn, hissing softly—idiot, fool
tubabs searching for an American adventure in Africa,
blinded by your own imaginations, missing the beauty of
what is really there. We talked, trying to deny it. We were not
American tourists staying in a fancy hotel with wooden masks
on the walls. Still, it seemed the very night had drawn away
from us—interlopers in the deserted village.

Dirk started a fire, and I set out my *pagne* for us to sit on.
We lit the candles inside the melons and set the faces in worn-
away window holes. They laughed and scowled at us throwing their shadows every which way, changing with the wind.
They lived and took on personalities of their own. We cooked
our meat and ate our fruit, caught up in the little tasks of
making a meal. They watched us silently.

I told Dirk about a college Halloween party I had gone to
with two friends, each of us dressed as one of the three pigs,
wearing pink felt snouts taped to our noses, and curly pink
tails pinned to our rear ends. We had made cardboard signs
that said "Go Hog Wild", and we each wore a word. No one
wanted "Hog", because it was going to be embarrassing if the
other two were not around. We drew straws for it, and I lost.

Dirk was wondering out loud what his friends would think if they could see him. They would freak. What a great letter home this would make. I pointed out he almost never wrote letters. We started wondering what the workers at the station would think. Dirk said he had not told Dabo because Dabo would have forbidden us to come, and then been horribly worried if we insisted on coming anyway. Dirk was sure they believed the village was haunted.

Our voices became softer and softer, and the night slowly returned to close around us. Complete blackness was broken only by the embers of our fire and the flickering expressions of the pumpkins. It felt as though we were at the end of the earth, the only people alive. There was so much space, so much open space stretching out in all directions around us.

Way off in one direction lay planted fields; in back of us was the short cut; and around us the walls, some standing solitary and dignified—refusing to crumble back to the earth—others softly rounded, their edges worn by time, wind, and occasional downpours in the rainy season. There were two houses which still had almost all their walls if not their roofs. In what had once been their windows sat our jack-o'-lanterns.

The walls surrounded us. We could feel them. What had they seen or kept hidden from others? Who had lived and died here, and why did they leave? What was the village's name? Walli Jalla meant "to spend the night laughing". What did this village name mean?

There had been laughter here, goats and chickens and donkeys, naming ceremonies, tired foreheads bowed to Mecca, and funerals. I had not yet seen a person born or die, and these walls had seen both. I thought of a Pulaar woman, quietly entering her house to produce life in an hour or two, with the help of a midwife. I could see a tiny baby wailing, or suckling, or sleeping, mother and child not allowed to leave the house until seven days had passed and the new life had proven its will to continue living.

Then there would be a naming ceremony, the mother and the father each giving the child a name, and the father would go to the *marabout* to get traditional medicine for the new-born baby. The *marabout* would write a verse or several verses from the Koran on a slate and then wash the words off with water into a cup. This liquid would hold the power of the words and would be rubbed onto the baby's skin.

The day of the naming ceremony, relatives and friends would come to the compound, and be told for the first time the child's gender. Gifts would be given, stories told of namesakes, and rounds and rounds of tea drunk. The women would all sit in one room and the men in another. A goat would be killed and rice and meat cooked and eaten that afternoon. What were the names of the babies born in these walls? Did they live? Did the *marabout's* potions protect them?

Or had they died? I had seen the men dressed in their best *boubous* coming from every compound in Walli Jalla, congregating on the paths to the cemetery, like small drops slowly coming together, taking strength, flowing, until the stream seems more than you could ever imagine the single drops becoming—seen the tired faces of old men walking with canes and the young strained faces who have made this walk at least once for one of their own children, or know they will, before they too grow old and walk with canes. How many times had the men put on their best *boubous* only to walk to a gravesite? Where had they buried their dead?

There was too much to the silence of these walls and Dirk began to speak. He told me of the great magic of the Mandengs. They were supposed to have the strongest powers of all the tribes of Senegal. He told me of a language professor in Thiès who swore he had seen a zombie sitting in the corner of one of the old battered public transport vans, being taken back to the land of his birth, his body capable of movement after death. Dirk told me a Mandeng's relatives would come to find the body, and breathe life into its cold flesh, so the body might retrace its steps to its birthplace. All Mandengs had to be buried in their villages or their souls would wander the earth with nowhere to rest.

Dabo was a Mandeng, and he had told Dirk this was true. We could not decide if we believed it. We thought it might be true. We fell silent again, and sat listening to the silence. There was a faraway howling that could have been the wind or hyenas or tricks of our imaginations turning the silence to sound. It made the silence deeper.

"Look!" Dirk whispered, pointing ahead of us, between broken walls. There were two dark forms there, where before the space had been empty. We sat and stared. The forms were not shadows; they did not leave, but neither did they come closer, become more easily identifiable. They were dark figures standing at the edge of our fire's light, watching us.

We sat frozen, staring harder and harder into the night. We had been fools to spend a night in the deserted village. I couldn't stand it. Why didn't whatever it was do something? I grabbed Dirk's hand. "I'll go see what they are, if you'll come with me," I whispered.

We stood up hand-in-hand and took very small steps forward, toward the darkness. I told myself if they were people they would speak or run or attack us and if they were hyenas then they would scatter; if they were spirits at least we would have confronted them. We inched forward until the forms began to take on lines—trunks and branches and tiny leaves.

"They're trees," I said with disgust.

"But they're making weird noises," Dirk whispered back. Rather, they were squawking. It was birds. We went back to our campsite, feeling foolish. We decided what had happened was that the moon had come up, making the sky lighter, outlining the trees against the horizon. It was a logical explanation, but maybe trees could be demons.

The next morning we woke with the dawn. Everything was clear and fresh as the sun touched the village walls with pinks and yellows. The silence was soft and beautiful, so clean you wanted to take hold of a piece of it. We built another fire for coffee, and took turns brushing our teeth. We didn't speak but sat on our haunches, steaming cups between our hands. There was something awesome in the dawn of the deserted village.

Three Wolof women came upon us and broke the spell. They were loud and pushy. They wanted the white people to give them a lift to the government post. One of the women picked up Dirk's jack-o'-lantern, turning the melon this way and that, dispassionately pulling it to pieces. Her fingers ground out the eyes and tore apart the mouth, as her face was turned to us, waiting to see if the *tubabs* were going to take them in the truck or if they would have to walk to Nianga.

We had forgotten to make tea for the spirits and I had thought to leave them sugar instead. It seemed important to leave something for them since they had let us spend the night within their walls, but to do so before these women would break the village's spell. The women would say something about it, laugh raucously at the strange ways of *tubabs*. So I kept the sugar, silently promising to myself that I would bring it back another time when there were no taunting eyes.

Dirk told the women we would take them and we packed up our things and left, the three women sitting in the back of the truck.

A month later we had to go to Dakar. I took twenty-seven sugar cubes out of the blue box of sugar sitting next to our coffee tin, and wrapped them in brown paper. Dirk checked the radiator and oil and hoses. We loaded our bags, locked the house, and drove to the village. We got out and climbed among the walls. It was already nine o'clock and the sun was high, beating the walls, the ground, and ourselves with its glaring heat. We went to look at our trees. There were three of them. We looked at each other.

"I only saw two," I said.

Dirk shook his head. We stood there a moment, lost in the feel of this place, wondering. Dirk turned and walked back to the truck. I took the wrapped sugar cubes from my pocket and stood still, surrounded by broken walls, the quietness of great time, and the whistling wind I felt had traveled the world 'round.

I stooped to leave the sugar in the dust, and as I pulled the paper free the cubes caught fire, a million pressed diamonds winking in the sun. I walked away then, back to the truck, smiling at the thought of the Pulaar spirits making their tea sweet with the sunfire cubes.

CHAPTER SIX

Taunting the White Woman

The river is the life blood of the Fouta touro. It is one strip of cool, sparkling wetness, cutting through a land dying of thirst. The people use it for everything—to do their laundry, their dishes, as their drinking water, to wash their animals and themselves. They gather on its banks and the young women wash their clothes, gossiping and laughing, while the children run naked, splashing each other, or try to catch fish with a scrap of cloth used as a seine. A little boy washes his father's horse, and a little girl her compound's dishes. An old woman sits half in the water and half out, her tired breasts reaching down past her waist, scrubbing the soles of her feet with the beach sand. In the pale evening light the village elders trickle down one at a time to remove their clothes and dip their dry brown bodies into the river's waters. The river is magic.

In Walli Jalla, a village path winds between walled-in compounds, past the *boutique* that sells little cans of Nescafé, down to a beach opening out on to the river. When the dry season comes, the water recedes, cutting steps into the banks, the river dwindling to a blue-green ribbon. I loved to watch the water flow. I thought it must have flowed exactly like this for centuries: unfettered by bridges, or trapped by dams, occasionally dotted by wooden dugout canoes.

This day I watched the water sparkle as the sun danced on its surface, and squinted my eyes at the smudgy lines of green across the opposite shore—rows of corn planted along the river bank steps. Everything was very bright and clear, as though it had just been washed, especially the sky. It was blue, but a blue that is not just a color, more a feeling—the coming of spring and wizards' crystal balls—as though if you

53

could look deep enough you could see what rests behind the sky. The cold season was coming and the temperature would no longer reach one hundred. The river brought out goose pimples in the early morning and late evening; in midafternoon it was perfect. I stood just where the river lapped against the sand, quiet and alone.

Alone. It had been so long since I had been alone. Only when I locked myself inside the house was I free of brown eyes forever staring at me. I had forgotten the luxury of standing by myself in a patch of sunlight.

I wrapped my *pagne* more tightly around my waist, took off my T-shirt and walked a little into the water. It was cool and soft, swishing around my calves as the sun warmed my bare back. A kingfisher that sat on a branch out over the water flew upward and hung in the sky, his blue and white body, hatchet head, and long quick beak silhouetted against the light. He plunged into the river and out, a thin silver fish parting his black beak as he returned to his perch.

I tried to fill my mind with nothing but the passing water, the kingfisher, and the silence. I wanted to forget my morning at the post office in Podor and hoped the river could help me—slowly wash away some of my frustration and anger.

It had been a bad morning. Dirk and I had driven to Podor, while the day was still pale and the post office locked, because we had heard there would be money. We had not been paid for a month. Fatu said if we did not pay her soon she would no longer be able to buy the food for our meals, and our *marabout* landlord had already come by five times asking for the rent. We had been to Podor three times before on similar rumors. We could no longer afford to walk across to the Sonadis, after the post office turned us away, to buy a soda.

There was no bank in Podor; what money came, came in *mandats*—postal orders—through the mail. Everyone needed money. It was seven in the morning when we arrived at the post office's wrought-iron gates, and already there was a little crowd of people standing, switching their weight from one leg to another, sitting on the three white steps or hunched down on their heels softly rocking back and forth in the quiet morning light.

There was one woman who didn't bother to squat. She sat in the dust to the right of the steps, and glared up at us as we joined the crowd. She was old and wore a ragged green *boubou* with a matching scarf tied round her head. Her eyes were bloodshot and squinty in her big wide face. They held hatred.

I glanced at her and then looked away at the rest of the crowd. I had seen her look before. There were tall old men in worn brown, blue, or white *boubous* leaning on canes, their necks and sometimes their heads wrapped in traditional Moslem scarves. Young Podor women, their *boubous* of bright satin cloth setting off their pretty faces and dangling earrings, chattered together in a small group off by themselves. Here and there the crowd was dotted with young men in slim western pants. Above everyone towered one old man, his face smooth with age, wearing a ragged *boubou* and a World War One pilot's hat. He looked very fine in his hat and I was thinking I had just learned how to say hat in Pulaar when the old woman spat out the word "*tubabs*".

Her Pulaar was ugly with derision. She said the word as though we were hideous fat white slugs. *Tubabs*, she asked, what were we doing here? We would take the money. We needed no money. Everyone knew *tubabs* were rich. They needed the money. They needed to eat. What right did we have to come to their country and steal their money? If we were paid, they would not be. There would be no money left for them, the Senegalese. Why did we come to their country, taking everything away from them?

I looked at her. She was fat—rolls of fat almost closing her small piglike eyes. She lived in Podor with electricity, water, and meat. I thought of my parents' house in Virginia with its plumbing and air conditioning, my soft suede boots, movie theaters, and pizza. I thought of Si, the bead lady, who sold the beautiful old porcelain trading beads I had slowly been collecting as treats for myself when things went badly. Things were bad, but I no longer had one hundred francs, thirty cents, to buy one of Si's beads.

The fat woman continued to spit her words out at us. I wanted to kick her, pound her face until she had to shut up. Her words hung in the crowd, the other people saying nothing, but you could feel they wanted to. They wanted to scream the woman's words, but did not have the courage, and I hated them for it.

Someone inside the post office opened the doors and the gates, making the people on the steps ripple as they rose to their feet. The crowd had grown and spilled itself inside the little room between the door and a counter which ran the width of the room's back wall. Behind the counter stood three men. Three men who would decide who would receive money—to buy rice or millet or pay the rent—and who would not.

The room was too small for so many people, and I was sandwiched between a huge Wolof woman and a skinny old Pulaar man. Dirk and I had been separated by the crowd and I could just barely see the top of his head pinioned against the far wall. I was swallowed beneath black arms waving *cartes d'identité* and *mandat* slips. Everyone was trying to stand taller, yell louder, push his neighbors to the sides—anything to be noticed by the men behind the counter, to be one of the chosen few to receive their month-late pay.

I was elbowed and stepped on. I elbowed and stepped on people back. The Wolof woman used her bulk to part the people in front of her and I followed in her wake, fighting for my place as everyone else tried to fill in the little gaps she left behind. I cannot remember if she got paid or not. She did make it to the counter and when she left there was a fraction of a second in which I could see an opening just in front of one of the three men. At least five people wanted to fill it and I pushed as hard as any Wolof and suddenly was face to face with the man behind the counter.

The man had a huge round head, teetering precariously on a long, skinny neck, and his face was pocked with acne. My hand was stretched forward to give him my *mandat* and passport. He looked at them silently, while I stared at him, all dressed up in Western clothes with a fancy leather belt. He spoke to me in French too quickly for me to understand and shook his head back and forth negatively. He wouldn't give me the money. He handed me back my papers and the people behind me tried to push me out of the way. I asked him why, and again he said something I couldn't understand.

I couldn't believe I had made it to the counter and still would not be paid. Again I pushed my way through the crowd, this time to its back edge to try and breathe. Everything was noise, confusion, and desperation, until all of a sudden it ended, as though someone had pulled a plug. Everyone stood down on the balls of their feet, returned their papers to their pockets, and silently began to file out of the room , one by one, back to the dusty roads surrounding the post office. The money had run out.

Dirk found me outside. I hated the crowd, the three men playing God, myself for not having understood the man's French. There was nothing for me to vent my anger on and words spilled out of my mouth hot with it, as I tried to tell Dirk what had happened. He hadn't made it to the counter and said he would go back in and ask the man why I hadn't been paid. I stayed outside waiting for him and he came back and told me I hadn't been paid because I was a government worker. Government workers would be paid last.

I stood silently watching the river bird fish for what seemed like a long time. The water eddied around my thighs and I hoped it had the power to soak away my anger, my wanting to kick an old woman, to slowly draw out the meanness festering inside me. This world took so much; wrung you out almost to the point of breaking, and then gave back a moment like this. I wanted to hold onto it and was afraid it would be taken from me. I needed it.

I felt eyes on my back and turned around. There was a whole tribe of little boys standing up on the bank, staring at me with shining, taunting, let's-watch-the-white-woman-wash eyes and jeering grins, sexual implications plastered all over their too-young faces.

When I had first come to Walli Jalla, Dirk and Dabo had told a story about a little boy they had caught and punished. They recounted with relish how Dabo had held him while he squirmed and pleaded and Dabo beat a portion of respect into his eight-year-old body. The next day, they said, the boy's mother came to thank Dabo. I had looked at them grinning while they spoke, at their obvious enjoyment in having beaten a child, and been horrified.

But no more. The children never left me alone. Never. They would line up along the outside of my compound wall—a row of black headless bodies chanting "*tubab*", yelling insults, and laughing because the white woman couldn't fight back. Every day, when I came back from the station, I was greeted by an overturned trash can and little pieces of paper and garbage they had strewn around the compound yard. They would come, their heads poking over the wall and watch me pick up all the pieces of trash. They would heckle and insult me, the village white woman, and try me just to the point of snapping. I would lunge at them, and they would run away in different directions—as impossible to catch as mercury.

The whole land seemed to jeer at me, the white woman who knew nothing, who did not belong in this country—but the children did it deliberately and wickedly, and they were as inescapable as the flies.

I asked them what they were staring at and told them to leave. That only made it worse. One started speaking in a high-pitched voice mimicking the white people's French. "*Qu'est-ce qu'il y a? C'est ça. Qu'est-ce qu'il y a? C'est ça.*" over and over. His high-pitched, mocking voice shattered the silence of the river and his small face was distorted with scorn. I wanted to wring his neck.

I picked up my soap from the bank and entered the river. I would ignore the little boys; maybe the river could give me enough peace to forget them. I soaped my arms, chest, and back with the big cake of peanut soap, dunked my head under, washed beneath my *pagne,* and got out to get my shampoo. After soaking my hair and rinsing it, I tried to recapture the feeling of the river, the quiet constant passing of the water, but could not. I sat on the bank and scrubbed my feet, rubbing off the dead skin and the dirt, and the whole time I felt those jeering eyes.

I got out and stood facing them, reaching for my towel. They started again. "*Tuuuuubab, Tuuuuubab, Tuuuuubab, Tuuuuubab.*" Over and over and over. "Leave me alone!" I screamed. The words echoed off the banks. "*Tuuuuubab, Tuuuuubab, Tuuuuubab, Tuuuuubab.*" Their faces grinned down at me.

I wanted to slap one of those faces, to hit and hit until it would never grin again. Grabbing my shirt and shrugging it on, I charged up the hill. I would teach these boys to have respect. I ran barefoot through the village in my wet *pagne*. I would catch one of those kids if it killed me. For once, they would see what it felt like. For once, I would win.

They were just barely out of reach. I would come racing around a corner only to glimpse one of them slipping around the corner ahead of me. This time I would not give up. I prayed to God to let me catch one.

I ran between compound walls, thinking of nothing but catching one of those little black bodies and pounding the impudence out of it. Someone called to me, but I didn't listen. I was around another corner, past another compound. The voice called again. It was a man's voice. I heard him, but couldn't stop. This was my chance. Don't ask me to stop! But a young woman could not refuse to answer an old man. In the ways of my village, that was unacceptable, so I went back and entered the compound's walls. A whole family was sitting out under a thatched awning, making afternoon tea. I looked at their faces. I didn't think they wanted to help me. They probably thought it was funny that the white woman had been worked into such a fury, running through the village like a mad woman. It would probably be the most exciting thing that happened that day. They wanted to hear the story first, so they could tell it to others around the night's dinner bowl. I would never be able to catch one of the children now.

I was shaking so hard it was difficult to go through the greetings. I didn't give a damn about this old man's health. I cut the greetings short.

"What bothers you?" he asked me. His face was deeply lined and tranquil.

"*Sukaabe!*" I threw the word at him. It seemed to hang there in the middle of all those quiet, questioning faces.

"Which children?" he asked.

I didn't know and that made it worse. I was sure I had greeted one or two of them moments after they had taunted me, but I didn't know their names and couldn't recognize most of their faces.

"I don't know which children. Boys. They always taunt me.

Bad. *Sukaabe moyyaani.* If I catch one, I beat him until death."
If nothing else, someone in the village would know I had had
it.

All the brown faces were turned toward me, eyes ex-
pressionless, faces smooth.

"Where did the children run to?" the man asked me.

"Toward the pumping station."

They would never be caught now. It would go on and on
and on. They would turn over the trash. I would pick it up.
They would throw rocks at my house. I would chase them.

I left the compound. There was nothing else to do, and I
didn't want to see amusement in these people's faces. I would
scream if I saw more laughter at the white woman in their
eyes.

I went back to the river to get my soap, shampoo, and towel
and tried again to recapture the peace, but it had been
replaced by disgust and bitterness. I had lost my control,
made a fool of myself. I had come down to their seven-year-
old level. The only thing they respected was a beating and I
was incapable of catching one to give it to him. I didn't
belong here. It was always the same, inside my head warred
the voices of America and the voices of Senegal, and I could
never seem to be true to either one.

I picked up my things and walked slowly back down the
path, toward my compound. I had had it with everything—
Senegal, the children, myself. I kicked at the dust with my
blue flip-flop.

I was almost back to my compound when the old man
called to me again. I turned around to see what he wanted.
He was walking along the path, dragging a little boy by the
arm. He had to walk slowly because the boy refused to walk
on his own two feet and was squirming in every direction—
arms and legs, his whole body wiggling one way and then the
other, like a writhing snake. I couldn't see how the old man
held him.

He had caught one!

I was excited; I had never thought the man actually meant
to help, let alone that he would be able to. Finally it would be
my turn.

No. It would not. I would not get the chance to see the boy

punished because I wouldn't be able to recognize him. The old man would ask me if this was one of the bad children; I wouldn't know, so he would have to let him go.

The boy was wailing and cringing and kicking at the open air. Surely, he was one of them. Even if he was not one of the boys from this afternoon, he must have taunted me another day. The Senegalese would not hesitate. Have him beaten and the daily tormenting will end, but what if he really wasn't one of the jeering faces on the bank? Can you have a child beaten when you aren't sure he did anything wrong? I hated the voice of American conscience. It should have no power in this land of thatch villages, dust, and flies; but it did.

The man stood before me. I had never seen such an act as the one this little boy was putting on. He did everything but melt away into the dust of the path. He rolled his eyes until there was nothing left but whites, whimpered pathetically, and shrank away from me as though I were a demon. Then I realized that this was the one boy I knew. His head was shaped like an egg. He always yelled the loudest, grinned the widest, and escaped the fastest.

The man asked me if this was one of them, and I said yes; and then I realized I didn't want the old man to hand him to me. I wouldn't know what to do with him. My anger left; I couldn't beat him. He was a child.

Luckily, all the man needed was my confirmation. I don't know if he let go of the boy, or if the boy finally wriggled free. The last I saw, they were running wildly down the path, the old man close on the little boy's heels, his rubber flip-flop swatting the air and infrequently hitting the boy's back.

I turned and walked back to my compound. This time I wore the grin.

CHAPTER SEVEN

Lion Country

I had dreamt of lions. I was sitting up on a little hill and saw two lions walking before me down on the plain. I caught my breath in excitement. I had seen lions caged at the zoo, and once in a wildlife park but never in the wild. They were a male and a female, all tawny and tightly muscled. Their bodies parted the tall savannah grass, their muscles rippling as though made of liquid. They walked almost leisurely, with the taught gracefulness of predators.

I watched them until they were out of sight. It was not at all like seeing them in the zoo. They belonged here in the savannah, out in the open. They were so threateningly beautiful. I had seen them as I sat up on the hill unprotected and alone; nothing but the swaying grass separated me from the lions. This was their land.

But then the cats circled and came around in back, climbing the hill. Now, they were hunting me. I jumped to my feet and ran and ran and ran, as they followed. I couldn't run fast enough and they were getting closer and closer, almost on my heels. I couldn't escape. No matter how fast I ran, the lions ran faster. In a moment they would catch me and I would feel wild claws and fangs and tearing flesh, my own flesh. I ran like a demon to save my life, my heart pounding faster, and faster. Just as the cats were about to pounce, someone drove by in the project truck and stopped. The driver yelled and I jumped into the back. The truck started with a lurch and I awoke.

I was safe, safe in the comforting Walli Jalla night. There were no lions. Nothing hunted me. I was drenched with sweat and shaking.

In March, a month later, Dirk and I camped on the banks of the Fallemé in southeastern Senegal. This really was lion country, only Dirk said they would have all gone south by now, this far into the dry season. Dirk said there could not be more than twenty lions left in Senegal, and our chances of seeing one nonexistent. The villagers told us lions did live here. One or two of them had seen a lion during his lifetime and said they were very frightful. We should not sleep out in the open, to stay close to the villages. But then they said the animals wouldn't harm us, that they ran from humans. I wondered if the animals wouldn't hurt us, why they warned us to sleep near the villages?

We didn't take their advice. Almost all the southern Senegalese were afraid to sleep in the open, some even on the Fleuve, and there were no wild animals to hurt one there. This was our great African adventure. We didn't want to be white tourists looking for African thrills with guides and rifles, air-conditioned vans, and hotels up on stilts that look down on salt licks. We wanted to be in the wild—the bush, the animals, and ourselves.

The banks of the Fallemé looked the way Africa was supposed to look. Waist-high strands of golden grass covered everything. It smelled sweet when it was broken, as though it had captured the smell of spring inside its blades and could hold it there through the dry season, in memory of the rains which had passed but would come again. It swayed in the wind, making the earth's lines, so harsh on the Fleuve, softly golden. There were trees and bushes and little hillocks. Herons sat in the topmost branches of tall old trees as the sun sank, a huge red orb, behind them. A fish eagle followed the curves of the river from high above and then dove down, down, down, a rock of feathers plummeting into the water, to rise again, a fish caught in its talons. Little monkeys came down to the water on the far bank to wash and drink and play. A lone hippo, the last to live this far north, surfaced with a great snort not a mile away. The sound of tam tams echoed off the river's banks and into the darkness as we sat by our fire that first night on the Fallemé.

This was our vacation, Dirk's and mine, and we had been

planning it for months. We had originally meant to back-
pack along the Fallemé for as far as we could walk in four
days. But the packs were way too heavy and we were already
caught up by this spot. There was one large watering hole
among black rocks, and here we had found wild boar prints,
as well as cats', and hyenas'.

I loved the days. The mornings were so clear—still cool
before the sun's vengeance. We made friends with one of the
fishermen from the village across the river and each morning
he would come in his dugout canoe and give us the fresh-
water lobsters he had caught and we would offer him coffee
or tea. We would sit on the soft sand beach that made the
river curve around it and which was planted with great
calabashes ready to be harvested, and talk of what we had
seen the day before, of what we hoped to see that day, of the
hippo and how lonely it must be, or of the deep beauty of this
place. It was as though the black rocks and the lone hippo,
the fisherman, and the calabashes on the beach had all begun
to seep into us, until the land had become a part of us and we
a part of the land.

For lunch we would cook rice, or eat dry Nar biscuits. One
day we ate Nar biscuits and a tin of pâté Dirk had bought in
Dakar as a treat. By siesta the sun would again own the land
and we would nap in the shade of the big tree we slept under
at night. In the afternoons, we would explore. One afternoon
we were awakened from our siesta by an angry baboon off in
the bush, barking his rage at us for blocking the path to the
river. I grabbed my camera, and we walked toward the noise.

A path led from the river into the bush until it was lost in
the undergrowth. There were no villages on this side of the
river. The track was made by animals on their way to drink.
Twenty feet from our camp the trail ran by an old tree that
had been hit by lightning. Sitting on it was a huge, angry
baboon.

He saw us and barked louder, jumping up and down, from
branch to branch and then back to the trunk. He did everything, but shake his fist at us. We were mesmerized by him,
his anger, his size, his humanness. He was so big. We stood
watching until we began to see other baboons in the bush,
recalled the stories we had heard of how nasty they could be,

and decided to go back to camp before we were engulfed by a tribe.

We thought the baboons would go to the watering hole. I wanted to get a picture of them. I took off my boots and rushed through the water along the bank thinking it would be faster than the meandering path. I was so excited about getting a good photo of baboons, that for a moment I forgot our discussion about whether there were crocodiles in the river or not. There were several rotting logs partly submerged that reminded me of the reptiles, sending me quickly back to the path.

I came to the watering hole, Dirk just behind me. The baboon tribe was there, as was the huge male. They covered the bank and encircled the water, jumping, barking, and fighting amongst themselves. There must have been more than a hundred of them. We inched closer and closer as I took photos. My camera lust faded and I retreated, the baboons looking riled. I didn't want one of them throwing me down and jumping on me as they were doing to each other.

We saw them at the watering hole several afternoons in a row, but never so many again. Other afternoons we would sit on the opposite bank from our camp, make tea and wait for the hippo to come. We could hear her from a long way off, as she came to the surface snorting water out of her great round nostrils and sucking down the clean air. For some reason we were sure she was female and named her Tina.

One afternoon she came directly in front of us, wiggled her ears in curiosity, as though to figure out what kind of creatures we were, and left us with a final snort.

The days were wonderful. I had never known such peace and felt as though I was part of the land, but the nights were terrifying. I knew there were lions in the bush around us, even though Dirk repeatedly said it wasn't so. The first evening we had slept on the beach, and just before we lay down we heard a deep growl on the other side of the bank. Dirk said it must be a hyena.

There had been huge round hippo prints, not far from where we had decided to sleep and I thought the lady hippo might step on us in the dark on her way to dinner. I tried to convince myself we would hear her long before we were stepped on, but I was not comforted. We heard all sorts of animals, some quite close to us as they came to drink. I pretended they were dreams and couldn't hurt me. In the morning there were tracks all about us, messages left in the wet sand, of the dreams that had come to drink at the water's edge.

After that we slept a little way up the bank under the biggest tree. I convinced Dirk we should at least put up the mosquito net. The first night we slept beneath it I felt safe and cozy and for once, slept well. By the second night, I was too aware of how flimsy mosquito netting was, and of how little stood between me and the night. I no longer felt safe under its gauze.

Half our vacation had passed the night we tied the net's corners to the branches and set out our sleeping bags. Dirk wanted to read by flashlight and I wanted to fall asleep while he was still awake. We crawled under the net and I balled my *pagne* up into a pillow and listened to Dirk turning the pages. It sounded very loud and I wanted to tell him to be more quiet.

Something tickled the inside of my leg, and I lectured myself about having too vivid an imagination. The tickling did not go away, however, and seemed to be crawling higher, inch by inch. I sat up, grabbed the flashlight from Dirk, and shone it on my thigh. A huge, hairy, frightened spider sat caught in the beam. It tried to get away from the light by crawling higher and I screamed, swishing him off the crotch of my underpants, as I yelled at Dirk. Dirk flailed after the spider as it ran here and there and finally became entangled in the net. He crushed it with his book.

The night was quiet again. Dirk went back to his book and I turned away. I never killed spiders. They were harmless and trapped flies in their webs. The spider had been as frightened as I and hadn't meant to hurt me. He had simply wandered into the wrong territory; climbed on a leg instead of a tree root. It was my fear that killed the spider.

Later, I awoke while the night was still black, and Dirk was breathing peacefully next to me. The night was full of sounds—grass breaking under foot, fish jumping, a bird awakening and going back to sleep, insects hopping and buzzing and talking, and the wind whispering. I could hear animals off in the bush, walking on the path where we had made our camp. One sounded as though it was just around the corner, on the other side of the sapling where we laid our heads.

It must be a *phacochère*, a wild boar, I told myself. *Phacos* are not carnivorous. Even if he walked right up, he would just sniff at me, realize I was not good to eat, and run away. But he would never get that close. The natives had all said wild animals were afraid of humans. Dirk had said they were much more afraid of us than we were of them. They could smell us from far away and we smelled bad. But, what if a lion started hunting the *phacos* and they stampeded and ran right over us; would we die?

Dirk continued to breath evenly. It made me furious. He had gotten me into this, convinced me to take unnecessary risks, and now he was sleeping peacefully. He had no right to be happily asleep. Maybe his sleeping noises attracted hunters.

I looked up at the Big Dipper. I had picked it out of the sky so many times. Dad and I had sat on the front steps in Potsdam, when I was a little girl, and he had pointed up at it and the Little Dipper. I had been safe; I had been a little girl, and Dad had known everything and protected me from all that was bad or scary. I thought if I stared hard enough at the Big Dipper I could recapture a shadow of that safety. The moon had set, and the stars were all very bright, the way they become when they do not have to share the sky. They were too bright for morning to be near.

I turned over on my stomach. I had read somewhere an analysis of sleeping positions. I thought it had said you felt safer on your stomach. I tried to tell myself not to be so scared, everything would be all right, but I could hear footsteps coming down the path. It must be a large animal. I couldn't see anything and the footsteps kept coming closer and closer. My heart pounded as it had never pounded before. I thought surely it would break open my body or I would have a heart attack. I was sweating and animals could sense fear. The steps stopped. The animal could not be more

than five feet away. We both seemed to hold our breath.
Then, it turned away.

I woke Dirk up.

"Dirk, I am so frightened."

"Huh?"

"Shhh. I am so scared. You can't fall asleep. You have to
stay awake with me. What time do you think it is?"

"Two or three."

"Dirk."

"Huh?"

"Don't fall asleep Dirk."

"I won't."

"Dirk!"

"What?"

"You were asleep."

"No I wasn't. I was just thinking about the price of building
Senegalese school houses."

"Dirk, don't fall asleep." But he did.

My heart had subsided, but not my fear. I didn't want to
die. I wanted to see my parents. It had been a year. I wanted
to meet my niece, eat a bag of Doritos, go to a grocery store, a
bar, a movie. I would die, and what for? for nothing, for an
animal I could see in a zoo.

I tried to think of something to make myself laugh. I tried
to think of things that were safe—of Walli Jalla and my
compound and my bed and my occasional boredom. I had
wanted an adventure, but now I was throwing away my life,
for some National Geographic idea of Africa. It was so stupid.

I prayed to God. I was such a fool I almost deserved to die.
How many centuries had humans spent training animals, or
hunting them, caging them, or killing them, and now they
risked their lives just to catch a glimpse of them. I was
selective in my beliefs in God, but if he would let me live, I
would do better. I would make Dirk sleep in the village on
the other bank with me tomorrow. I would not sleep at the
watering hole as we had planned. I would not go out in the
bush tomorrow morning looking for the *phacos*. I would have
more respect for God's beasts.

I could hear what sounded like a pack of dogs, far off in

the distance. Hyenas. They were supposed to be worse than lions. Dirk had read an African mammal guide that said hyenas would eat the faces off people sleeping in the open.

If I lived to morning, I would not forget all of this. It was not something to be forgotten, to let evaporate with the morning light. I will remember, God, if you let me live. I will remember what you have taught me, but I did not know if I would ever feel safe again. I wouldn't forget this night but I wanted to forget that I would die, if not this night, some night. I had felt this great, black, cold nothingness and I wanted to forget it had ever touched me, to push it from my mind. Death was a terrifying, gaping hole that I must enter completely alone, with nothing from this world. I had never known death before.

The sky looked almost gray. Hadn't the stars begun to dim? Dawn had finally come and it seemed not so much the beginning of another day but the gift of a second life.

The next night we slept in the village. It was late afternoon when we walked between the huts. Men were gathered in a cluster making the mortars women used to pound millet. They were in all forms of creation—the thick, still barked, slices of tree trunk, slabs of trunk with their middles hollowed out, and the finished mortars smooth and practical standing on their bases. The men stopped working when we walked among them. They came and spoke to us, asked if we wanted to buy their mortars, told us they had heard of us staying on the other bank. We spoke for a while, but the reception was cool, and no one asked us to stay. Men started going back to their work. Dirk wanted to leave. I would sleep in the village, invited or not. If I had to, I would sleep right there in their village square. Finally, a well-dressed man reluctantly asked us to come stay in his compound.

We didn't know why they were so cool. They had told us their chief had died the week before, that was why we had heard the tam tams. Did they think our presence and their chief's death were somehow connected? They told us other white people had come before us, some with rifles to hunt the boar, and one woman who spent months looking at rocks.

I stretched my Pulaar to its limits. They said they had never spoken to a white person who knew their language. We spoke of lions and hyenas and the bush. When the women brought us our meal, I spoke with them of millet and leaf sauce and goat's milk. A young woman with a pretty face brought us a bowl of millet and milk and I told her it was my favorite of all food, that she was the best of hostesses. She laughed. A white woman who liked *lacciri e kosam*.

We held each other's hands and I told her I was afraid of lions. When it was time to sleep the woman said something to the men and they told us not to sleep on the bed they had originally given us, but to sleep inside. We said we were more comfortable under the sky and they brought us a wooden bed.

In the middle of the night I awoke, felt the hard slats of the wooden bed and listened to the night sounds. Dogs began to bark, and I turned on my side. I was safe, in the village compound.

When dawn came, I felt disoriented, finding myself surrounded by an unfamiliar village family with their morning routines. Dirk and I wiped sleep from our eyes and someone brought us water. A woman came selling milk she carried in a calabash on her head. Rougi, the woman who had spoken to me the night before, bought a little milk and I tried to tell her to buy more. She sent a child to bring the woman back, but she didn't understand I wanted to buy the milk for her, for her sharing of their meal the night before. The woman returned and I bought a big bowl of the rich white liquid. Rougi told me how sweet and cool it was and that it would be good for me. I said, no, it was for her, for sharing her *lacciri e kosam* with white strangers. She did not want to accept it, saying I should keep it for myself, but I insisted.

Our fisherman came and found us in the compound. He held at arm's length the antennas of three lobsters, leaving their bodies to swing delicately back and forth in the air. He presented them to me very seriously, his body twitching with happiness and excitement at having tracked us down. He was Malian and spoke almost no Pulaar. I said we had already eaten breakfast. He shook his head no; he did not understand. He was so pleased with his crustaceans. I smiled and reached out, as he graciously passed the antennas from his hand to mine; everyone in the compound silently watching the ceremony.

We gave the family what was left of our powdered milk, tea, and mosquito repellent, and thanked them for their hospitality.

It was our last day, our last night, and Dirk wanted to spend it at the watering hole. We took our leave of the village, saying we might come back, but most likely not. We wanted our last day to be everything.

We wandered the banks and swam in the river. We spoke a little of things ending, but tried to make it not seem so. Dirk wanted more than anything to spend the night on the little peninsula sitting out like a finger in the watering hole. He said animals were afraid of water and that we could make a barricade across the point where the peninsula joined the land. We would keep a fire burning after the evening light had faded.

I still wanted to go back to the village, but the walk was long and I had a fever. We slept by the water and saw no animals. Only one hyena came down to drink and he stood off in the dark barking at us, and then went to drink at a puddle.

The dawn was beautiful, an African morning, with the huge pale sun shining through the black lace of the trees' branches. We didn't want to speak. We didn't want it to be over. When would we sit on the banks of the Fallemé again?

We made a fire and coffee, using our voices to break the spell. Our time was up. We had to go. Again, I said there were lions here, I could feel them. They were off in the bush and they had come close to us the night I was so frightened. One of the villagers had said he could take us to where they came to drink. Dirk said it would be nice to think of them out there, but he didn't believe it.

We packed our belongings. We were completely out of food, so the packs were much lighter, and I was glad because the original walk from the truck to the river had been almost unbearable. Our skins were burned red-brown from the sun, and our hair streaked to match the grass. We were hungry and tired. It would be good to drink a cold soda.

We started up the path to the next village, where we had

left the truck. We had lived a fantasy. I chattered about the photos I had taken. I was very proud of them. I half-wanted to become a wildlife photographer, but now I wondered. I had been terrified and didn't want to feel like that again. Did wildlife photographers get scared? Dirk said he would miss the hippo. It was sad she lived here all alone. The bush was slipping away as we walked along the well-marked path. Soon we would be at the village.

"Dirk!" I stopped dead, pointing to the ground. He came up beside me. There were tracks in the dust. Huge tracks, as big as both my hands put together. They were big round pugs deeply imprinted in the sand.

A lion had walked the path before us.

CHAPTER EIGHT

Dabo's Birthday Party

Dabo wanted balloons, not just any balloons but lots of red ones. He wanted them for his birthday party, and asked me if I could buy them for him when I went to Dakar. I looked at Dabo's face when he asked me, looked at him hard, and thought of his conversation with Abdoulaye and Demba in Wolof, telling them we were white people who came to their country only for ourselves, to make them work long, hard hours on our fish program, a crazy white-person's fish program—growing fish like millet—ordered them to work for us at the wrong hours at the wrong times without buying them motorcycles or uniforms or giving them housing, like the forestry program did in Podor.

Balloons always seemed to me like little bright scraps of dreams tied to strings, and so I went from store to store in Dakar looking for them, packages with a lot of red, thinking of Dabo—his muscles bunching under his skin tight and deft as he had built a chair or shelves, his face, which became smooth and wide-eyed when he lied, his wanting red balloons and knowing I would get them for him.

The big department store was out of balloons. I finally found some in a grocery store. I checked very carefully for the red spots of color in each plastic bag and remembered the afternoon Dirk, Dabo, and I had been riding in the cab of the truck and Dabo had been listening to his Walkman. He had bought the bright yellow waterproof tape player, from a Peace Corps volunteer just before the volunteer returned to the States and wore it almost every day.

This time he had been sitting between Dirk and me listening to a Bob Seger tape. Dirk knew the tape; he had given it to Dabo. I remember at first Dabo sat with his earphones on, far away, the only one allowed into his music world. Then he very deliberately looked at Dirk and then at me, pulled a second set of earphones from his bag, plugged them in, and handed them to Dirk. Dabo helped Dirk put the earphones over his head as he drove.

I picked the package of balloons with the most red and went to the check-out counter to pay. I was remembering the time Cindi, Kevin, and I went to the station on a Saturday afternoon, to fish with the home-made fishing poles that were kept in the workers' room.

Dabo was there when we arrived and I asked him where the little stick poles with their fish twine were? His face smoothed over like a deep lake swallowing a stone and he shook his head back and forth, to show he did not understand. I repeated the question. It was a simple one. I repeated it five times and Dabo's face became smoother and smoother. He spread his hands wide, his fingers extended to show he was trying his best to understand, but my French was simply too garbled. Finally he said in a condescending tone, "Suzanne I cannot understand your French. What is it that you want?" The week before Dabo and I had used those poles. He had understood my French then.

Still, I bought the balloons. I bought them and carried them as though they were precious stones instead of bits of colored rubber. I walked back to the Peace Corps administration building thinking of the afternoon I had tried to tell Dirk what Dabo was doing to me.

We had been sitting in the kitchen of the Walli Jalla house sweating and watching the dust, and I had tried to tell him how Dabo could make me feel—the Walkman, and the French, and the time I loaned him my red sweat shirt and he took it home over the weekend and said I was rude when I saw him in the *marché* that Saturday and asked for it back.

Dirk had watched me as I spoke, the words spilling out, and tumbling over each other. Parts of me broke loose and I had to stop speaking to control myself.

"Let yourself cry," Dirk had said.

But I would not cry. I hadn't cried for the skinny man and his dead baby, who we took to Podor one afternoon. The man sat in the back of the truck cradling the tiny corpse, thinking white-man's medicine could save it, while I sat in the cab, silent and empty. No, I had not cried for the child or the father; I would not let Dabo make me cry for myself.

I brought the package of balloons back to Walli Jalla and the next day gave them to Dabo. When I agreed to buy the balloons, it had been on the condition Dabo pay me back. Somewhere between Dakar and the station, I decided I wanted them to be a gift because no one before had ever given Dabo of the Mandengs balloons. No one before had ever told Dabo about birthdays—until he lived and worked with Americans.

It was Dirk who told him, the year before on Dirk's birthday as they sat in the Walli Jalla compound with the dust dancing around them, turning the world and the sky into nothing but a million pinpricks of drab brownness. The stars were lost first to the dust, and then the neighbors' compounds, their own walls, and finally even the neem tree.

It was Dirk's twenty-fourth birthday. He spent it working at the station the way he did every day, covered with mud, seining, and fixing dikes, with no one knowing this day was any different from the others. He waited until the work was done, keeping his secret to himself, thinking about the secretary's office at S.A.E.D., Societé l'Exploitation et d'Aménagement de la terre du Delta, where he received his mail, and about birthday cards and maybe a slip saying he had a package at the post office in Podor.

When they finally got to S.A.E.D. the secretary's office was locked and Dirk had to go and find Ebu to open the room with its treasure—a little wire bin of letters. There were at least twenty envelopes—blue aerogrammes; silver-gray, long, thin rectangles with planes flying across their bottom corners; and plain brown Senegalese envelopes that had *"par avion"* stamped on them, but none of them were for Dirk. He looked through the pile twice to make sure.

He and Dabo thanked Ebu for opening the room, and went back to the truck. Dirk decided to go by Bautch's to see if he had any beer to sell, and he collected the cold green bottles and took them to Walli Jalla. He and Dabo sat on the front step in the dust, drinking the beer and talking. Dabo said there was a white woman in Podor who wanted to sleep with him. They talked about what it would be like when they lived in Podor: the electricity, the meat, the Sonadis with its beers and cold sodas. They talked about the house they would find, but not about how they would afford it. Dabo told a story about when he was a little boy in the Casamance, the southernmost region of Senegal, and he had to act as a human scarecrow in the millet fields. Dirk talked about living in Nigeria where the women wore choker necklaces all the way up their necks and if you cut the necklaces the women would no longer be able to hold up their heads, and they would dangle like buds too heavy for their stalks. Dabo wanted to know about America, not another African country, so Dirk told him stories about American birthdays.

He explained that in America the day you are born becomes a holiday. Each year your friends and family throw you a party on that day. They put all sorts of bright balloons and crepe paper up, and buy you funny cards, and sing "Happy Birthday" when you walk into the room. Then someone brings out a cake with fancy icing and "Happy Birthday" written on it, and it has as many candles as you have years, and if you can blow them all out in one breath you get to have a wish come true. There are lots of gifts all wrapped in special paper with designs and pictures and ribbons, which only you get to unwrap to see what is inside, and everyone laughs and claps and treats you as though you are king for a day.

Dabo liked that story, and pictured bright colors and gifts all for himself out of the dust which had swallowed their world.

Dirk ended his birthday by vomiting into the trash pile that collected in the far corner of the compound. He vomited beer over the scraps of paper and tin cans and one broken rubber shoe. He couldn't remember if Dabo was sick or not. He didn't want to remember anything about that night.

Dabo remembered. Half a year later he began to ask about birthday parties. He wanted to know what he had to do to have one. Dirk told him he had to know what day he was born. Dabo didn't know how old he was. There is a naming ceremony a week after each child is born, but the date is not written down, and it is not celebrated again. Dabo said he would try to figure out the day he was born, and a week later told Dirk he had been born on the 27th of December. There was one problem. Dabo wanted to have a big birthday party for himself, with Dirk and I there, but we had to be in Dakar on that date.

He was very upset, so Dirk stretched the birthday rules a little. He told Dabo he didn't have to have his party on the actual day of his birth, lots of people had them months later. Americans did it that way all the time.

This made Dabo happy again and he set his party for the 11th of January.

The day before Dabo's party was a Friday. Dirk decided to stay home to work on reports, and I drove to the station by myself. There was a lot of work to be done and I was hoping for once Dabo would be there on time, and that he and Demba would just do the work without complaints, fights or tricks.

There was no longer any peace at the station. Always, there was an underlying tension like when the air is pulled tight just before a thunderstorm. It didn't break, but grew and grew, infecting everything, only seeping out in small ways that led to no relief. Dabo almost always came to work late, walking up the driveway with loose fluid movements in his fancy city-boy clothes, acting as though we were the ones breaking the rules by expecting him to arrive on time; Abdoulaye, Demba, and Dabo repeatedly told stories of how things had been different when Steve was there—he had given them money for tea, and sometimes meat for a special meal. He had worked like a man. They said he spent all his weekends with them, drinking tea and talking in the heat. I knew that was not true because he had a girlfriend who he visited in Guidakhar. I told them that angrily and then was sorry. They worshiped Steve.

Nothing was ever done voluntarily. Only after Dirk and I suggested and then ordered and then badgered was anything accomplished. Then it was done sullenly and in the most inefficient, uncaring manner—simply so it could be said it was done. More and more often their faces became closed, like the oily masks the merchants wore in the Dakar markets. Hardly ever now did the wind pass by the station to find laughter and carry it off into the *waalo*.

Each morning I woke up hoping that somehow things would be better and I'd try to think of one small thing that would be good during the day. The hope left, but still I would try to find something to shine before my eyes in the early morning light, even if it was only the thought of watching the rainbow rings of oil spread on the surface of a pond as I washed my hands after lunch. The morning before Dabo's party I could think of nothing. I only hoped the day wouldn't be too long.

When I pulled into the station, Demba came to greet me. Dabo had not yet arrived. Demba asked of my health and tiredness and I asked of his family and his family's health. Demba's face was wide and placid; he made me think of a cow. There was a story that he had been nice to Dabo, when Dabo first moved to the Fleuve, and Dabo got him hired. He followed Dabo around like a puppy. Demba had been working at the station for two years and still managed to trip over his own feet when he was pulling the seine. I wouldn't have hired him. If Dabo didn't come to work today, we would never get the work done. Demba hadn't stopped speaking and told me he was too sick to work this day.

He held up his bare foot to show me. It was dry and cracked, deep painful cracks that went into the sole. He showed me his heel. Here it was so dry the cracks had connected and a whole chunk of his flesh was beginning to come away from his foot. He pulled it as far out as possible, to demonstrate, wincing with the pain. Underneath it was bright red and rough like raw meat. Looking at it made my insides contract. He showed it to me five times.

Demba said I should take him to the S.A.E.D. doctor, as though it was my duty and he would die if I didn't. I was to drop all work and look after his heel. He was a grown man, who had somehow survived before the coming of white-people bosses. His heel was bad, I saw that, but he made such an act out of it, was so happy it meant at least one day off from work that I was tempted to tell him he could sit and wait while Dabo and I worked and then I would take him to the doctor. What was happening to me that I could treat a man like a plow horse? I said I would take him as soon as Dabo arrived.

The day hadn't started, no work had been done and there was so much to do. Now half the day would be spent with Demba at the doctor's and the other half was already ruined because Dabo was late. I would have to tell him if he came late he must stay late, the way I always told him, and then we would fight, always the same fight and no one ever won. Sometimes I wanted to just drop it, so it wouldn't color the rest of the day, but then Dabo would have won.

At nine o'clock he walked up the driveway whistling and swinging his bag. Demba and I immediately climbed into the truck. I said I was taking Demba to the doctor, but would be back soon. Dabo smiled as though it was a new day, untarnished, and we were all great friends. I was not ready for the fight yet. First, I would take Demba to the doctor.

When I returned three hours later, Dabo still hadn't changed into his work clothes. He was making tea, squatting in front of the charcoal burner, wearing his fancy jeans with the pockets and zippers, an old St. Patrick's Day t-shirt Dirk had given him, and a baseball cap that was red and white and said "Coke" on the crown.

I said nothing to him as I climbed from the truck and went into the office to change into my pond clothes. They were still wet from the day before. It seemed I was constantly muddy and wet. When I stepped out of the cinder-block room I almost fell over Dabo as he poured himself a glass of tea.

"Dabo we're going to finish harvesting pond number three."

He looked at me blankly, and continued drinking his tea. I walked off alone with the dip net. I didn't want to play Dabo's games today. I was too tired. I would start the work myself. The hell with Dabo.

I walked through the brown water in the bottom of the pond, water left where it was too low to drain and wasn't deep enough to seine. There were still fish in it and they had to be taken out. The only way was to try to catch them one by one with the dip net. It was hard work, hard, back-breaking, dirty work. Before it had been different, and I still had that picture in my head. It mocked me, that image of what it had been, could be, but was no longer.

That other time it had been Dirk, Dabo, and I working together and there had been four inches of the opaque water like a brown lid covering twenty fish. It had been one of those rare days when the sky was blue, touching us all, making us feel more alive. I don't remember who first thought of catching the fish with the dip net; it was probably Dabo.

We had turned it into a contest, two people sitting up on the bank, the mud hardening on their skin as though God had just created them, looking now and then at a watch as the minutes slipped away, watching the third person desperately scoop at the brown water with the little net, trying to catch more fish in twelve minutes than the other two could.

It was tricky. Occasionally, a fish would come to the surface to pipe, sucking air into its mouth and leaving behind a telltale bull's eye that would grow and grow. But we couldn't wait for these because they came up too infrequently. We had to walk up and down the pond, bent double with our hands in the water, feeling for the slightest ripple of a fish with fingers and feet, and an intuition which was slowly born of working with fish day after day.

The easiest ones to catch were the ones that panicked when they sensed our prowling. They would go wildly skittering up on the mud flats, flapping desperately. As long as they shot up on one of the flats close by, we could go running through the water and land on them with the net before they returned to the cover of the brown water. But even when one was in the net it wasn't a sure thing, because the netting was coming away from the frame and they could wiggle through and swim away leaving us kneeling in the mud empty-handed. After each fish was caught there was a triumphant grin thrown to the spectators and a march to the bucket of water where we kept them until we had enough to weigh.

We had felt like such hunters, running and diving, filthy with mud, drops stinging inside our eyes and noses, with the sun shining clear and we had each boasted about who was the best and then tried to prove it. I think Dabo caught the most. I caught the least, but was the most proud, because I had been afraid I wouldn't catch any.

That seemed a long time ago as I walked up and down the pond with my net, while Dabo whittled away the time and the tension grew. Finally he came, wearing the red shorts, he always wore in the ponds, armed with another dip net and he and I each walked the pond in silence, scooping at the water with no excitement. Dabo had lost his sunshine smile of this morning. Now he was sullen, and I wondered how it could be when all he had done this morning was drink tea.

You could feel the hostility between us. It hung in the air, as obvious as the dust. I was sorry I had given him the balloons. When I handed them to him, he had taken them without a word and I never got to explain they were meant as a gift, that he did not have to pay me back as he had promised. He would never pay me back and my desire to give him a gift turned sour, eating at me, making me dislike him more.

I was so tired of it all. This would be another day with nothing but bad emotions, with no work done. It was already two o'clock and we had only caught five fish.

I said in a light tone, as though Dabo might hear just the tone and not the words, "Dabo, you were late this morning. You will have to stay late this afternoon and work until five."

He stopped pretending to hunt for fish, set his net down, and faced me.

"Suzanne, that is not fair."

"It is fair, Dabo. You came an hour late; you will work an hour later."

Those words were like a spell which always conjured up a whirlwind of talk, talk that seemed to have a life of its own, twisting around and around, then finally drifting off leaving us exhausted and with nothing to show for our efforts.

Dabo said things were not good here, that Dirk and I did not know the ways of Senegal. We rested our dip nets in the mud and moved to sit on the bank.

He said he could get another job whenever he wanted it. He didn't need to stay here. Dirk used the project money as though it was his own and he didn't care about the workers, neither helping them nor sharing. Steve had been different.

Dirk said things and then did not do them. He had said he would move to Podor and live with Dabo, but he never would.

I half-listened to Dabo's words having heard them many times before. I had too many words of my own to say now. It was a lie that he could get another job any time he wanted it. This was a good job that paid well. It was Dirk who had made Dabo the manager, not Steve; Dirk who gave him a raise and more responsibility. It was Dirk who had made the workers S.A.E.D. employees so they would have health benefits, but instead of thanking him for this, they used it against him, said he was not following S.A.E.D. rules. Dirk had said he would move to Podor, but he didn't. He had been best friends with Dabo and now he was best friends with me. Dabo had wanted me, confided in Dirk about it, and then Dirk turned me against Dabo and kept me for himself.

Everything went round and round and the refrain from Kipling's poem, "East is east and west is west, and never the twain shall meet" wove its way through the words, repeating itself over and over in my head. Still, I believed in words, in the Western sense, that everything could eventually be talked out, so I tried harder to listen to what Dabo said, to catch glimmers of truth.

Dabo said he thought the three of us should sit down and talk about the problems. I thought that was a good idea and it shocked me to think it had never happened before. We washed and changed our clothes and drove directly to Walli Jalla. Of course, Dabo did not work late to make up for starting late, but I had forgotten all about it in the hope that finally things might get cleared up.

Dabo and I drove into the Walli Jalla compound just as Dirk was bringing out our little charcoal burner and setting it next to all our camping gear. We had planned to go to the monkey place tonight and I had forgotten. Dirk had everything packed up and was ready to go.

We greeted him and he looked unhappy. We had planned this trip for weeks.

"Dirk, Dabo and I were speaking about the problems at the station. We thought maybe if the three of us all talked about

them, we could work them out," I said in French and Dabo
nodded his head.

"Sue, what about the monkey place?" he asked in English.

"I know. I'm sorry. I forgot."

"You know there is no way we can have this discussion and
still get out there before dark?"

The station seemed to seep into every crack of our lives,
dominating and coloring even the time which was supposedly
our own.

"I forgot. What do you want to do?" I asked.

Dirk turned to Dabo and went back to speaking in French.
He told Dabo he thought it was a good idea, but this was a
bad time. Would it be all right if we came to his house
tomorrow to talk about it?

Dabo nodded his head.

"Are you sure?" I asked.

He said yes, that would be fine, smiling and laughing as we
were packing up. He thought it was funny that we were going
to go sleep in the bush to try and glimpse monkeys.

We had to go to the *marché* in Podor, and dropped Dabo at
his house. He got out of the car, waved, and we drove the five
blocks to the open-air marketplace.

I thought maybe something good had happened.

"Dirk, what do you think? Maybe we'll finally work things
out."

"You can never tell with Dabo," he said.

We bought food for our dinner that night, a feast of eggs,
onions, and potatoes. I decided to bake Dabo a birthday cake
and bought cocoa, butter, and sugar.

I asked Dirk, "Don't you think Dabo will be excited to get a
cake? It's too bad we can't get any candles. It's important to
make a wish."

Dirk didn't want to talk about Dabo or the station. He had
spent the afternoon getting things ready for this trip and he
didn't want to think about other things.

We had a wonderful night, saw a jackal as the sun was
setting, a scorpion in the light of our cooking fire, and
monkeys in the morning. The quiet of the dead forest
seemed to catch inside of us, and we tried to hold onto it as
we drove back to Walli Jalla.

We had said we would come to Dabo's at twelve and it was only ten, so I decided to bake Dabo's cake. I had never baked a chocolate cake in Africa. Dabo would see that we cared.

I baked it in an old bent tin pan that we sometimes used to boil water. As the cake began to cook, the house and Walli Jalla seemed permeated with the smell of it. For the thirty-five minutes it took to bake, we talked about our favorite American sweets.

I removed the cake from the oven and set it to cool on the stove. We left the house quickly and drove the truck to Dabo's compound. He rented a room in a small building set apart from the others with electricity and access to a refrigerator. We entered the compound walls, greeted the family Dabo lived with, and left them to go to Dabo's room.

His door was open so we knocked on it and walked in. Dabo was sitting on a metal chair in front of a little table where he had set his boom box, which was playing Cat Stevens. He motioned for us to sit on his bed—an old metal frame with a rubber mattress, and we sat down and greeted each other. I looked at his walls which were covered with glossy pin-ups from Playboy and Hustler interspersed with a few of his own drawings—a picture of two women pounding millet, another of a village, and one of three men pulling in a seine.

Before we began to speak, Dabo said Malik Si had called a meeting and we must be there by 12:30, bringing Demba and Abdoulaye too.

Malik Si was the coordinator of the fisheries program for S.A.E.D. He lived in a fancy house at Nianga Cité, and his father was very rich and powerful. He had wanted to be a musician, but his family had said he would be a *fonctionnaire*. He used to work for Eaux et Forets, but they didn't want him and couldn't fire him, so they traded him to S.A.E.D.

We rarely saw him as he didn't come to the station to work. Occasionally he would show up, if there was some form of publicity, and he would talk about the program as though he knew it very well. Every other month we would have a meeting at his house—Dirk, Malik, and I—and everyone would speak in flowery French, and Dirk would tell Malik the things that had happened in the program, and occasionally Malik would tell us something that was happening at S.A.E.D. headquarters, a new rule or stipend that must be paid and we would all nod our heads politely.

This wasn't one of those meetings, and as we drove the road back to Walli Jalla, past Guia to get Abdoulaye, and on to the Cité, I wondered what it was for and why he had wanted Demba and Abdoulaye to come. It seemed unfair that he could call a meeting on a Saturday afternoon and I was thinking I would have a hard time being civil through French chatter when there were real problems at the station we needed to take care of.

We knocked on the back door of his house, which he opened for us, ushering us past the kitchen, which was practical and Senegalese, into the fancy living room. It was long and quite large, filled with cheap Western furniture. There was a red carpet, over-stuffed uncomfortable red chairs, an empty fake-walnut china case, a large-screen TV, and even a plastic rose in a plastic vase made to look like cut glass.

We greeted each other, sitting stiffly in the uncomfortable chairs. I looked across at Demba and Abdoulaye, who looked especially uneasy dressed in their *boubous* and *kaalas*, so out of place in this Western room. It seemed ironic that Malik had the power to summon us to sit and waste time when he did not seine the ponds, get spined or muddy, or become exhausted from trying to fix a dike which refused to be fixed. Demba, Abdoulaye, Dabo, Dirk, and I were the real workers. What could Malik have to say to us that could possibly mean anything?

Malik began to speak quietly in French and I swore I would really pay attention this time instead of asking Dirk what had happened later. This time I would have listened anyway. Malik was reading the rules of Senegal, telling us what we could and could not do at the station, how the workers had to be treated—could only work so many night hours, must be paid per diem if they took any work-related trips, had to be provided with some form of transportation. . . They went on and on, and whenever Malik seemed to forget one, Dabo would ask a question to help remind him.

Dabo had gone to Lac du Guerre the year before to get brood stock. He wanted to go this year, but Malik told us if he went he must be paid per diem. We were not paid per diem. These were not rules formed to help a project run, they were formed to strangle a program, while the workers looted what they could.

I watched Dabo harder and harder with each question, while his face became smoother, and my dislike crystallized into hatred.

Finally the meeting ended. There were polite nods and good-byes, hand shakes all around, and Dabo asked—again all smiles—if we were coming to his party that night and Dirk said we would.

Abdoulaye went to work in his fields. We dropped Demba at his house on the way home, and Dabo said he would catch a ride into Podor with Malik.

My anger erupted like magma from the earth, acid words, burning the air, tumbling out, over and over.

"It's a betrayal, Dirk. Dabo has turned against us. He is bad, evil, manipulative, slime, nothing but slime. We should fire him. Why did you say we would go to his party? I won't go. He slapped us in the face and then we turn around and take it?"

"I think we should act as though nothing has happened," Dirk said quietly.

"I won't act like that! I hate him. They're trying to take the station away from us."

"I'll go to the party," Dirk said. "and I think you should too."

We opened the green doors and went to sit across from each other, over the broken-down coffee table. Dabo's paintings from the year before, when he and Dirk had lived in Walli Jalla, danced on the walls as though taunting us. There was a fat woman carrying a basket on her head, a wolf and a fox fighting, and a man boxing, all painted largely in black against the white-wash of the walls.

I walked to the stove to get Dabo's cake. I put it on the table between us and we broke it apart into huge chunks of sweet chocolate and ate it. We ate it all.

That night we went to his party; Dirk and I and SiSay, who was the night watchman at S.A.E.D., and lived in Walli Jalla. I felt sick. I had been sick a lot lately, but since Dirk seemed to think it was very important we both make an appearance, I went.

We parked outside his room and went in to greet him and his guests. The room was overflowing with people. They sat on his bed, the floor, and in his two chairs. There were young women with long corn rows and fancy Western clothes, and slim-waisted men in polyester pants. Everyone was drunk. One man was fondling the breasts of the woman to his right, while she was flirting and rubbing the thigh of the man on her other side. There were cases of beer and soda and billows of cigarette smoke. Between the people on the floor sat plates of fried potatoes and meat. Dabo's one light bulb glared off of the green walls and the glossy naked women pinned to them.

I told Dabo "Happy Birthday" but couldn't stand the noise and the smells and said I would wait in the truck. I tried to curl up into a little ball on the front seat. I had a fever and started to sweat. The music was thumping loudly and hurt my head. I wanted to be back in the quiet of Walli Jalla.

Getting out of the car, I walked to the other side of the road. I was going to be sick. I could hear the music very clearly, the drunken laughter, and all the people crowded into Dabo's room. It seemed as though there was no one else alive but me and the people at Dabo's party. I looked at the ugly brick houses with tin roofs, the magical electric lines, the trash in the dirt street, then bent over and vomited. I couldn't stop retching. I was exhausted and kneeled in the dust, staring at my vomit—all that was left of Dabo's birthday cake.

CHAPTER NINE

Paper and Numbers

I sat in a brown upholstered chair waiting to see the embassy doctor. To my right was a small coffee table covered with the latest issues of Time, National Geographic, and Sports Illustrated. There was a woman standing behind a counter with a sliding glass window, and a man was speaking to her as he held the hand of a small boy. The boy had a cold and the man was complaining of the awful dust in Dakar. Everyone was speaking English and everyone was white.

I played with my hair in its pony tail. It was stringy and sun-bleached. I thought about how I must look. I knew I had lost a lot of weight, my arms and hands were all bone and sinew, showing the veins. They looked like someone else's—a marathon runner's or an anorexic's. I didn't own a mirror, but there was one in the Peace Corps bathroom. I had looked into it that morning to see a face that looked old, old and drawn.

My pants were made of Senegalese material, baggy and loose and my shirt didn't match. I had meant to wear my sneakers, but had forgotten them, and so wore my plastic flip-flops. I had hennaed my feet the week before, and a pattern of rusty red fish swam around their edges. I tucked one of them under me.

Dirk and I had left Walli Jalla the day before. We had awakened early, taken down our mosquito nets, packed the truck, and locked the green doors of our Walli Jalla house. Mbinté, Fatu, Samba, and Oumar had all said good-bye, telling me to greet Dakar for them. We went by the station to leave directions for the work to be done while we were gone, then drove to the paved road. I loved this road, having traveled it so many times that I knew all the villages and curves, the horizon, the gas station in Richard Toll, the mosque which sat surrounded by sand dunes—its minarets silhouetted behind tan semicircles. I never tired of traveling it, but I liked it best from Walli Jalla to St. Louis.

After St. Louis the land didn't feel so much like a part of me. Then we were out of the Fleuve region and things were a little greener and baobabs grew. The villages were thatched round huts instead of square clay houses and the people were Wolof, not Pulaar.

Now I sat in the doctor's office at the American embassy, and I was afraid. I was afraid if this was real, the Fleuve was not. I was afraid that Samba's cracked old hands, the light of Fatu's cooking fire as she prepared millet and leaf sauce, Mbinté's little girl, Huley—these things would cease to exist, unless I held onto them very tightly and did not believe in this place. The quietness of the river, mornings watching the sunrise, the Podor *marché*—these things were real and alive. This office, this whole building seemed too clean, too fixed— a world all neatly pressed, with the pulse of life having been pressed out of it.

A nurse came and called me back to a smaller room with a gray examining table. She told me to change into a white paper gown and pulled the door shut behind her. I took off my clothes and folded them. For a moment I was naked and then I opened the stiff paper gown and put my arms through its holes. I sat up on the table. It was cold and I pulled my legs up to my chin and sat hugging my knees, trying to hold onto my warmth against the coldness of the air conditioner.

The nurse came back and took my temperature and pulse. She asked what region I lived in. When I told her the Fleuve, she didn't know where it was. She asked me what I did, and I said I managed a fish station. She smiled politely, saying the doctor would be right with me, and walked out again, quietly closing the door.

I looked at the little room. There were wooden tongue depressors, one of those things you hit people's knees with to get their responses, a clear plastic container of cotton balls, and another of syringes. The walls were painted off-white and hung with framed prints by famous artists, making windows of contained color where nothing moved.

There was a knock on the door and the doctor walked in carrying my folder. He was young and tall and wore a yellow button-down shirt and brown pants with penny loafers. Over the button-down hung his lab jacket with three ball-point pens neatly hooked into its breast pocket.

He asked what was wrong with me. I told him I had been losing a lot of weight and felt tired and woozy. My hands and feet tingled, my stomach was always horribly bloated, and I vomited regularly. I could feel my pulse throbbing. I was so tired I could no longer do my work.

He listened to my heart with his stethoscope. The cold metal made me shiver. He pressed the little silver circle hard up under my breasts, readjusted it, and listened again. He listened to both sides, my back, and then returned to just under my left breast. He asked me if I knew I had a heart murmur, and I told him a doctor had heard it before, but said it was benign. He looked into my eyes and down my throat with one of those medical pinpoint flashlights. He made me say ahhhh.

"You have no other symptoms?" he questioned.

I felt I should. The way he asked, it seemed mine were inadequate to have taken up his time.

"No. I mean they are hard to explain, but I feel bad all the time, as though I might pass out. I haven't been able to do my work. It's been getting worse. I think it must be parasites."

I looked at him. I had thought he would know without my putting into words—I have been afraid; otherwise I would not have come to him. In my home of Walli Jalla there are people who care for me and ask me every day if I am well and send me food when I am sick. But I have been so afraid that I have come to Dakar, which I hate, and left behind my world where things are slow and hard and mean something to me. I thought maybe the doctor would know these things without my saying them, but he did not.

He told me, "Many people feel sick from the heat."

"I don't think it's the heat," I said.

"Your symptoms are very vague. They could be from anything—stress or heat, possibly parasites. There is no blood in your urine, your stools? No fevers?" he asked.

"Sometimes, I think I have a fever. It feels that way, but I have never taken my temperature. I've never passed blood."

"And your stools have already been checked for parasites?"

"Once. They didn't find anything."

He looked down at me and closed my folder. He had written a few words in it.

"I find nothing wrong with you, although the Peace Corps doctor will probably want to see you himself. He should listen to that heart murmur and can run more parasite tests on you."

"All right," I said, and he left.

I had to stay in Dakar for a week before the Peace Corps doctor returned. He provided medical care for three other countries as well as Senegal, and was away visiting another country's sick. Dirk left for the Fleuve without me while I stayed in the little building they called the health hut. It was a fake hut, like those on the beaches for tourists. It had been built in the Peace Corps parking lot for volunteers who were too sick to be in their villages, but healthy enough to get their own food and look after themselves. There was no bathroom. You had to run across the compound to the first floor of the Peace Corps administration building. On the third floor of the same building was an old shower that sometimes worked and sometimes didn't, but had when it did work only a trickle of cold water.

I spent the days and nights lying on clean sheets under the beat of a fan reading American novels. Outside the compound's walls was Dakar and Dakar's people—people selling oranges, nuts, and chew sticks, driving taxis, or catching buses, hawking material or prayer mats, braiding each other's hair, running *boutiques* or roadside coffee and bread stands, sitting in the street or on the sidewalk broken and bent or blind and begging. Mixed in with these people were tall beautiful women with long plastic cornrows and eye makeup wearing the latest fashions, tired white women who looked unhappy and bought boxed cereal at one of Dakar's three

Western stores, and oily men in fancy embroidered *bou bous* who stood in line to put their money in the bank every Monday.

Once a day, I left the walls to walk the main street and buy food. Next to the Peace Corps compound was a row of wooden shacks with tin roofs. Stacks of tires were in front of one and couches and armchairs in various stages of completion in front of another. The others were full of instant coffee, sugar, powdered milk, and tea. Men sat in front of the shacks, as permanent as the sidewalk, talking or making tea, hiking up their *boubous*, squatting on their heels as they rocked on the smooth surface of the concrete.

I would walk past the men and past the woman selling hard-boiled eggs and peanuts, past the fancy furniture store with picture windows, the bakery, the bar reeking of urine and spilled beer, the movie theater, the fancy walled-in compound that had a wrought-iron gate guarded by two Senegalese men in sailor suits holding semiautomatics. Children would ask me for money, and someone would try to convince me to buy bananas—following me almost all the way to the Score.

The Score was a real grocery store. It had a butcher's counter and seafood, fruit and vegetables and post cards and Snickers candy bars. I would buy cheese and bread, apples and Seven-up. The cheese was in wheels kept in a glass case guarded by two young Senegalese women behind the counter. I could only afford to buy thin slices of the cheapest cheese, and would ask for it in imperfect French. The girls made it obvious they did not like waiting on poor people.

I would try to remind myself of how much I longed for these luxuries in my village. One day I felt so scared and alone that I bought a huge hazelnut chocolate bar. I ate the whole thing that afternoon, but it was missing the taste of forbidden sweets. I could not gain weight.

Finally the Peace Corps doctor returned, listened to my heart, and gave me miff kits for my stools. I asked him if I could leave, but he said I must stay. He wanted to get the results back from the tests and listen to my heart at different times to see if the murmur changed. I had planned on being in Dakar for three days and so had brought only one dress, a *pagne*, my fish pants, and a T-shirt which I washed out by hand in a metal bucket.

That Sunday was Easter. Everyone left the Peace Corps compound except the guardians. That morning I walked quietly to the bathroom and vomited into the toilet. I did not care about the vomiting, but couldn't stand being alone anymore and decided to go to the beach.

There was a beach where admission of 300 francs was charged and almost the only people there were Lebanese and whites. In Dakar that meant you could lie on the beach undisturbed and unworried about having anything stolen. At free beaches you would be surrounded by Senegalese children and adults demanding money and gifts, wheedling or threatening, badgering or grabbing. I thought maybe the sun would feel good and I wanted to look at the ocean.

I took a taxi and sat by myself in the sun watching Lebanese men doing push-ups and beautiful young Lebanese women watching the men. I was so tired. My skin prickled at the slightest touch. Even the water hurt. I felt more alone surrounded by these people than I had in the hut with my books. After an hour I walked out to the street and took a taxi back to Peace Corps.

In another week, the doctor had decided my heart murmur was benign, I had read *Marjorie Morning Star* and *For Whom the Bell Tolls*, written everyone letters, and studied my Pulaar. No one had found anything wrong with me. And I wanted to go home. Maybe I just needed rest and food.

I couldn't wait to get back to Walli Jalla. I was painting a mural of our camping trip on the kitchen wall. So far there was a lion, a river, baboons, and the tree we had slept under. Each weekend I tried to paint another animal, and now I was two weekends behind. I wanted to hear Fatu and Mbinté and Fatiim say, "Mariyata, *aa fooyi, aa fooyi, moyyaani*," "You lose weight, you lose weight—bad," and hold my tired hands in their warm ones as they shook their heads in mock anger and real concern. In Dakar no one called me Mariyata; no one knew my Senegalese name.

Dirk had to come back to Dakar for a meeting and the doctor said I could leave with him. He brought me different clothes, and I swore I would never wear my Thanksgiving dress with the blue fish and purple water lilies again. We went to the Rustique for beers and ate schwarmas and French fries from the Lebanese stand two doors down, sitting under the awning over the sidewalk, watching the people pass by.

I told Dirk about the embassy doctor—how cold he was. Dirk told me things were the same as ever at the station, Dabo was still late, and at the Cité he had seen Oumar, who greeted me.

He asked me if I was well, and I said I didn't know. I felt a little better, but didn't want to speak about it.

For siesta we returned to Peace Corps to take naps, and I knew I was still sick. My stomach was huge and bloated and I went to gag into the first-floor toilet. My hands and feet ached; my head felt weird and I wanted to cry. I was so scared. What was wrong with me? Why could no one find anything? I never used to be afraid and tired and weep. This was some other person, who was so worn out she couldn't dream and plan and do the things she wanted to do. I lay in bed punching my pillow and crying. Dirk took his nap.

We drove back to Walli Jalla and into the compound two days later, bringing some other volunteers with us.

Fatu, Aisata, and a growing pack of children came running, all chanting, "*Haayoo* Mariyata, *haayoo* Mariyata, Mariyata, Mariyata." They surrounded me, chanted my name, and clapped their hands. There were excited smiles on their faces, and everyone hugged me. The Diengs popped their heads over the compound wall, clapped their hands also, and smiled.

I walked over to hold their hands and greet them. Samba asked of my health and my stomach and old Maimoun smiled behind him, Oumar grinned and asked after Dakar, and Fatiim held up pudgy two-year-old Racine. He always called me Ha Ha. I shook his little hand and then Huley's and little Maimoun's, who wanted to be held up too. Everyone wanted to know if I was well, and if the white doctor had cured me.

I smiled and nodded my head, but felt so tired. Why wasn't I happy? I told Fatu and my family I would come visit them the next day. I wanted them to know how much I had missed them. I thought maybe they could see it in my face. Fatu told me I had lost more weight. Bad. She would have to cook me lunches and dinners to fatten me up.

I was a little embarrassed in front of the other volunteers. It was such a scene. Cindi said her village had never welcomed her with such a hullabaloo. I said this was the first time it had happened to me. Later the Diengs sent over *gosi* for all of us.

The volunteers left the next day and I was happy to have my home to myself. Dirk had moved to Podor two months before, and I had thought maybe that I would be lonely, but I loved it. I loved having my house, my village, my friends, and time to sit on the front step by myself and look up at the stars.

I went to Fatu's for dinner the next night. After Dirk moved I had started eating my meals with Fatu or the Diengs and sometimes Ya Ya or the Aans. I never knew who would be in Fatu's compound. Bautch, who ran the restaurant in the Cité, lived there and sometimes he stayed and drank tea while other young men came to eat and drink and speak with him. They would ask me if I wanted to get married and they would ask about America and how to say things in English. Then they would teach me more Pulaar words than I could ever remember. At first I didn't like them much, and told Fatu I liked it better when they were not there.

This night it was just Fatu, her husband, and her old mother. I sat on the mat while Fatu stood over a pot stirring the millet and yelling to her oldest child to bring her more water. Then she came to the mat, sat close to me, and held my hand. She wanted to hear all about Dakar, and her eyes rolled with excitement. She said Dakar must be so much grander than Walli Jalla. Walli Jalla was nothing—a small village of dirt. She didn't know why I lived here.

I tried to tell her that I liked Walli Jalla better than Dakar. I had told the people of Walli Jalla this over and over, and at first they wouldn't believe me. I could not tell Fatu of the peace I found in the village and make her understand. I told her there were so many people in Dakar that no one knew anyone, no one knew your name or greeted you.

But there are so many things there, she answered. People are rich and live in huge houses. There are autos everywhere and people eat meat every day. She said she knew I went there and stayed with rich white people. That was good, she said. I must like that better.

I told her about the embassy doctor. He had tools and learning but he didn't care; he never sent me bowls or hugged me or held my hand. I told her the people of Dakar had lost their hearts; they worked with paper all the time, paper and numbers, and maybe that was why they had forgotten people have hearts. It took me a long time to find the Pulaar words.

When I finished, she thought for a moment. She said she would not want to live somewhere where people had forgotten their hearts, and shook her head back and forth.

The men were served their bowl first, then the women. We sat on a mat around the bowl, dipped our right hands into a small dish of water, and then made little balls of the millet and leaf sauce and ate them.

I loved *lacciri e haako*, but hated *gosi*. These were virtually the only dinners my village ate. They ate *lacciri e haako* or *liddi* when they could, and *gosi* when they could not afford millet. Sometimes they would eat the thick white pudding every night for weeks. I don't think anyone else liked it much either; we would all complain.

I was not very hungry, but Fatu insisted I keep eating. She kept pushing the millet from her side of the bowl to mine. I told her over and over, "*mi haari,*" I am full, but she would not hear of it. She said I was too thin and that was why I was sick. Finally, I could eat no more and she let me stop. The water bowl was passed again and this time we washed our right hands with soap.

I sat for a little while with the fire still burning, talking to Fatu and her mother and then left. I was exhausted.

I set up my mattress, put a sheet on it, and began to hang my mosquito net, tying its ends to the neem tree's branches. My neem tree was in bloom—covered with tiny perfect white flowers smelling of spring. It was very beautiful, and I could think of nowhere I would rather sleep than under its boughs.

I went to sit on the step to brush my teeth, and look up at the stars. There was so much space here, so much room. I felt as though the places in me that had become closed in Dakar could again unfold. It felt good to sit, listen to the sounds of the village, and smell the neem tree.

I was about to go to bed, when Fatu's little girl ran into the compound and handed me a small metal bowl. She was very shy and ran back out before I could thank her. I removed the woven cover. Fatu had sent me a bowl of pure meat.

CHAPTER TEN

Dirk's Sweater

I felt more comfortable sitting on the carpet than on the couch or chairs. The carpet was thick and soft and gold. I leaned my back up against a blue sofa, and faced the picture window that looked out onto the trees in my parents' back yard. They were towering and green and gave so much shade you could barely see the sky. Now and then a cardinal would whistle. Each time it took me by surprise and I would stop and wonder what made that sound.

I was knitting and listening to rock and roll, as I recorded it from the radio to cassettes. I had just bought a pale green radio and tape player from K Mart. It had taken me too long to choose which one I wanted. I had stood, overwhelmed, in front of the glass-enclosed display, looking at all the different types, while the man behind the counter looked at me. I knew I was taking too long.

I told the man I was in the Peace Corps in Africa and needed something that could hold up in a lot of dust and heat. He was not sure which would do best under those conditions. I finally chose the green one, mainly because it was small enough to fit into a goat bag. I handed the man sixty dollars. It was more than a quarter of my month's pay.

It was exciting to own something that could play music. My Walkman had broken months before. It boggled my mind to think Americans could listen to music any time they wanted. I listened to the songs as I tried to knit the sleeves for Dirk's sweater.

I had decided to knit him this when I was first medivaced. I thought it would be a good going-away present and I wanted the comfort of having something to do with my hands while I

98

was on the bus to D.C., sitting on the metro, or waiting to see another doctor, who would do another test. Somehow this sweater, and my completion of it, had gotten mixed up in my mind with my chances of getting back to Senegal. I felt if I could finish it, within the forty-five days Peace Corps gives you to get well and diagnosed before they terminate you, something would be found in all those tests, or I would simply stop being sick. I was convinced if I finished the sweater then I would get to go back to my life in Senegal, and if I did not, then I would be trapped here in this world where everything was so easy, clean, and plastic.

Today was my forty-third day in the States. The pieces to Dirk's sweater were now all finished and I had started to sew them together. The arms were too long and didn't fit correctly into the yoke. I hadn't used a pattern. It was Friday and I had an appointment on Monday which would be my forty-fifth day. Still, no one knew what was wrong with me.

The phone rang and I was afraid to answer it. I thought it would be the Peace Corps nurse, who would tell me I was medically terminated. Terminated. Why did anyone other than God have the right to terminate me? Termination meant I could not go back to my village, to Samba and Fatu and Mbinté, to my half-finished mural on the Walli Jalla kitchen wall. I would never get my chance to drive the truck or to run the fish program. I would remain imprisoned in the comfort of cream-colored walls and gold carpet.

I did not live here, even the walls must feel I did not belong. I belonged seining muddy ponds with cut-up hands, eating millet around the bowl, swishing flies, sleeping out under my neem tree and the stars, complaining about the dust. That was my world. How could anyone terminate me from it?

When I was on the plane from Dakar to New York, I woke up the man sitting next to me at 4 a.m. because I was hoping he was Senegalese and maybe spoke Pulaar. I didn't know how I had gotten myself onto an airplane with blue reclining seats, magazines in English with articles about making money, and stewardesses who came with little plastic trays filled with eggs, sausages, and a roll with butter. I so much wanted to hear Pulaar, something familiar, something to remind me I had not dreamt my last year—I really did live in a small village on a tributary of the Senegal River.

The man was from Nigeria and lived in D.C., but he was very nice when I told him I was in the Peace Corps, had gotten sick, and was scared to death of coming back to the U.S.

When we landed in New York, I had two hours to kill until my next flight to D.C. Everything was so large and clean. There were red stuffed seats and red carpets and red fake-leather covered doors. There were a lot of people, but they were all separate. No one gathered in a clump to squat down on the floor to make tea and laugh.

I watched the women. They wore such nice clothes, I felt shabby. My drawstring pants were almost worn through and hung with no shape. My white shirt was still a little brown with dust and had sweat stains under the arms. But these people were not real to me. So many of them were fat; I didn't find them attractive. Pulaars were more handsome, I thought. These people were so white.

I understood everything they said, conversations, usually just a blur of French or Pulaar or Wolof, about the cost of dog food, a traffic accident, someone's divorce. It was incredibly easy to find out when my flight left for Washington, check my baggage, and ask someone where I could find the ladies' room.

It didn't seem I was sick enough to have been sent across an ocean, but when I ran into the ladies' room to lift up my shirt and look at my stomach, I could see it was still greatly distended.

The doctor in Senegal had asked me if I wanted him to send my parents a telegram telling them I was being medically evacuated, and I had answered no. I didn't want them to think I was dying. Now, I called them collect at 7 a.m. this Sunday morning. I told Dad that I would be in National Airport in three hours and that I was a little sick. He said he was not surprised. They had known I was sick for some time now. They would meet me at the airport. He called me Susie, and didn't ask a lot of questions over the phone.

Within twenty-four hours of leaving Senegal Mom and

Dad had put me to bed in my old room with the needlepoint of wild flowers on the back wall and the seagull mobile twisting in front of the window. They brought me a tray with French toast and syrup and bacon and a glass of milk. We laughed and they hugged me, and Mom only said once how thin I was and exhausted-looking.

My Mom and Dad were rich, unbelievably, luxuriously rich, and I had never realized it before. Their house was better than the most expensive hotel in Dakar. Mom prepared roasts, chicken, hamburgers, and turkey. The chickens were fat and didn't look anything like village chickens. They had not been killed for a special occasion. We ate vegetables—cauliflower, broccoli, beans, and carrots. Mom made my favorite cranberry upside down cake and they bought me a Baskin-Robbins fudge cake, with "Welcome home, Senegal Sue" written on it in green frosting. I ate almost the whole thing by myself and they bought me another one. They bought me five altogether and by the last one they had stopped asking the person behind the counter to write anything on it in frosting.

Mom and I had silly conversations in French. I could not afford to let my French slip while I was home. Not only could it not slip, I greatly needed to improve it, because when I returned to Senegal I would be coordinator of the program and Dirk would no longer be there to translate words I did not understand. I made long lists of new French words to memorize and went over them in my head—*piste*—a small road; *rubrique*—heading; *moyens*—means—as I walked from the bus stop to my parents' house.

Mom and I would sit in the kitchen making nachos and trying to speak French. She would tell me not to speak so fast, and we would say things such as, "Where is your father?" "Have you seen the cat?", or I would walk to the fridge, looking for the sour cream, poke my head inside its shelves filled with American food, and ask, *"Ou est la crème?"* I never could remember the name for sour cream, even though I had once gone to the big store in Dakar to look for it. I wanted to know the country I was living in at least had sour cream, even if I could not afford it. *"Ou est la crème?"* I asked from the refrigerator. Mom came and pointed it out to me. It had been sitting behind a bowl of blueberries. "*Voilà la crème,*" she said and we both started giggling and couldn't stop.

Never did my parents say I shouldn't try to return to Senegal, or that I was killing myself, or that they were worried. But when I would get up in the middle of the night to be sick, one or the other of them would come and hold my hair out of my face, standing in their pajamas, sleep making their features soft and their eyes squinty, stroking my hair and handing me tissues or a glass of water when it was finished.

Night was the worst. My bed had both headboard and footboard, a mattress, and a pillow. I had not slept on a pillow in a year. It smelled of Mom's fabric softener. She had mailed my sweats to Senegal during the cold season and they had smelled the same way and so I had refused to wash them for a month. The smell was so wonderful, so American. I hadn't been able to bear the thought of it being replaced with the almost rancid odor of peanut soap. I sat in the kitchen of the Walli Jalla house with my red sweat shirt held up to my face, soft and warm and smelling like Mom's laundry. I sat there for ten minutes thinking of America.

Now I lay on a mattress, on a pillow, and under sheets smelling Americanly clean. I lay there and looked at the ceiling yearning for the stars. My stomach was always distended with gas. My lower back was cramped, my middle back felt weird, tingly. It was always hot to the touch as though a little fever lived just there. My arms and legs had begun to ache terribly. My left hand and arm were shot through with small lines of pain, starting in my hand and streaking up my arm. The pains had kept me from sleeping and finally, I had asked the doctor for a painkiller.

Sometimes I would lie in bed knowing I was going to be sick and then I would go and vomit in the bathroom. It had an off-white toilet and a marbleized sink and countertop with a dish of soap in pastel colors shaped like shells. Over the toilet hung an oriental print of a cat sticking out its paw to bat a spider. The toilet bowl was not filthy, the floor was not covered in dust. There were no smells—only the perfume of the soap.

I didn't have to go to the kitchen for a pot of water, to fumble for matches to light a candle that would flicker and had to be protected from the night breeze as I lit my way to the latrine. There was no heat to beat my aching body. My parents' house had air conditioning and I could be sick in beautiful coolness. I tried to remember feeling this bad in the hundred degree heat of the Fleuve and couldn't imagine how I had stood it. How had I survived in a desert wasteland with no one to wake up in their pajamas, stroke my hair, and stay with me?

I did know I had to go back. I would lie awake in the darkness, returning to Walli Jalla in my mind. There was a digital clock by my bed glowing the hour in red numbers. It was 12:00 here; it would be 7 a.m. there. The sun would have risen but not quite awakened to its burning power. It would still be peaceful, and I would go and buy *beignets* from the woman who lived in the compound behind mine. Someone would be pounding millet in the Diengs' compound. I would hear Fatu's voice scolding a child. There would be birds in my neem tree and I would sit on the step drinking coffee, and watching them, and listening to the mourning doves coo. The doves always sat on the edge of the house's tin roof. When I slept inside, during the cold season, I would curse them as they hopped up and down sounding like a herd of elephants. But more than any other sound they made me think of Senegal's morning.

Dirk had written that everyone in Walli Jalla greeted me, asked after my health, and wanted to know when I was coming back. I would lie in my refinished antique bed in my parents' air-conditioned house and think about a Pulaar village where people were worrying about me and wondering when I was going to come home.

I kept thinking about Mada, the wife of the weekend guardian. She cooked our lunches at the station and was my friend. The first day I met her she had come there to have Dabo take a thorn from her foot, but it had hurt too badly and she had left before he had pulled it free. She came back the next day and stayed until he had finished. The thorn was an inch long. It had hurt very badly, but she never cried out.

I left because it hurt me too much to watch. The next day I went to her village. She wasn't there, but I left salve and bandages with her husband.

She came by the station a lot after that and she and I would joke about Dabo and men. She said she was my older sister and I said I had never had one before. I asked her about the clitorectomies done on little girls and she told me if they were not removed the girls would grow penises.

One day at the station, before I was medivaced, I had felt so sick, that I had gone into the office, curled into a small ball on the concrete floor and slept. Earlier I had tried to fix the dam in the canal which always needed fixing. I had dug deep into the bottom of it for the best clay and tried to stop up the holes between the plastic feed bags filled with dirt.

Mada stood at the edge of the canal doing her wash in a big green plastic bucket. She didn't ask if I needed help, but walked into the dirty water that came up to her waist, and bent over to pull the clay from the bottom, as I was. She took the dripping clay in her hands and tried to push it into the holes of the dam. There were too many holes to ever stop them all, but we had to try. The level of the canal without the dam was too low to get water to the station.

Mada and I saw something in each other that went deeper than black or white, American or Senegalese. One day she walked from her village to the Cité and back to find fish for our lunch. Another time she made a necklace of beads from special roots and clay that smelled like spices for me to send to my American mother. Mom, in turn, gave me a long necklace of gold and dark red glass beads to bring back to Mada. I would lie in bed and talk to God. He had to let me go back to take those beads to Mada.

These people taught me, fed me, and laughed with me. I have to give them a little of what they have given me. I love these people the way I have only loved my American family. You must know that I have to return, God. Please.

I would lie there in tears and everything would be very quiet. The windows were closed because the air conditioner was on.

One night I lay in bed and watched the sliver of light under my door and knew Mom was still up, reading a book in the guest room. I was frightened. My body was not getting better. I would be talking to Mom in the kitchen, standing on the tile made to look like bricks, and then just sit down—like a balloon having let all its air escape with nothing left to hold it up. I was always tired. The days were turning into weeks, and the weeks into a month.

I climbed from bed and went to the guest room. Mom moved over and I crawled in beside her and wept. Why was God doing this to me, why couldn't I get well, why did a Peace Corps nurse have the power to take away my life—the things most important to me? My body was not mine. It was turning to stone and I was trapped within it. Was I dying? They had done all those tests and no one knew what was wrong. I curled up on my side and sobbed while Mom rubbed my back.

The mornings were better. I would pretend I felt better, that the doctor's latest medicine had helped. We tried attabrine and flagel. I wanted the flagel because I thought I still had amoebas. It made me very sick, but I continued to take it for five days because I was willing to live through ten days of anything if it would make me well, and I could return to Senegal. Finally, I called the doctor and he said I must be allergic to flagel, a lot of people were. It took me a week to get over the effects of it.

One day, I watched my heart beat on a computer screen, and saw my intestines on another. They looked like harmless blobs of gray and it seemed impossible they were ruining my life.

Another time, between doctor's appointments I went to the McDonald's on K street. I wanted a Quarter Pounder.

I stood in line waiting to speak my order that would be punched into a machine by people dressed in brown polyester with matching caps and turned into paper packages on a plastic tray. I could not stop thinking of Fatu. What would she think of all this?

I wished she was there with me, I would try to explain it to her and then she would laugh and roll her eyes. But really she would be scared and overwhelmed by all the white people in tight-fitting clothes, the different smells, the language everyone else spoke. McDonald's was a part of where I came from, but with Fatu was where I belonged.

When I first came to the Peace Corps medical building in D.C., I was handed a printed sheet that welcomed me to Washington, spoke a little of medivac procedures, and told of the reasons why volunteers were not allowed to return to their countries. In three paragraphs they concisely justified why they might take away your life. Each volunteer had a Peace Corps nurse who set up doctor's appointments, filled out bill vouchers, paid you your per diem, and was the person who would tell you if the Peace Corps medical team had decided you were too great a health risk to be allowed to return. She also sent telegrams back to the volunteer's country, keeping the administration there up to date with what was going on.

My nurse was old, with white hair pulled back into a bun. She smoked cigarettes and ate her lunch out of a brown paper bag at her desk. She never seemed to remember my name, what country I was from, what papers needed to be filled out, or whether it looked like I would be able to return or not. She seemed pleasantly incompetent, and was probably just overworked. I hated her because she would say sympathetic things to me. I thought she was weak—she would not last a day in my village. She couldn't possibly be the person who would stand between me and returning to Senegal. I tried always to act healthy in front of her, and continuously talked about my work and how much I needed to get back to the station. I could not believe how much weight I had gained back, how energetic I was feeling, how much I liked Dr. Parker, and was sure this medicine I was taking now would do the trick.

I did like Dr. Parker. I was assigned to him, and then he farmed me out for a lot of tests. He was slim and perpetually tanned with dark hair and a mustache. There was a caricature of him as a doctor propped up on the window sill in his office, and finger paintings by his daughters had been framed and hung in one of his examining rooms. He did not seem to think I was dying, was business-like, and understood the goal was to get me back to Senegal.

His receptionist watched my sweater grow from balls of yarn to a back and front and arms, beige with blue fish swimming across the chest in a line, wavy lines on the top and bottom of them. Everyone watched my sweater grow. Strangers on the metro would ask me about it, who it was for, how I had thought of the pattern, and where I had learned to knit.

The week before I had been knitting in yet another reception room as I waited for an upper G.I.

An old man and woman came in and the old man, skinny and white with age, was trying to read the small print from an insurance form out loud, saying it obviously had not been written for an eighty-year-old.

They seemed out of place in this underlit modern waiting room. Their faces belonged in a two-story frame house that would smell warm from having been lived in, and the woman would make pumpkin pie from scratch. I thought they must have seen the world change a great deal, and felt very close to them.

The woman saw me knitting and came over to look at my work. She liked my pattern and I explained I was making it for a friend of mine.

She returned to her seat and told her husband almost word for word what I had said, except at the end she added she thought I was knitting it for a boyfriend. She said all these things to the man as though she were whispering, but she was speaking as loudly as she had spoken to me.

It made me feel warm to listen to them. They were something to hold onto in a world of cold metal tables they strapped you onto, of men and women dressed in white coats, doing things, using machines I didn't understand and speaking to me as though I was either very young, very old, or mentally retarded.

Now I was sewing the pieces of Dirk's sweater together with a yarn needle, listening to the radio. The cap on the arms was wrong. I had pulled it out once already and now it would have to be pulled out again, and the arms shortened. I wanted to scream with frustration when the phone rang, screaming in my head. I didn't want to answer it but I picked the receiver up. The voice was the Peace Corps nurse. She told me the latest test results had come back from Dr. Parker and they were negative. He had been unable to find anything definitive. They were worried about my health and simply could not let me return to Senegal. I would be terminated and my case sent on to Workman's Compensation. She was sorry.

"Are you there? Are you there, Susan?"

She did not even know everyone called me Sue.

I hated her. She could not take Walli Jalla and Mada and the fish station away from me. I had fought for these things. They were mine. I had made curtains for the Walli Jalla house. I was planning on buying contact paper to cover the kitchen shelves. I had a flea and tick collar sitting in my room as a present for Sahné, and a box of milkbones.

"Did Dr. Parker say he thought I shouldn't go back?"

I had to ask the question, and I knew to speak would make me cry. I would not cry over the phone to this grandmotherly woman who wouldn't last a day in my village and who would try to comfort me with stupid English words.

"Yes, the doctors have agreed; you really are too much of a risk. You are quite sick and they have no idea why."

She was sorry.

She needed to get some information to fill out a new set of forms. She was asking addresses and birth dates while the tears were streaming down my face. If she had known anything, she would have pretended not to hear me but she had to tell me not to cry, and that everything would get better.

"After you get well you can always join the Peace Corps again if you want to," she said.

"Don't cry, Susan."

She had no right to tell me not to cry, and I hung up the phone.

I went back to my spot on the gold carpet, and sat down with my back against the couch. There was no sound but the radio. There was no sound for my pain. There were only tears that never seemed to stop. They came not from my eyes but were wrenched out of somewhere deep inside me, a quiet dark pool I had just begun to discover which swallowed the bad things I couldn't understand or fight.

I tore at the sleeves, pulling them apart and into little ravels of yarn. My mother came home and found me surrounded by pieces of Dirk's sweater, the unraveled yarn, and my tears streaming down my face and splashing onto the needles.

CHAPTER ELEVEN

My Return

The Dakar *gare* was overwhelmingly alive. There were parked vans and cars and seven-seaters painted blue and red and yellow and white in different stages of disrepair sitting like exposed stones in a torrent of flowing people. There were people selling bananas, apples, cola nuts, crushed ice flavored with *beesop* in little plastic bags, hard-boiled eggs, mangoes, bags of raw peanuts, boiled shrimp. Driver's assistants asked anyone carrying luggage where they were going and propelled them toward a car they said was going to the town or past the village named. Drivers sat behind their wheels as their cars slowly filled with human cargo—women holding crying babies, men in flowing indigo *bou bous*, others in polyester pants, slick shirts, and fake eyeglasses, interspersed by children with colds and young men in ripped church-group clothes threading in and out of everyone else selling plastic watches, cassettes, sunglasses, and Marlboro key chains.

The Dakar *gare* was one of my least favorite places in Senegal, but this day I embraced it—the smells, the noises, the crushing humanity. I arrived in Dakar late that morning, and spent most of the afternoon trying to sleep away the weariness of my eight-hour plane trip. I couldn't stay asleep though and by five o'clock I was at the *gare*. It was silly of me to travel so late, trying to reach the Fleuve the same day I arrived.

I knew that, but it didn't matter. I had not fought to come to Dakar; it was unimportant. I wanted to hear Pulaar, see the dust, smell the nearness of the river. It was the Fouta Touro which infected my blood. I felt I couldn't live without it and needed to get back to it the way salmon return to their spawning grounds. I would leave this day, if only to get to St. Louis, the city on the edge of the Fleuve.

One of the driver's assistants saw me carryng my bag and badgered me into telling him my destination. He propelled me by my arm, while trying to take my luggage from my hands as I gripped tighter—not wanting to pay for services rendered. He directed me to the corner of the *gare* where the cars going to St. Louis parked. There was a seven-seater and I sat down in it, protecting my place by the window, waiting for the rest of the car to fill.

Everything was bright with my triumph and I grinned. I had made it back, even after they said I would not; I was in Senegal. I had lived through a weekend of endless open gray space when they had said I was medically terminated. I had nothing to hold onto and the only thing still real was the sweater for Dirk. I pulled out the sleeves, reknit them, sewed the sweater together, and knit the neckline as though my life depended upon it.

It was finished Sunday; a miracle happened on Monday. I had my last doctor's appointment with Dr. Parker and he said another parasite had been found, *B. hominus*. It had been found in stools sent long before from Senegal, which had been misrouted and not arrived in the U.S. until I was there too. Then the results were sent back to Senegal because someone did not realize both of us were in Washington. Peace Corps Senegal had just returned them to Dr. Parker.

He explained all this to me matter of factly and hope stirred out of the grayness, but hope which was crushing because it would be doubly hard if it was unfounded. I was afraid to speak. Too much depended on it. Finally, I asked quietly if Dr. Parker thought this parasite could be the cause of all my problems? He did. I asked its treatment and he said thirty days of Iodoquinol. My days, however, were all spent. I had none left to spend in the U.S. and still return to Senegal.

I had a round trip ticket to come back here in a month for my brother's wedding. I explained this to the doctor, my words all in a rush because I had to know his answer. I asked him if he thought I could go back to Senegal to take the medicine, check in with him in four weeks, and if I was still no better be terminated then. There was a momentary silence after which he said slowly, yes, he thought I could. I asked him more details, to make sure he meant it, and asked him to tell my Peace Corps nurse. I tried to betray nothing of what I felt, because I had learned to show how much something means is to lose it.

My nurse didn't believe it. I sat across from her gray metal desk while she shuffled some papers. She had spoken with Dr. Parker but still acted as though I was not going back. She said Dr. Parker had not told her I could go, and she had just been on the line with him. I suggested she call Dr. Parker again and held my breath, as she let hers all out in a disapproving snort. It was true. I would go back to Senegal.

That was five days before I arrived in the Dakar Airport and the A.P.C.D., Assistant Peace Corps Director, for fisheries came to pick me up, and shook his head back and forth saying how they had been told I was not coming back, while I watched for my luggage to appear on a creaking conveyor belt that went round in an oval. No one could believe I had made it here and Terrice, another volunteer, told me they thought I had been terminated and given my job to Kevin Turner.

But I would not think of that as I sat in the *gare*. I would not think of my job, my health, or that this might only be a month. I had longed too much for this to lose it to worries. I was home, and nothing could take that away from me.

Slowly the car filled and finally we left the *gare* for the road. Now I wanted to whoop, could barely contain myself as the hot wind blew against my face. The scenes which passed by us were the ones I had in my memory, the same ones I had thought about during the last month to make sure they were real—there was a country named Senegal across the ocean with a road between Thiès and St. Louis cutting between red-tan earth and over-sized baobab trees. I knew this road, knew the big curve with the three black baobabs, knew the little village just before the huge hollow baobab which commanded everything around it as though it were king, knew the acacias, the donkeys, the goats, the sheep, and the little roadside stands.

I photographed everything in my mind, because now I

knew what it was to leave. I greeted the land, the sky, the wind itself. We drove past a herd of grazing camels and it seemed they had been waiting for me and I wished I could yell out the window, "Hello, I am home! Thank you for waiting." It was all so big and open, so much space, everything inside of me expanded with it until I thought I might burst if I didn't get to whoop, and had to satisfy myself instead with crazy grins.

The sun began to set, and I watched its pink turn liquid and flood the sky. For a moment there was nothing in the world but the flat tan earth covered by vermilion and orange and silver which slowly leaked from the sky to the thirsty dust. I felt the sunset was for me; it so perfectly reflected my own brightly fierce emotions at having returned.

Darkness took the sky and some of my triumph. The car windows turned to black rectangles and I had to remind myself that I was in Senegal. I laughed out loud wondering what my American friends would think if they were in my place: in Africa traveling on public transport cutting across the night.

It was pitch black, broken only by lightning, when we arrived at the *gare* in St. Louis. For a moment I was afraid I would not get a taxi and have to walk the bridge to the Hotel de la Poste. A man had his neck slit from ear to ear walking the bridge one night the year before. I thought of him and shivered. I had been a fool to travel so late. Luckily there were two taxis sitting waiting at the *gare* and I caught one of them, paid the driver and was out in the light of the Poste's patio.

The Hotel de la Poste was more than one hundred years old, run by a French family, and still had the flavor of a time when people had come to the Fleuve for safari. It was something of a white people's hotel, and to me always stood for all that was rich and luxurious—a fantasy land. Dirk and I stayed at the Poste when we had to come to St. Louis for work and once for a vacation. All the waiters were Pulaar and they knew us, knew we came from the bush and spoke their language, and once one of them gave me free French fries. One night Samba, my village father, had told me he had a brother in St. Louis, that I should find him in the city and stay with him when I had to travel. He said his brother worked at a hotel, and it turned out he was one of the cooks at the Hotel de la Poste, so each time I passed through I would ask for him and we would chat in Pulaar and I would tell him news of the village and our family.

The familiarity of the hotel wrapped around me like a cloak, as I walked to the desk to greet the clerk. He broke into exclamations and smiles when he saw my face. I told him I had been in America because I was very sick and he nodded his head up and down saying he knew, he had spoken to Dirk. He wanted to know if I was better now and if my family had been happy to see me. We laughed with excitement at seeing each other. He kept saying "Suzanne" and pumping my hand and a waiter came out of the restaurant to see what was causing the commotion and set down his tray to also laugh and pump my hand. Soon Samba's brother and all the waiters I knew and the little gray-haired Pulaar man who cleaned the rooms had surrounded me and were pumping my hand, laughing with excitement. They all knew I had been very sick and had been across the ocean in America. Everyone asked if I was better. I felt like a Pulaar princess. Inside I smiled, all warm down deep at the feeling of Pulaar again on my tongue.

Triumph never lasts long in Senegal, and mine had begun to fade by the next morning as I sat in the St. Louis *gare* waiting for a twelve-seater to fill. I had to wait for three hours, and when the driver took my money he seemed to think I would not miss my change. A woman with a wailing baby sat next to me and demanded in Pulaar that I buy them cookies. An old man in front said I should buy him a gift. The baby had nowhere to go to the bathroom and urinated on the floor of the van. I raised my feet to escape the puddle and the afternoon was lost to the smell.

It took five hours to get to Torregi, where I caught another car to Podor, which would drop me at Guia. Luckily, I only had to wait half an hour for the second car, and the trip was no more than fifteen minutes. I clutched the seat and yelled to the driver to stop as he almost passed the little thatched awning which marked the Guia *gare*, and usually provided shade for an old woman who sold squash and tomatoes and sometimes cantaloupes.

The driver slammed on the brakes, screeching the tires on the pavement, and I climbed out of the car amidst a cloud of dust. My bag was handed out after me, and the car accelerated quickly, again leaving me in dust. I stood perfectly still for a moment. Somehow, I felt lost. It was late in the afternoon and the old woman had packed up her things and left. There was no one to be seen and the wind blew as though through a ghost town.

Guia was across the road from me, a handful of earthen houses with thatched roofs. The houses were raised from dust and would return to dust. It seemed there was nothing but dust and the horrible heat. The village looked very ugly, dilapidated and ramshackle, something existing only to prove the harshness of the Sahel. This was Guia, I told myself, the village next to Walli Jalla, where Abdoulaye lives, and felt surprised to know this scrap of African desolation. It was so barren, with no color, no trees, and seemingly no people. Did I really fight to return to this? Would anyone?

I picked up by bag, which was heavy with a big box of Bisquick, two packages of Chef BoyArdee Pizza Mix, a bottle of wine in the shape of a fish, and a Duncan Hines Brownie mix, and started to walk. It seemed my bag would dislocate my shoulder before I arrived in Walli Jalla. When I saw a little boy drive by in a *charrette*—horse and cart—I stopped him and asked him to drive me to the village. He was not anyone I knew, but he knew of me—said he had heard the white woman was away, and agreed to take me. He dropped me at the pumping station and I walked the block or so to my compound.

My compound was the destination of my dreams, what I had held onto deep down inside during the tests and questions from the men in white lab coats and the women in white dresses, the blood given, the times I vomited into my parents' clean off-white toilet in the middle bathroom, when I sat across from my Peace Corps nurse with her white hair held back in a bun. It was nothing but crumbling clay with chipped white-washed mortar. It was filthy, shabby, with little pieces of trash strewn around the yard. This was my home with the flower bud curtains, the half-finished mural, the fireplace drawn on the kitchen wall. The house was closed and locked, and it looked as though no one had lived in it for years.

The moment I entered my compound gates, it seemed Fatu, Aisata, the Diengs, and a million village children materialized out of nowhere, surrounding me, holding my hands, and chanting "*Haayoo* Mariyata, *haayoo* Mariyata." I was near the cane bed under the neem tree and I sat down fast as though their words had pushed me over, and the crowd rearranged itself around me like a hoop skirt. Everyone asked a dozen questions all at once and I couldn't think, could barely mumble Pulaar greetings. It was too much.

I asked Fatu where Dirk and Kevin were. I thought I would walk back to Guia and catch a car to Podor. I wasn't ready for Walli Jalla, not yet. I wanted to tell someone, who would understand, about America, the horrible doctors, and how they had almost not let me come back, but I had fought. Dirk would understand and I wanted to give him his sweater and tell him how I had known if I finished it I would get to come back. Even when they told me I was terminated I would not stop working on it.

Fatu was saying something about Bautch telling her they had taken the truck to Bakel, something to do with fish. It took me ten minutes to translate her words into the basic Pulaar words I still remembered. Dirk and Kevin were in Bakel at the end of the Fleuve.

Everyone was saying with glee that I had forgotten their language. "*Aa waawaa* Pulaar," they said—you cannot speak Pulaar, and laughed. Fatu said I had a heavy tongue and Aisata said I had forgotten. I wanted to scream. I thought of the nights lying in bed aching for this village, these people, and now they were too much. The heat beat against my skin and my sweat made little rivers of dust.

I told the crowd I was tired, and they began to trickle back out of the entrance to my compound. I felt each person take a piece of how I had dreamt of this homecoming with them as they left, until I sat alone and empty on the cane bed. My house was locked, and I did not have the key. Dirk had suggested I leave it with him. I sat and stared at the faded green doors. I had crossed an ocean, left behind a world to get back to them, and did not have the key to unlock them.

One of the shutters had been lifted from its hinges by a child, Oumar Ndiaye, so he could enter my house and steal. He stole little things, a hat, a broken watch, a belt. At first I thought I had misplaced them, then that it was the ghost, until the son of my landlord came and told me there was a thief. All the village knew. Fatu had told me Oumar was bad, but I had liked his face. I was too sick then to really care. I didn't need the things, but the villagers would not understand. They would no longer respect me if I was so rich I didn't mind a thief and so I'd spoken to Oumar's father. He told me Oumar had already been beaten and Oumar still told me he had not done it.

Oumar came back with me to the compound to try to prove his innocence and we gathered a crowd of women and children as we walked. He stood in front of my shutter as I showed him where it had been taken from its hinges and he told me it was not him and the women and children repeated it was not him. I said if it was not him then I would bring the policemen to the village and they would question him and all the other children until they found the thief. Then the women and children turned away from Oumar and said it was he, and his eyes finally lost their hardness and defiance, replaced with a flicker of fear. He said it was him, and slowly the worthless things were returned to me and Oumar was sent to live with his mother in Thiès. Everyone said he was bad, like his mother; he belonged with her.

The shutter had never been fixed and so I pulled it from its hinges, climbed up on the cinder blocks used to hold the doors open and entered my house as Oumar had. I pulled my legs up under me and squatted on the window sill looking down into what had been my kitchen. Half of it was gone. There was no broken coffee table, no bright blue gas burner, no shelves—the ones I had thought I would buy contact paper for in Dakar. Everything was covered with inches of dust, as though there had been a disaster long ago and the earth was slowly coming back to claim the remains.

I jumped down and sat on the broken concrete floor. Everything was ugly and broken. I let my fingers play in the dust. It seemed no one had ever lived here, certainly never loved it as a home. It was no brighter than the earth and thatch houses of Guia. I thought to cry, but I was tired of tears.

I stood and opened the doors, went into the middle room and pulled out my mattress to put it under the neem tree. I took my *pagne* and Dirk's pillow. For now I would sleep.

That night I ate *lacciri e haako* with the Diengs. It tasted very bad after all the American food I had eaten. I gave them their gifts, not for them, but for me. I had wanted to bring them gifts from America. To each woman I gave a necklace, to Tiijon notebooks, Oumar a watch, and Samba a pen with a clock on its side. Still, it didn't seem real. I was a foolish white woman giving an African family, who lived in a small Senegalese village, gifts from K Mart.

The next day I cleaned my house. I swept away forty-five days of dust from my bedroom, the little room with its line to hang things to dry, the room we named the library, the middle room, the kitchen, the room with the fireplace and my half-finished mural on the wall. I looked at the fireplace and remembered Dirk and I making it that first Christmas— so there would be somewhere to hang stockings. We had argued for a long time over what type of fireplace we wanted and finally decided on brick with an arch and a white mantel. I had bought two prints to hang over the mantel at The National Gallery of Art. I hung "Ville D'Avray" and "Winter Harmony" and thought they looked very fine.

I scrubbed the metal stove, dusted the door on cinder blocks which I used as a kitchen table, set out my mixes, my wine, and the two wine glasses I had brought back from America, stood back and smiled. I went through the things in my armoire, straightening and dusting, surprised at what was there. I found the flea and tick collar Cindi had brought for Sahné from the States, and wondered why it had never been used. Just for a moment I was again surrounded by gray emptiness, thinking something had happened to her, but I put that away as silly. Dirk forgot things. Oh well, now Sahné would have two.

It felt good to clean my house, and when I was finished I

went to the river to clean the dust from my body. The river was everything I had remembered, and I silently thanked its waters as I dried myself and returned to my compound.

Both Samba and Demba were standing in front of the green doors waiting for me. Samba explained he did not understand how the watch worked on his pen and looked very distressed. I showed him which buttons to push and he said he was going to give it to Tiijon, since he could not write and walked back out of my compound holding the pen before him as though it might bite, staring at the blinking digital clock.

I unlocked my doors and Demba entered, sitting in one of the broken chairs. He asked after America and my stomach. I asked about his family. He said Sahné was dead. Sahné was dead and so were the cats, Dabo was sick, and Dirk would not be back for three days. None of the workers' salaries had arrived and they all needed money.

"Sahné is dead?" I asked.

He said yes and tried to explain to me how she had died with Pulaar words I no longer understood. It did not matter; I was not listening. I was thinking how Sahné had run with me in the mornings and how soft her black velvet ears were to the touch of my hands.

She had lived in Walli Jalla with Dirk and me, but then Dirk moved to Podor and we sent Sahné to the station. The reason we owned a dog was for killing rats in the warehouse and keeping goats off the dikes between ponds. I watched Sahné catch rats once. She would pounce on them, hold them softly to the ground, look into their eyes, and wag her tail. She would let them go, because she wanted to play, and then look pained when they did not.

One night I was sleeping inside the house because it was the cold season. It was very dark, and I was deep in sleep when I heard an animal in the house, its claws against the floor. Before I was really awake, I had grabbed my flashlight, jumped out of bed, and tackled what I thought was a sheep. I flashed the light into Sahné's brown eyes. She was lonesome.

Mbinté and Fatiim called her my child and she came once with me when I went to the Diengs' to eat and sat patiently off the mat as we sat around the bowl. Mbinté gave her what was left of the afternoon's rice because Sahné was family. Sahné was someone to love and to hold. I had a box of milkbones for her.

I wanted Demba to leave because he would not understand loving a dog. I told him I was tired and went to get the digital watch I had bought for him. I started to take it from its package and Demba screamed for me to stop. The package proved it came from America. Watches without packages could be bought in Dakar.

Dirk came back and brought with him K.T., Kevin, Cindi, and Jon. There were more greetings and hugs and a lot of English. I felt almost as overwhelmed as I had with the villagers. Everyone wanted to know if I was here to stay but I didn't know. They couldn't believe I had convinced the Peace Corps to let me return. They had been sent a telegram saying I was terminated and Dirk and K.T. had sold half my belongings to Bautch for thirty beers. Now they were trying to buy them back.

After awhile I talked to Dirk alone, gave him his sweater and tried to explain the parts of me I had sold to get myself back here, soft parts I would never be able to buy back—not even with time; and how afraid I had been in the airport waiting for my flight to Senegal, because I knew I was still sick. I said I had heard Sahné and the cats had died, and Dirk said yes, it was true. S.A.E.D. had put down poison for the rats, and the animals we had taught to kill rats died because of it. Sahné died a terrible death by poison, Sahné who never hurt a thing.

Dirk explained everyone was here because there were two new fisheries trainees and in three days they would be coming up to the station for their indoctrination to fisheries on the Fleuve. Everyone wanted to be a trainer and I wondered who would be posted at the station.

Linda came. Marsha stayed in Dakar because she was sick. We worked at the station and seined a pond. It felt good to feel the brails and the mud and the spines and bad to hear K.T. and Dirk speaking of the station the way Dirk and I always had. I thought of the day in Washington when I had gone to the statue garden and spoke with the ornamental carp in their marble ponds. I told them I had fish in ponds, lots of fish in eight different ponds in an African country far away and I missed them, catching their silver, blue and red bodies in the net as their scales caught the sun, watching them feed in pale dawn and early dusk.

I felt like a ghost returned from the dead. It seemed I did not really have a place anymore, like a wound that heals. Things were taken care of. I don't know what I had thought, maybe that everything would grind to a halt without me. I couldn't complain. I didn't know if I could stay or even if I was well. Everyone said I looked stronger, healthier and yet I was still so tired. Linda had five trainers to show her around; she didn't need me, so I slept while the others went to the station. It made me sad. I had thought myself more important.

I was still sick. I could feel it in my bones. It was a Senegalese sickness, and I began to think maybe the Senegalese could cure what the Americans could not. I remembered Mbinté telling me her uncle was a *marabout,* a Moslem religious man, and healer, and that if I ever needed a *marabout* I should speak to her and she would take me to him.

He lived just across from my compound and his children were brats. Mbinté took me to see him the next night, and when we walked into his compound all his *tallebés*—young boy students—were gathered in a circle around a bonfire chanting words from the Koran. The night was very black and the red tongues of the fire flickered orange on the boys' faces and made them all look the same, glazed brown faces with glass eyes, as though the words they chanted were not Arabic but some sort of spell.

Mbinté and I walked to where the *marabout* and his wives had put out mats in front of their houses and sat under the stars. We took off our shoes, shook hands, and greeted everyone and joined them on the mats. Mbinté spoke first in very fast Pulaar, I assumed explaining my problem. When she had finished he asked me why I had not brought a present for him from America.

I looked at Mbinté's uncle. He was a big man with a heavy face and neck and rings on his fingers. He wore a pale blue embroidered *boubou* and expensive pointy-toed Arab clogs. I said I had no money left over to buy more gifts after the gifts I bought for my family and the men I worked with. The *marabout* looked disappointed. He asked what was wrong with my body, just as the doctors with stethoscopes, white lab coats, and pale nurses had. I spoke of my stomach, my aching hands and feet, and my back with the little fever. He stared into my face as I spoke, and I thought he had a little of that oily expression worn by the Senegalese I did not trust, and maybe a little merriment in his eyes that he couldn't hide.

He told me I must give him a one-hundred-franc coin for him to understand my sickness, and I wondered what had happened to toenail clippings and snips of hair. I handed him the coin and he told Mbinté to bring me back the next night. Our interview was over. Mbinté and I took our leave, telling the *marabout* and the people of his compound to pass the night in peace as we walked past the little boys being lapped by fire.

The next night Mbinté came to my compound and we walked the short distance to the *marabout's*. I asked Mbinté what I should pay her uncle. I wanted to know beforehand. We stopped for a moment on the dirt path to speak in the darkness of the night and she said 1500 francs, and to pay more later if his medicine worked. That made a lot of sense to me and I nodded my head, wishing it was that way in America.

This time we went inside the *marabout's* house to speak with him and found him sitting on a mat with pillows in the light of a kerosene lamp speaking with another patient. They spoke very earnestly together and their faces shone, their words accented by the tick tock of a wind-up clock.

The other patient left, and again we took off our shoes and sat across from the *marabout* on his millet stalk mat. I wondered what magic the other man had asked for, and if Mbinté's uncle could really give it to him. Walli Jalla's *marabout* looked especially big this night sitting crosslegged with his back straight and an indigo blue *boubou* spread out all around him.

He said he knew what was wrong with me. He would make a potion and a charm, very strong medicine, which he would give to Mbinté who would explain how I should take it. Mbinté nodded her head in silent agreement, and then said I must take the medicine exactly as she told me and not forget. She tried to impress on me how important this was, and her Pulaar words were the English words of my mother. The *marabout* said he would tell Mbinté what was wrong with me the next day when he gave her my medicine. He asked for payment and was not pleased with my 1500 francs. He had foreseen a gold mine. I told him I was not like white people. I was poor, and Mbinté said quietly, "Yes, it is true, she is poor."

The next afternoon Mbinté came to my compound and told me the *marabout* had said my illness had been caught from trees by a river. I had been sick since sleeping on the banks of the Fallemé. He had made a black potion which was in a large plastic cup Mbinté set into my hands. She said I was to say, *"Bisimilla"* and take three small sips and then rub the black water all over my skin morning, noon, and night for five days. She repeated the directions to me twice until she was satisfied I really did understand them and then she left to go back to cooking her compound's dinner.

When I took my medicine at night in my bedroom, the candle I set on my armoire would throw strange shadows and I would say *"Bisimilla"* to the silence, and then watch the light play on my naked body as I coated it with the cool magic liquid, wondering if I believed in it or not. I knew it would only work if I believed, but sometimes I laughed at the flame sending out sinister shadows while I, college-educated with a biology degree, seriously plastered a black potion over my skin after saying welcome and sipping three times. I took my medicine for five days, taking very small sips, and it seemed maybe to have helped. I was not quite as tired as I had been before.

My month in Senegal slipped away as quickly as my forty-five days in Washington had. I hennaed a moon and star on my palm for *Tabaski* and thought my mother would disown me if it had not worn off by the time I returned for my brother's wedding. Aisata saw it and remembered the fish I had had when I first came to Walli Jalla. She asked if I could make a fish on her palm in honor of *Tabaski* and I spent an afternoon after lunch pasting pieces of bandage tape to her hand, patting the cool green henna over it, and then covering it with a plastic bag and a sock. The fish came out well and Aisata liked to say she would always have enough to eat because she held a fish in the palm of her hand.

I bought a *boubou* and headwrap and went to the Diengs for *Tabaski* because I wanted this *Tabaski* to be everything the last one was not.

Fatiim made millet and milk especially for me because she knew I loved it. I had to tell her I couldn't drink it because she had used untreated river water to mix with the powdered milk. It made me feel separated from my family, but I could not afford to get more parasites.

We drank many rounds of tea in the heat, slurping the foam off the brown sweet liquid while Aisata held the bright blue fat-bellied pot over the coals to make more. I played with the children, doing "this is the way the horsy trots" for Racine and Maimoun and Huley, and answered some questions Mbinté and Fatiim had about planes, such as, "Is there anywhere to go to the bathroom on one?" and "Does that just fall from the plane to the earth like a bird passing feces?"

It was a good afternoon. I had my family. Speaking Pulaar tired me and soon I excused myself to sit back in my own compound, under the neem tree, writing letters in English about my African holiday. Fatu, Ya Ya, and the Aans all sent over bowls of meat so I could share in their feast. I wanted to feel successful and proud but just felt tired.

A week before my flight back to the States I hennaed my feet in honor of Jim's wedding. Pulaars henna their feet and hands for all special occasions. I had bought a Mauritanian teapot as a wedding gift. It was very beautiful, pewter and bronze, with memories of men in turbans, sitting behind sand dunes dotted with darker dune-colored camels, holding their pot up high to pour out the steaming tea into an afternoon surreal with heat. It was a thing that felt good to hold in your hands, almost as though by doing so you could be touched by the hands which had held it before.

A week before my flight back, I became sick. I got a fever

and began to vomit. Dirk and I wrote up a list of my options and priorities. I wanted to finish my two years, stay in Senegal, and get well. Dirk said his Dad knew specialists in Washington, to call him. I should ask if I could take all my vacation days to buy myself more time. Dirk said to get a letter from the A.P.C.D. saying he expected me to return and that I was instrumental to the program. Dirk would talk to the administration and would stay and work an extra month if it would help.

I no longer knew what I should do. It was bad to know the States were so close. I had known that before, when I first arrived in Senegal, but then they had drifted farther and farther away—a world away, instead of a plane trip. I could leave if I wanted to. I knew that now and thought of it each time I was sick, or there was a dust storm, or the flies seemed too much.

The day before I left, someone asked Kevin Turner, in front of me, if they could get a ride in the truck up to the Fleuve for the party in Bakel. The party was in three weeks. I would be in Senegal by then—if I came back.

Somehow that one question settled everything. Too many of my days had been lost to the station, colored brown with mud and exhaustion. There had been leeches and water snakes and rats. I had learned to use a *coup coup*—machete—to cut the weeds on the banks, learned to drag the seine and pull in the lead line, worked to make three Moslem men respect me as their boss, always trying to overcome the terrible handicap of having been born a woman. The days at the station changed me: little pieces of me were lost to them, and parts of them remained in me, like an improperly cleaned cut where the skin heals, growing over small pieces of gravel until those pieces become a part of you.

I had spent my days at the Nianga fish station, paid a price, and wanted their reward. The truck was part of it. It was the prize of the coordinator. I could not give it up. I had worked too hard for it. One question, overheard, decided me, like a chemical catalyst turning murky fluid to crystals: I would return.

CHAPTER TWELVE

Mada

Pulaar mornings, those in Walli Jalla, had a quiet luminescence to them. There would be light when you still could not see the sun—a pale other-worldly light, eggshell before pearl, which started in a corner and ran across the sky. Each day the sun rose behind the thatched roofs of the Aans' compound, and when it was still behind them, just broken free from the curve of the earth, it would bring the pale light to life, shooting it through with quicksilver, pink, and lavender, before turning it to white light broken only by the yellow orb of the sun sitting up on the edge of my compound wall. I thought I should wake then, when the sun had climbed far enough above my wall for its rays to touch me as I lay sleeping under the neem tree.

Instead, the strident ringing of my alarm blasphemed each dawn. It shattered sleep while the sky was still black, and I would turn over slowly to reach out my hand from under the mosquito net to turn it off, to save a few of the precious moments between sleep and wakefulness. Those moments were as elusive as mist, impossible to hold. Each morning they were shredded by the list of things which needed to be done that day, that week, that month, and the weight of having become *la Coordinatrice de la Projet du Pisciculture* sitting on my chest, unbearably heavy, threatening to suffocate me if I did not get up and move.

I lay in bed staring up at the spider web of my net and the stars and wished my alarm had been wrong, that there was no pale light to the east, it was still night and I could go back to sleep. Slowly, I climbed out into the darkness, undid the corners of the net, folded the mattress, sheets and netting and carried them into the house. I pulled a large plastic

125

cupful of water from my *loonde,* emptied it into the bent pan sitting over my gas burner and lit the flame. I pulled a second cup to take to the wall with a piece of peanut soap, my towel, and toothbrush to wash my face and brush my teeth—spitting the foaming blue spots of toothpaste over my compound wall into the dusty path. A third cup I pulled and poured into a white container to take to the latrine. When I was finished I sat on the front step to watch the lighting of the sky and because my energy seemed to be seeping away already, like water in a leaky vessel.

Everything ached, as though I had been beaten in my sleep, a slow burning ache that made my movements heavy and my brain dull. It was going to be one of my bad days. I stood and went to turn off the water. I had better not drink coffee; it made it worse. The *beignet* girl came, her metal bowl, covered with a woven trivet, sitting on her head. She took it down, removing the cover to show the rich brown *beignets,* which tasted like doughnut holes, nestled together in the bottom of the bowl. They had become the highlight of my days and I bought ten.

When she left the sun had reached up to my wall and still I sat unmoving on the front doorstep. I shook myself as though I could shake the slow burning from my body or the thickness from my thoughts. It would have to go away. That afternoon there was a meeting in St. Louis with a S.A.E.D. director, the new S.A.E.D. coordinator for fisheries, the Peace Corps administrator in charge of fisheries, and me.

I had been dreading the meeting for weeks, holding onto the thought of finally getting to see Mada in her new village as though it were a talisman that could ward off the evil of this day. I was not good at formal meetings. I cared too much about the program, did not have a good French accent or the appropriate fluency, was a woman, and young. To see Mada would give me something to look forward to in a day otherwise colored with nothing but anxiety.

It was Jeuldé who told me Mada was in Figo. He said she was staying there, but that she wanted to come back to live in the village behind the station. He said she wanted to return because she had heard I was back from America. I had gone to see Jeuldé in his village because he hadn't come to collect his salary at the end of the month. Jeuldé was the guardian at the station and a miser. Mada had been his wife, but she finally left him when he refused to give her money for cloth to be made into a *complète* for *Tabaski*.

I had driven to the little collection of huts where Jeuldé lived. His was run-down, sticks and trash strewn about, with a goat walking freely in and out of the door. At first I thought no one was there, when Jeuldé walked out of the door, bent almost double, and then stood as though dazed dabbing at his eyes with the edge of his dirty pink *boubou*.

He looked terrible. He always carried his age about him like a mantle: his white hair shaved close to the head, his face marked by wrinkles which pulled at his yellowish Mauritanian-tinted skin, leaving his eyes looking sunken and tired. But now there was an emptiness to him as well, as though his skin was nothing but a loose sack barely holding his bones together.

He had to be at least seventy and Abdoulaye and Demba told me he was very rich and powerful, an elder, but he did not carry himself as such around white people. He had lived in a different era and reserved an ingratiating act to be taken out and put on for *tubabs*. He had sagging breasts the men at the station loved to joke about. They said he was impotent, that was why Mada had no children, and also why he might threaten to bring her back but never would. Abdoulaye said if Jeuldé made Mada return, she could ask for a test, where Jeuldé would have to prove his manhood to the village.

He came to the window of the truck to shake my hand with his own dry and lifeless one, drawing his lips back into a grimace of a smile, while he greeted me in Pulaar. I asked him if he was sick, and he said he had been but was better now. I gave him his money for the month and said if he became sick again he must send someone to the station and I would take him to the *dispensaire* in Podor. He said that was good. I was worried about him and thought of the day he had worked in place of Dabo and I had made him seine one of the big ponds with me five times—I had a fantasy of actually accomplishing all the work on my list that day—and later felt guilty because I might have killed the old man. I wanted to help him.

I told Jeuldé he was family, everyone at the station was family, and if he needed help to ask. The look on his face was as desolate as the ruin of his hut, and I wanted to give him something, a piece of warmth. He told me he and Abdoulaye, Dabo, and Demba had become my children. I said he was three times my age, he could not be my child. Yes, he said, but I took care of them.

Then his face changed, and his eyes became eager. He told me he had heard from Mada; she was in Figo. That was very close, he said, it was the village with the mosque along the short cut to the paved road. He said Mada had heard I was back at the station and that she wanted to return too. He wondered if I could take him to see her sometime and then the three of us could come back together.

I looked at Jeuldé. He was so tall, but bent with time, and the wind seemed to be tearing at his eyes. I wanted his words to be true. I could feel the same eagerness in his eyes stir somewhere down inside myself. It felt like a small green plant trying to break through hard-baked dust and I was surprised. I had felt no emotions since Dirk left, except those which were connected to the station and the program, and the soft flickering memory of something more felt strange— almost frightening. Jeuldé's words opened the place where I held my loneliness: the afternoon Dirk and I drove away from Walli Jalla knowing he would not return, Sahné's velvet ears, my longing to hear Mada's soft laughter at the station.

Mada was special. She made me think of the water lilies which grew after the rains came, like small white miracles amidst puddles in the desert. She was beautiful, fragile yet hardy, like the lilies. You could see it in her face. The harshness of the Sahel had not been able to bake her, turning her to shell. Her eyes were different, softer, and it was as though a little of her soul shone forth in them and her soul was warm and good. She was the only precious thing Jeuldé had ever owned and he had never known her worth.

I spoke to him, saying that what was between them wasn't my business. I thought of how the lilies died if you picked one and put it in a bowl. I shook my head.

It would be a terrible thing to help bring her back to a place that made her unhappy. Still, Jeuldé had planted that

The hollow baobab, just north of Thies.

My house in Walli Jalla.
The Diengs' compound is on the other side of the wall.

Dirk, myself, and Dabo at the fish station
in front of one of the thirty-three arc ponds.

A typical scene between Thies and St. Louis.

The mosque near the turn-off for the shortcut to the fish station.

The fisheries volunteers in 1985. *From left, bottom row:* Kevin Wilson and John Bell; *top row:* me, Cindi Horton, Dirk Bryant, and Kevin Turner behind Dirk.

Mada (*standing, far right*) with her sisters and their families in Tivouanne.

Thanksgiving dinner in my compound, under the neem tree, with *(from left)* Demba, Abdoulaye, and Dabo.

Aisata on my front steps, helping me pluck the chickens for Thanksgiving.

Mbinté and her daughters, Huley, Mariyata *tookosel*, and Maimoun.

Amadou and Dad teaching each other how to say "one" in their language.

Fatiim and her son Racine.

The women and children of the Dieng compound making tea. Mariam is to the far right (*second row*).

stirring of hope and I decided to go see Mada, myself, to ask if Jeuldé's words were true.

Jeuldé now looked miserable and I wondered if he still considered himself my child. As I drove away I looked in the rearview mirror to see him standing in front of his hut, which was no longer a home, a corner of his *boubou* to his eyes, and the wind whipping the dust higher and higher as he stood bent and alone.

I had held on to my eagerness to see Mada, only to find it gone as I sat on the step thinking of the afternoon's meeting, and the previous disastrous meeting. That had been my first conference as coordinator, my first without Dirk to translate the French words I didn't know, and it was held at the C.R.S., Catholic Relief Service, headquarters in Dakar. Before the meeting, I had spoken with both Peter and Sarah and updated them on the program and its needs.

The secretary called us to say Suleyman Fall had just arrived, and we went to meet him. He was the director of all S.A.E.D. livestock programs. He was small with a bobbing head, and quick keen eyes. His teeth seemed a size too big for him, and one of the front two was chipped. I had never seen him wear anything but plaid shirts, jeans, and brown leather shoes. He had studied in the Soviet Union and spoke fluent French. I liked him.

We exchanged greetings. He was wearing a *grande boubou* all of white eyelet material. Its traditional Africaness was accentuated by the small black briefcase he held. The *boubou* made Suleyman look much bigger than he had in jeans.

Peter ushered us into a conference room with a huge oval wooden table polished to a bright shine. We chatted a little as we waited for Howie to arrive from Peace Corps. He was standing in for the fisheries A.P.C.D. When he arrived there were more polite greetings and Sarah handed me a sheet of paper. We were all to sign our names and titles.

"Susan Lowerre, *Coordinatrice*"—that was all I had to write but I couldn't do it. I wrote my name, although it sounded a little funny because I was beginning to think of myself as Mariyata Dieng. I tried to write *Coordinatrice* but it looked wrong. It was the responsibility of carrying the title; it left me in a constant state of nervousness which raced through my blood disorienting and scattering my thoughts. It was as though I had always just finished drinking way too much coffee.

I couldn't think. Out of the corners of my eyes I looked to see if anyone noticed me as I held the paper tightly and seemed to have lost my mind. I was supposed to run a program, be responsible for three workers and five volunteers, a floating fund, the truck, an experimental fish station, produce fingerlings, ensure the project did not fail and I had trouble writing my title. I passed the sheet to the man on my left.

Everyone else signed quickly and the meeting began. S.A.E.D. had written up their own budget proposal with an introduction, some thoughts on the future of the program, and then clearly typed line items with allotted C.F.A.—Senegalese currency. Suleyman had a small pile of budget proposals which he passed around the table for each of us.

I strained to understand all that he said as he read from the typewritten sheets. They proposed building a fifty are (approximately one acre) demonstration pond in Dagana and thought there should be another fish station. There were also motorcycles figured into the budget for nonexistent people and what seemed like some type of canoe for our small ponds. The S.A.E.D. budget was ten times that of what C.R.S. had proposed.

Suleyman had not written this; it seemed he hadn't even seen it before that morning. It had to be the work of Daoude Ba. Daoude had become the new S.A.E.D. coordinator for fisheries at about the same time I became coordinator for Peace Corps. He had spent a semester in the U.S. at a training sponsored by the Agency for International Development, A.I.D., for third-world fisheries personnel. Before that he had worked at the old fish station in Richard Toll.

Daoude had a wide, blank face, with a receding hairline and reminded me of a hippopotamus. He seemed to know nothing of aquaculture. We had unending sincere conversations about raising fish along the Fleuve. He would make suggestions such as having two growing seasons, being very adamant about it. He couldn't understand why we had not thought of it before and would look at me accusingly. It was a good idea, except that during half the year the level of the river became too low to pump the water to the irrigation canals, let alone to the fields and ponds they fed.

Once, I had suggested if he was going to be coordinator he be posted at Nianga, where he could actually work with the program and get hands-on experience in the ponds, instead of staying in St. Louis in his little air-conditioned office reading and writing about aquaculture.

Suleyman had finished reading the proposal and a silence fell around the table. Everyone was very polite. Peter and Howie nodded their heads, said a few diplomatic words about its construction, and then were quiet. They had learned better than I that paper and words did not necessarily mean actions. Things would pass. It was important to be polite. The typed words on these sheets of paper would not happen.

Suleyman's words were burning inside me. We had spent the last year working as I had never worked before. We got the fish station to produce and three village ponds stocked with viable fingerlings. When we had arrived the program had no stocked ponds. The other volunteers had looked at us with pity, thinking our program would die, but we had pushed and labored, keeping scientific records until we had a station pond which had produced 2.5 kilograms of fish per hectare, improved feeding regimens and stocking ratios, good-strain fingerlings, three village harvests, and a consultant from Auburn who came to look at our records and suggested C.R.S. continue our funding.

I prayed that Howie, Peter, or Sarah would tell Suleyman we could not do the things he suggested, unless we wanted to ruin all we had worked for. Their French was good; Suleyman would listen to them. No one spoke. My French was so rough. It was a handicap, the same as having a speech impediment. I knew it sounded unprofessional but I had to speak.

I spoke, looking down at the shiny surface of the table. The program's objectives were to stay small, I said, not to expand until we had the ponds that were already built, producing. Overexpansion had nearly killed the program once; we could not afford to make the same mistake again. Ponds bigger that twenty-five ares were impossible to manage.

There was an uncomfortable silence. I looked at Suleyman. He was looking at me and it was obvious what he saw: a young white woman with a ponytail wearing pink pants and sneakers, who knew nothing of the ways of the world. This young woman was speaking against him—the director of a branch of the Senegalese government. My words were the equivalent of the annoying buzz of a fly. They should be flicked aside with the same indifference, and yet these white men listened to me as though I actually had something to say.

Peter finally spoke and explained that C.R.S. simply could not fund a large project, but he hoped compromises could be made. The meeting ended with nothing accomplished. Everyone was out of sorts. Three days later I realized I had left out the second "o" in *Coordinatrice*.

Two months had passed since that meeting, and I had studied French every day for an hour between washing in the river and going to eat with the Diengs. I saw what power language held. I was beginning to realize many things, not the least of which was my deficiencies. The program had to survive. What if it failed because of my incompetence? We needed to hire a coordinator, not use a Peace Corps volunteer—someone older who really was a fish expert, spoke fluent French, did not live like a native, someone who the Senegalese administration would listen to. However, it wouldn't happen because to do so would double the project's budget.

I sat on the front step, paralyzed by the attributes I thought a good program coordinator must possess, which I did not. Coumba Si broke my thoughts. She had come to the compound to see if I was ready to leave. The village always knew when I was going somewhere and one or two people always wanted to come with me. Coumba Si wanted to go to Richard Toll to sell her bananas and Moustafa Aan needed to visit relatives in Thilé Boubacar.

I checked the oil and the radiator, filled my canteen with water, picked up my leather folder that bulged with the paper work of the fish program, found my French/English dictionary and loaded them all into the cab of the truck.

We lifted Coumba's huge tub of bananas into the back and set it next to Mustafa's little suitcase. Moustafa and Coumba started to climb into the truck bed to sit with their belongings and I told them to sit in front with me.

Coumba untied her baby from her back and sat him on her lap. We drove the winding gravel road past Kodite and Nianga, the turn to the fish station, and then out into the openness of the short cut with its hopeless flatness, dust devils, and sand dunes to the north. Coumba's baby was wailing. She and Moustafa smelled and I wished I had just let them sit in back. I needed to go over my French words in my head for the meeting, and it was impossible to think with the noise and distraction.

We were almost to Figo, when I explained to my passengers that I would stop there to ask after a friend. They nodded their heads and I wished I felt something other than tired and a longing for the day's end.

We saw a man standing in front of his hut wearing *chias*—a cross between a skirt and knickers—and a *tingaadi* hat that was pointed and made of straw. I stopped to greet him and ask if he knew where I could find Mada Si. At first he shook his head, looking blank and then his features lightened and he said she was in Tivouanne.

Part of me was disappointed: of course she is in Tivouanne; I was a fool to hope to see her. But another part of me was relieved. I told myself I didn't have the time and was surprised at my relief. It was almost as though I had been afraid to see Mada, and I didn't understand why.

Moustafa said Tivouanne was only a few kilometers from Figo. I said I didn't have the time to go to another village. Moustafa insisted Tivouanne was so close I could easily go and visit my friend. He didn't see the signs of my relief, and said Tivouanne was close so many times I finally said we would go, if only to shut him up.

In five minutes we were there. The town had round thatched huts instead of the square clay houses of Walli Jalla.

I climbed from the cab and walked to the nearest compound, whose surrounding wall was made of sticks stuck into the ground. Two women squatted next to their cooking fire, looking at me suspiciously as I asked after their health and tiredness. Their faces were closed to me. They had never met a white woman who spoke their language. I asked them if they knew Mada Si. Like ice melting, their expressions changed and they began to greet me again, only this time with warmth and smiles. In answer to my question, they pointed to the opening in their compound wall and I saw Mada standing next to the truck greeting Moustafa and Coumba and Coumba's baby. She turned just as we did and smiled.

I loved Mada. Had I known that before? It hung in the air, sparkling like dew in a spider web. We walked toward each other and Mada hugged me. I had not known adult Pulaars hugged.

We stood back and laughed. We couldn't stop. It was as though there were springs bubbling up inside of us, which had to be let free to run out into the dryness of the Sahel. Mada's eyes looked so happy; her face was younger. Abdoulaye had told me if a young woman marries an old man then she too will become old like her husband. I had thought Mada at least forty until one afternoon she told me she was twenty-seven, three years older than myself. Now she was growing young again.

Mada invited Coumba and Moustafa to come to her compound and we walked back a little way to one of the round huts. Inside was a wooden bed, which sat up from the floor, and there were decorated gourds hanging from the walls. Mada said I must sit on the bed while Moustafa and Coumba sat on a mat on the floor. Mada slipped back out of the hut, as women from her family came in one by one to meet Mada's white-woman friend.

They shook my hand, greeted me, and smiled Mada's shy, pretty smile. Several of them sat on the mat and the hut was crowded when Mada returned with the things for tea, milk, and little dry Mauritanian biscuits. After Mada had started the coals in her *feurnot* and was mixing the milk with water in a calabash bowl I left the bed to sit on the mat next to her. All the women said I should sit back on the bed because I was an honored guest, but I said it was too far away, I wanted to sit next to my friend. Slowly they smiled and looked at Mada as though words she had told them were true.

She passed the milk and the biscuits to Moustafa and Coumba, telling Coumba she must take extra for the baby. She asked me for my water, which I got from the truck, and she made a special bowl of milk with my treated water because she knew my stomach was "afraid" of theirs. We spoke of our friends and the station. I told her Sahné had died and she understood. I watched her make the tea. So many people had come to honor Mada's guest that it was becoming very hot, and it seemed as though the people pressed closer and closer until I felt I was suffocating.

I said I only had a very little time and that we could not stay for tea. Mada said we must, at least, have one cup. She seemed to see the tension growing in my eyes. I said I had come because I needed to speak to her and that I must speak to her alone. She handed the flip-flop used to fan the coals to the woman next to her, took my hand, and we walked to an empty hut. This time we both sat up on the bed next to one another our bare feet hanging over the edge.

For a moment we sat in silence, the words trying to slip away from me, to hide. Dirk, Sahné, and Mada were the three things I had loved most. I had thought they had all gone away, only to find Mada. I wanted the days back touched by her: the afternoons we would sit and laugh in the office, making jokes about men, the Ramadan lunches she cooked for us while she fasted, the time I took her to Podor and she drank an orange soda—the first of her life—and the carbonation made her nose feel funny, leaving us both in giggles.

I said I had spoken to Jeuldé and he had told me she wanted to return. I had come to see if Jeuldé's words were true. I didn't look at her.

"No," Mada said slowly and carefully, she would not return. For ten years she had been Jeuldé's wife. She had worked hard and he had given her nothing. She was tired; she had not been well and it wasn't good to be sick. She had completely closed her heart to Jeuldé. She was happy in Tivouanne.

I looked at my feet, my toenails still stained red with henna, and saw Jeuldé standing in front of his hut wiping his eyes. I thought maybe God had cursed him for having been given Mada only to lose her. I felt his emptiness and was glad when another woman walked in to tell Mada something so I could turn my face to the wall and wipe away the tears before they were seen.

After a few minutes the woman left and I tried to tell Mada in Pulaar something I did not have words for in English— what she meant in my life, how she had made it softer, better, the loss I felt without her. I hugged her again. Little Huley and Maimoun and Racine were the only Pulaars who had ever let me hug them.

"It is right you are happy," I said. "I can see it in your face and that is good. It makes me happy to see it."

We went back to her hut and drank the first round of tea. I said I was sorry I could not stay longer but I would try to stop by the next weekend. Mada handed Coumba the bag of biscuits to take for her baby on the trip, and we walked back to the truck, waving good-bye as we pulled out onto the paved road to St. Louis.

I had meant to go over French speeches in my head for the meeting, looking up the words I didn't know in my dictionary as I drove. Instead I thought of Mada. The meeting was the insistent ringing of my alarm and Mada the quiet dawn. I knew why I had been afraid to see her. I had become like the animal corpses by the side of the road—their skins preserved by the dry heat while their insides turned to dust. For three months I had completely lost myself in the title of *Coordinatrice*. Seeing Mada broke its spell.

CHAPTER THIRTEEN

Thanksgiving

The trees my niece draws look a lot like my neem tree did. They have straight brown trunks shooting up from a flat world, lost in a semicircle of bright green leaves. Dee takes a lot of time and colors the leaves in very carefully. My neem tree was like that. It was a picture-book tree: alive and green, blooming in the spring, which always seemed a miracle.

I could not imagine it ever being two pale green leaves breaking through the hard-baked earth of my compound floor: one tiny spot of green surrounded by dust. The weight of the leaves would bend the fragile stalk over almost double. That would be too vulnerable for this world, too tempting for the goats. How would it survive? Instead, I thought someone had looked at the barren dry yard, the crumbling walls, the brown houses, and found the view too desolate. The picture was too harsh to bear, so someone drew a fully-grown tree, making shade, with birds sitting in its branches, like one of my niece's drawings.

The neem tree had delicate leaves. They were narrow and grew one on either side of the branches all the way down to the point where the branches became twigs, and they swished quietly in the wind. I liked to sit under it, in the shade, with my feet up against its trunk and write letters, and I always wondered what people who did not have neem trees tied their mosquito nets to. For Christmas I decorated it with the fancy ornaments I had cut from cardboard and painted white, red, and green. I parked the truck underneath it, standing on top of the cab to reach the higher branches. A village boy climbed higher than that to hang my star of tinfoil and cardboard. He climbed way up into the neem tree, up to where the branches were so slender they could barely hold a

137

little boy's weight, and grinned down at me as he hung the shiny silver star amongst green leaves.

The station's Thanksgiving dinner was held under the neem tree. I wanted it to be perfect and had been planning it for months. At first I had thought I would bring the saw horses from the station, set them under the tree for legs, using my old broken door as the table top. But the truck broke down the day before my *fête* and I had to make do without the saw horses. I could have the dinner inside, but it would be hot and cramped, and I didn't know how I would seat five people. No, it must be under the neem tree.

I lugged two broken-down desks out into the compound and pushed them together at different angles under the chandelier of green branches. Finally they sat the way I wanted them to, and I tried to think what would make the best tablecloth.

I had three *pagnes*—one with a green background and big orange fish, one tie-dyed purple and blue, and another, white with a pattern of intertwined dark blue lines that looked very African. I decided on the blue and white one, and ran to get it from my armoire. It looked wonderful, very neat and clean and tableclothish, transforming the desks into a dining room table.

Next, I set out the plates. I had inherited them with the house—metal with a blue and white enamel design. They matched the cloth. I wasn't sure if I had enough silverware for everyone, and had to scrounge through the plastic kit in the kitchen. I had enough, if someone used my Swiss army knife. I set the forks and knives out with the jam jars I used as glasses. The table needed a centerpiece—something to add just the right touch. I ran back inside the house to get the fish bottle I used as a candle holder.

I had not known you could buy wine in a bottle shaped like a fish. It was pale aqua all scalloped with scales, standing up on its tail, holding the neck of the bottle in its mouth. I felt I had stumbled on a great treasure when I saw it and brought it back to Walli Jalla to drink the wine with Dirk.

It set the table off perfectly but its candle was soft and bent from the heat so I went to the village *boutique* to buy another that stood straight. I exchanged it with the old one and stepped back to look at my table.

The edge of the tablecloth fluttered in the breeze, the glasses, silverware and plates holding the rest of it down, while the fish stood tall and solitary, beautiful in his glittering scales. The neem tree's branches hung down over everything in a delicate canopy of green. I had never imagined anything so pretty and formal in Walli Jalla. It made me think of when Dirk and I had gone to see "Out of Africa" in the Dakar movie theater. I had watched all the luxuries, shaking my head back and forth trying to make sense out of their Africa and mine. The only part to touch my world was when Karen Von Blixen said good-bye to her servants. It gave me a horrible ache to know I would leave too, and I cried—partly for the woman on the screen, but mainly for myself. I was not thinking of good-byes as I looked at the table. I was thinking the baroness had nothing on me.

The only problem was I did not know if Dabo, Abdoulaye, and Demba would see what I saw. I had baked cornbread in a low flat pan and planned to cut it into squares, had cleaned and stuffed two chickens, surrounding them with potatoes and onions. There was a wheel of Camembert I had brought from St. Louis, and French bread to spread it on. I had even made an apple pie, with apples from St. Louis, and butter from Matam. I had baked everything in the small white gas stove that looked like a child's toy, left behind by a previous volunteer. My only disappointment was I had not gotten the recipe to make relish from *beesop*. Thanksgiving dinners should have relish.

I didn't have time to sit worrying about relish and piled all the dirty dishes into the red plastic bucket I carried on my head to take them to the river. I changed into my *pagne* and checked my watch. Everything was on schedule. I took the bucket outside and locked my doors.

I liked the way it felt to walk in my *pagne* and flip-flops balancing a bucket on my head with one arm. It felt like the early morning sound of women pounding millet, as though the village sound had come to rest inside me and moved me to its rhythm. Usually people would tease me as I walked to the river, calling out "Mariyata, you are a real Pulaar woman now," and I would laugh and greet my neighbors who lived along the path.

This afternoon everyone wanted to know if my guests had arrived yet. The whole village knew I was having a *fête*—half of them having been involved in my desperate search for eggs and bread. They seemed as excited as I, and grinned at my nervousness as I said, no, not yet, but soon, soon.

At the beach, Mariam Aan was trying to pull her compound's drinking water—to get out to where the water ran cold and clean without getting herself soaked. I offered to take her huge plastic bucket out, since I was going to wash anyway, and returned to the bank with it full. It was very heavy as we lifted it to her head and I used two hands to keep it from sloshing down over her dry clothes. She asked about my American *fête* and I told her it was called Thanksgiving. She tried the word on her tongue, giggling at its funny feel.

I took my shirt off, setting it up high on the beach, and dove under the water. The river was cold in November and I gasped a little when I came up for air, feeling very bright and alive. I went back to the bank for my soap and shampoo, washing my hair and body, wondering what I should wear. I liked my black pants best, but even with the parasites, they weren't loose around my waist. I wanted to eat a lot of food, but in comfort. I decided to wear my pink shirt from The Gap and my gray jeans.

I rinsed and climbed from the water, laughing at myself. For a year I had done everything I could to make the men at the station forget I was a woman. Now I decided to cook them stuffed chicken and wear pink. I only knew the men in terms of pulling a seine, weighing buckets, fixing the dikes. Dirty and sweaty, maybe wet and muddy, with a pickaxe, machete, or brails in our hands I felt comfortable. It was hard to imagine us in fancy clothes around the dinner table eating Camembert and bread.

I was a little afraid; it might be horribly awkward, a foolish white-woman idea to share Thanksgiving dinner with workers who she had hated the year before. I thought of Demba tripping over his own feet, Abdoulaye's face going oily as he massaged my shoulder when I shook his hand, Dabo who manipulated us and would sell his soul for a Sony Walkman and clothes with lots of zippers.

Only two months before, Dirk and I had parked the truck in the station's driveway, to look through the clear rectangles of its windows at what we thought was the future. The ponds were completely overgrown. Weeds, scraggly and tall, ringed each oval of water, virtually obscuring their liquid surfaces. Thick green plants had been allowed to grow up from the bottoms of the feeder canals, where the earth was still damp but the water didn't run, and you could just make out a few of the wire socks, used to filter the water, dangling from their inlet pipes. They had not been cleaned for weeks and sagged heavily with mud and twigs and trash. One had broken through. Debris, caught on its wire edges, hung there in tatters over the pond.

Slowly Dirk and I had climbed from the truck and walked the ponds as though we shared a nightmare. I undid one of the screens, dumping the refuse on the bank in a lump. A drowned rat fell out with the mud, and I stood back disgusted. As I watched, it came to life—skittering in the mud to get over the bank and down into a hole in the drainage ditch. The water in all the ponds was low. The canal to the 33-are ponds had broken through and been left unrepaired. A gaping hole yawned where the water had escaped and there was a little ravine down the side of the dike where the water had run unchecked to meet the overflow from the perimeter canal.

We turned back to the station building. No one had come to greet us. It was Friday and there were always two workers scheduled on Thursdays and Fridays. The station was never to be left unguarded, under any circumstances. In an emergency the workers had been told to get Jeuldé or Si, the man who lived in the hut across from the canal, to stay at the station until someone could relieve them.

The wind blew, pelting us with dust that mixed with our sweat, and then passed us by to continue across the ponds, across the flat land, across the river to Mauritania.

We looked into the workers' room. Abdoulaye lay asleep snoring on a pile of feed bags. We turned away and he woke up, ran to us and grinned, shaking our hands, trying to pretend everything was normal. He trailed after us as we went to see the damage in the warehouse. The big seine we used to harvest the ponds lay in a wet heap in the wheelbarrow, infested with red ants. To hang the net was the other cardinal rule. It was the only one we had, the mesh having come from the States. If it was left unhung it would rot or be eaten by rats.

We had only been gone three weeks—I at my brother's wedding and Dirk as a trainer in Thiès. Abdoulaye poured forth a stream of excuses, as though in defiance, amongst them that Dabo was sick and in St. Louis.

I told Abdoulaye I was leaving, but would be back in three days. If everything was not fixed when I returned—the net hung, the dike filled, the weeds cut, he was fired. He had pleaded then, but still with an odd expression in his eyes, almost of contempt. He said that was not fair. I no longer cared.

Dirk and I returned to the truck, backed away from the station and drove away from it all. We went to a volunteer party in Bakel. For a long time we did not speak of what we had seen. When we did, we said we had seen the future—this was what would happen when the white man left. We had worked to the point of exhaustion, all those days, for nothing.

I thought things had changed since then. We had a station meeting after I returned from Bakel and I said I would no longer be the person who worked the hardest. This was a Senegalese fish station. It did not matter to me. I would leave in a year. It was they who would remain, still need jobs along the Fleuve, still have families to feed. This program could fall through. If they had learned no skills, then they would have no means to find other jobs.

I said I would teach them everything I could in one year; they would have a pond to manage themselves, to plan the stocking and growth samples and harvest, and to keep the profits. We would all work together. There was twice as much work to be done this year as last. Anyone who did not want to work would be fired. I did not want to hear about S.A.E.D.

rules. If I could not run the station with workers who worked, then I would go back to America right away. I had come to Senegal to teach Senegalese about fisheries. I was tired of working with three old women. I had thought they were men.

Most of the meeting was in French, Dabo translating it into Wolof for Abdoulaye and Demba, but the last I said in Pulaar, and the men looked nervous and then laughed, and Abdoulaye said fisheries was a man's job.

Since that meeting we had changed the locks on the station, made posts for each pond to mark the evaporation rates, fixed the old motorcycle, cleaned out and inventoried the storeroom, repaired its floor, built a thatched awning for the station, set up a system with the butcher in Podor by which we could get cow's blood to mix with our feed each week, stocked a seasonal flood pond in the neighboring village of Guia, and set up one of the small brood ponds for the workers to manage by themselves.

I had not quite believed that much work could ever be accomplished at the station. I was hard on the men—no sick days unless they were validated by the doctor, no drinking tea when there was work to be done, no spending a whole afternoon watching the water drain from a pond. And I was hard on myself. I had said we were family and so I helped Abdoulaye and Demba harvest their rice fields, went to meet their wives and children, helped them out with the truck when I could.

Still, I did not quite believe it was real. It was too close to what I had wanted, hoped for, and I worried it might only exist in my head. Maybe it would be short-lived, just another game to get more from the white woman, and then I would be that much more of an idiot for having tried to thank the men. It made me think of watching Peter Pan, clapping my hands to save Tinkerbell. If you believed, really believed, could you make things come true or were you just a fool?

It all raced through my mind, good and bad, trusting and not trusting, as I squatted at the edge of the river washing the bowl I had made cornbread batter in, the heavy cast-iron frying pan dirty from stuffing, and the only pot I owned big enough to hold boiling water to dip chickens into before they were plucked.

I hurried because I was afraid the men might arrive while I was still at the river and it would ruin everything if I met them while I carried dishes on my head wearing my wet *pagne.* So I rushed, trying not to hear another voice whispering that the men would not come. I had saved and stored, cooked and hoped, for nothing because the men would never come. I would be left with a feast and no guests, the little table under the neem tree, which had looked so perfect, becoming a mockery.

I finished my dishes and packed them in the bucket. I walked the path in quick steps now, torn between hoping Abdoulaye or Demba would already be in my compound—so I could know they really were coming—and that no one would arrive until I was properly dressed.

I walked through my compound walls and no one was there. The table sat perfect, empty and waiting. I put my dishes down in the kitchen and went to my bedroom to change and decided to use a little of what remained in the precious bottle of perfume Dirk's Mom had given me.

Still no one had arrived and I could no longer stand waiting by myself. I ran to Fatu's compound to see if I could borrow a chair and if she would help me carry out the plastic sofa from my middle room, but she wasn't home. I was disappointed. She would have felt my excitement and nervousness, shared them with me, so it would not be so hard to wait.

I walked back to find Demba and Dabo standing next to the table. They both looked very shy, Demba in his best pin-striped *boubou* and Dabo in fancy Western clothes. They shifted their weight from one foot to the other and smiled nervously. We greeted each other awkwardly and Demba said he had brought his tape player, and Dabo had bought the batteries.

I explained I still had some things to do, that they should sit, and went inside the house. I needed to keep my hands busy, and decided to cut the loaf of French bread into slices for the cheese. When I finished I carried one plate with bread and the other with cheese out to the table under the neem tree. I tried to explain it was an appetizer, and brought my Swiss army knife to cut it.

I checked the chicken as it cooked in the oven, cut the cornbread into squares, and pulled water from my *loonde* in a huge plastic cup, which would have to do as a pitcher. I was running out of activities. I could not sit with Demba and Dabo trying to make small talk while we waited for Abdoulaye to arrive. I checked the chicken again, letting go of the oven door when I heard clapping, yells, and laughter.

I stuck my head out the door to see what was happening. Abdoulaye was dancing. He wore his old green raincoat, which looked as though it had come from the Salvation Army—God only knows how it made it to Guia—and his *tingaadi* hat. Really it was a fake *tingaadi*, the type they sold to tourists, and it had hung on my kitchen wall. Abdoulaye had seen it there, pointy and made of straw with a leather rim and leather chin ties, and asked if he could have it. Since then it seemed he never took it off, except to work.

Demba had turned on his tape player and Abdoulaye was dancing to the music, spinning around on one leg, the other one up in the air, the flaps of his raincoat flung open as he spun faster and faster, Demba and Dabo clapping, while Abdoulaye laughed as though he was burning up inside with the happiness of being alive.

I took the last things out to the table, joining the clapping and laughter. After the song had ended, Abdoulaye and I greeted each other and he helped me get the sofa from the house and we all sat down. I thought we should start on the cheese and bread while we waited for Linda, the new volunteer at the station. She had left to spend Thanksgiving in Thiès, but said she would try to get back in time for the *fête*.

It was fun to watch the men eating Camembert. Abdoulaye ate the most, holding my Swiss army knife in his work-worn hands as though it was sterling, patting down the cheese delicately onto his bread, with exaggerated manners. Everyone seemed so sternly formal I almost giggled.

Demba saved me by saying they had brought his tape player to record our conversation—to have something to remember the holiday by. He asked if I had a blank tape and

I went to look in my room. I had found an old tape left by the volunteer before me. It was the closest thing to a blank tape I had.

Demba put the tape into the player. He wanted to hear what was on it before we began to record. It was Baaba Maal, the Pulaar musician. Demba and Abdoulaye became bright with happiness, singing the words of the song, and then looked at me accusingly. There were tears in Abdoulaye's eyes. He sang along with the tape, in a clear voice, pure and sad.

It would have been sacrilege to tape over Baaba Maal, so instead of recording we listened, and I told Abdoulaye he could have the tape if he liked.

The sun was beginning to set, everything turning pale. There were only three slices of bread left and the cheese was gone. We decided Linda had not been able to catch a car in time and we should start the feast. I brought out the roaster heavy with the two stuffed chickens, potatoes and onions, setting it down in the middle of the table, and then went back for the platter of cornbread and the apple pie. I wanted to see what it looked like, all that food together, and made the men wait while I took a photograph.

I lit the candle and Dabo cut the chicken, setting pieces on our plates, saving a slice for Linda and another to be taken to Jeuldé. I told of the stuffing inside the chickens, how important it was, that you could not have a real Thanksgiving without it. We had almost had to, I explained, because I got up too late to buy village bread. Luckily Jibi, the treasurer at S.A.E.D., had heard I needed some and sent his little girl to my compound with a huge loaf of Podor bread. As I spoke, we each put a little of the stuffing on our plates, which we ate solemnly, as though it were a rite in a religious ceremony.

We ate the stuffing, the chicken, and huge squares of cornbread with melting butter. Dinner was serious and we barely spoke as we ate. I was worried we would not have enough room left to eat the pie, but was wrong. Again Dabo cut it into slices—saving one for Linda and one for Jeuldé, and we ate the rest. Apple pie in Walli Jalla—sweeter and richer than apple pie had ever been before. I was glad I had not broken down and eaten the apples as they sat in my kitchen tantalizing me—fresh and ripe, the only apples for miles around.

We pushed our plates away and settled back into our chairs. It had become dark; the flame of the candle glowed and threw shadows on the remains of our feast. Samba called to me from the wall and I went to speak to him. He had killed the chickens for me, as women were not allowed to kill animals in my village, and wanted to know how my dinner had gone. I told him it went well, and ran back to the table to get him some of the cornbread, a slice from Linda's piece of pie, and what was left of the chicken.

It was good to have my stomach full of fancy food, and to look at Dabo, Demba, and Abdoulaye and know they were full as well. It felt like Thanksgiving, and I was glad I had stayed in Walli Jalla. I felt very close to them, but Dabo shattered my contentment.

"It would be good to be rich and eat like this every day," he said, not wistfully, but as an accusation.

I watched the candle burn and the faces of Abdoulaye and Demba and Dabo shining in its light. I looked at the remains of our meal, what was left of two months planning, a quarter of my month's salary, and a day's worth of cooking. Dabo could ruin things. He had a talent.

"No," I said, "that is not true. The meal was special for the very reason that we cannot eat meals like it every day."

"But wouldn't it be wonderful if we could?" Dabo asked. "If we were rich like white people, who do eat this every day."

I looked at him.

"You know I don't eat like this every day," I said. "I eat fish and rice with you at the station and millet in the village at night." Did he really think I ate chicken and pie all the time? Two nights before had been the actual night of Thanksgiving, and I had made stew for the Diengs and gone to bed hungry. Dirk had told me once Dabo's heart was flawed; that he would always want more.

"Maybe that is true," he said. "Maybe you do not eat like white people, but all other white people eat like this. They say they come here to help the Senegalese but I know they really come to make a lot of money. Money is all that is important. If you have money you have everything."

Dabo's face was greedy. To give him something was to remind him of everything he still did not have.

"That is not so," I said. "The things you have, when you have no money are the important things—people, family, and friends, people who help you when they know there is nothing to gain."

Dabo turned to Demba to support him. They spoke together in Wolof and then Demba said to me in Pulaar, "It is true, Suzanne. If you have money you have friends and you can have anything."

I watched the flame flicker in the glass fish, throwing soft candlelight over the table. Something wonderful had been beginning, something delicate and new. Dabo had poked a hole in it and I could feel it slipping away.

I said in Pulaar, working to find words that would mean something to Demba, "Those are not real friends. Real friends are the ones who you have when you have nothing, the ones who stay when you need help, who lend you millet until next month's salary, who help you harvest your rice fields."

Demba listened, as though he already knew the words I would speak, had heard them a thousand times before, and no longer believed them, and then something happened. He sat forward, looking hard at my face as though he saw me for the first time. His face was bright with understanding and he spoke very fast.

"You are right Suzanne," he said. "When I have just been paid everyone talks to me and pretends to be my friend, but when the money is gone so are they."

"*Aa haali goonga,*" he said. "*Aa haali goonga.*" You speak the truth.

He kept looking at me in that bright way, as though he had just found something special. Abdoulaye spoke. He said real friends are family. They stay when you need them even after everyone else has left.

Dabo had meant to ruin what was happening, the closeness, the trust, and instead he had made it stronger. I was white and a woman, but it was he who stood on the outside. It seemed such a lonely place to be and I wondered how little was left inside him that he could not be touched by honesty or friendship. Who had made him that way? Was he flawed or did white people ruin him?

We played Baaba Maal again and Abdoulaye danced, his blood on fire. He twirled and jumped and flipped in the air. His face glowed from sweat and the light of the candle and his grin was full of excitement.

After two songs he sat down and it was Dabo's turn to dance. He danced to the reggae tape he had brought and we clapped our hands. He danced and then finished, sitting back down in his chair, and they said it was my turn to dance. I went inside the house to get one of my tapes, and we played Rod Stewart. Abdoulaye's fire had caught inside of me and I twirled and jumped, laughing out loud at being young and alive.

We tried to get Demba to dance. We all got up and danced around his chair, teasing him to join us. We tried to pull him to his feet, Abdoulaye and Dabo on either side holding an arm, and finally he stood. He shuffled his feet a little, looking down at his shoes as though they could save him, his face bewildered and shy. Abdoulaye, Dabo and I were lost to the music, and didn't notice when he sat back down. We danced, twirling each other around, clapping our hands to the beat until the music ended.

Abdoulaye offered to make tea. He made the best tea of any of us. I scrounged for my charcoal burner in the storage closet and finally found it, along with the charcoal. Abdoulaye brought the coals to life, fanning them with his flip-flop, making glowing red embers burn under the blue tea pot. We drank our three rounds without many words. The tea was sweet and hot and I felt it warm me to the pit of my stomach.

It was getting late and the men needed to leave. I didn't say anything, having hoped they would stay longer. I walked each of them to my compound wall and wished them peace for the night. They thanked me for the *fête*. Demba, just before he left, held my hand in his, which was big and rough, looking seriously into my face as he told me this was the best station *fête* they had ever had.

After they left, I went to sit on my doorstep. I needed to clear away the dirty dishes, blow out the candle, and put the fish back in his place on my kitchen table. I needed to remove my *pagne*, put it with my clothes to be washed, and bring the desks back into the house. But for now I just wanted to sit and watch the warm light of the candle on my Thanksgiving table under the neem tree.

CHAPTER FOURTEEN

The Morning Star

I awoke an hour before my alarm went off. Every morning for a month now, my last hour of sleep had been stolen. I needed that last hour to be oblivious to the things which needed to be done that day, that week, that month. Liquids passed directly through me: in the mornings waking me, and in the afternoons leaving my body dehydrated, causing terrible headaches. I could bear the headaches. I could not bear losing that last hour of sleep.

This morning I had been awake for twenty minutes. I was determined not to leave my bed, not to light a candle and run to the latrine just because my bladder no longer functioned correctly. I would not be ruled by my body. After half an hour, I lost the fight, the way I always lost it, and climbed out from under my mosquito net.

The morning star hung in the sky just in front of me, a fiery diamond in the night. It did not seem real. I had never seen a star so large, so close. I always watched the desert stars. They looked as though someone had taken time to polish them, and I wanted to get to know them this way because they didn't look the same in Virginia.

But I had never seen a star like this, such bright light, huge, pulsing with life against that vast blackness. It seemed more than a star and I thought of the three wise men.

The chance to see it seemed a precious gift, and I smiled a little in the dark thinking I had the most beautiful ceiling in the world.

When I returned from the latrine, I sat back on the edge of my bed to look again at it. I hoped to look long and hard enough to capture a piece of its beauty to hold inside myself. It would be a tiny part of something beautiful only I knew

151

was there, and I would take it out when I needed to look at it during the day. It would be a charm against the routine work: mixing the cow's blood with the fish feed, getting into my muddy work clothes, dipnetting, weighing and being spined by the fish. All these things would become easier with the magic of the star.

Just the night before I had been writing in my journal and realized I could not name one beautiful thing I had seen that day. That felt bad, and it scared me because I thought maybe I was forgetting how to look. This morning I had seen the star the moment I climbed from bed, and I could not help thinking somehow my day would be touched by its power.

I made coffee and sat on the doorstep reading about Oliver North in my Newsweek sent by the Peace Corps. Youmise, Ya Ya's wife, appeared before me. She was wearing her fancy tie-dye *boubou* and had her baby, Daoude, tied with a piece of cloth against her back. She greeted me and then stood silently waiting for her ride to Podor, watching me with patient eyes, as I closed the magazine. I didn't want the day to begin yet, but collected the things I needed for Podor and was ready to leave.

The night before Ya Ya had come to my compound just as I was about to stop studying French and go over to the Diengs' for dinner. He told me he needed a ride to Podor. His wife's younger brother was sick and staying at the *dispensaire* and he wanted to bring him a few things.

I had looked at Ya Ya and shook my head. That morning I had waited to drive Mbinté to the Cité so she could take Huley to the doctor, worked eleven hours harvesting pond number three, given Aisata and the egg girl a ride back to Walli Jalla, leaving just enough time to wash in the river, write in my journal, and study a little French before dinner. I hated the egg girl. She was rude and saucy and I was sorry I had given her a ride. When I dropped her off at her compound I told her she could give me an egg in return and she had pretended not to understand me. I had looked at her in disbelief, when she said she did not understand, *rokkam*— give me. It was the first Pulaar word I had ever heard, and since then I had heard it over and over again. The egg girl refused to give me an egg and I told her I would never again give her a ride in the truck.

Everyone wanted something, even my friends. Everyone wanted to be taken somewhere in the truck. I had not realized what a problem it would be. In the beginning, people just flagged me down as I drove by, and I would let them climb into the back of the truck if they wanted to go where I was already going. Then people would hear when I was planning to go to Richard Toll or St. Louis and come and ask if they could go with me, and I would say yes because they were from my village and it seemed wasteful for me to drive to these places alone.

I wanted to become a part of Walli Jalla and did, but I was a villager who had a compound to herself, owned fancy furniture, was rich, and drove a truck. Someone always needed help and I never knew when to say yes, and when to say no. I couldn't help them all.

The night before, I had told Ya Ya I would not take him to Podor. I was not a taxi service. He could walk to Guia and wait to flag down a car coming from Torregi if it was urgent, or he could wait until morning, when I had to go to Podor anyway, and I could take him then. He did not seem particularly disconcerted or disappointed by my answer and said he would send his wife over the next morning. That was the problem. I could never tell when someone really needed help, or just thought it would not hurt to ask the white woman, because she had so much and she might say yes.

Youmise and Daoude and I drove to Podor. Daoude was a year old and already his face was Ya Ya's. It was wide and open and he had an impish grin. Dirk and I had gone to his naming ceremony the year before, sitting on mats eating millet with milk and drinking round after round of tea. Daoude seemed like a small connection to Dirk, and I smiled at him thinking that I would buy him a gourd rattle the next time I went to Dakar.

I dropped Youmise at the *dispensaire* and she asked me if I could pick her up on my way back. I parked the truck by the school and walked behind it to where the butcher slaughtered his cows in a square cinder-block building. The air was heavy with flies and the sweet smell of blood. Cows' heads and feet, tails and intestines were everywhere. Dabo met me on the path, and we walked inside, greeted the butcher and his workers, and waited for our bucket of blood.

Usually the butcher's did not bother me. It wasn't pleasant, but we needed the blood to make pellet feed. The rough pellets were more efficient than the dry meal we had used the year before—half of which was always lost to the wind, before reaching the fish. Already we had seen improved growth rates.

Usually, picking up the bucket of blood was just part of my week but today it was horrifying. The flies were thicker; the blood more putrid. The glassy eyes of the severed cows' heads looked up at me, as though I personally had taken their lives. One of the butcher's helpers was rinsing out long strings of intestines with a hose and what was left of the dead cows' bowels collected in puddles at his feet, covered over with a layer of flies. I thought of the times I had been glad to eat intestines in the lunch bowl, and decided I never would again.

Usually I stayed and chatted with Jean who saved the blood for us as a favor. This time I could not; I couldn't stand the blood and the smells; the flies rising up from the carcasses and puddles to crawl on my arms and face and in my hair. I was too tired and I felt as though someone had beaten me in the night. I was feeling this way more and more. When I was rested I could stand this world, even find it beautiful, but when I was tired I had no energy to make it better. All I could do was survive.

I knew I had parasites again. Soon I would go to Dakar to have stool tests done. The doctor would not be happy. I wished only that I was at day's end, and not its beginning.

We put the bucket of blood in the back of the truck and Dabo and I climbed into the cab. I was thinking Dabo had better not be in a bad mood or begin to complain that he did not have a *mobelette* or motorcycle. I wasn't going to fight with him this day.

Youmise was waiting for us and she climbed in to sit between Dabo and myself with Daoude on her lap. Dabo picked Daoude up and sat him on his own lap, facing him. He held

Daoude's little hands in his big ones, smiling at him, jostling him up and down. The lines in his face went soft as he looked at Daoude with a tenderness I had never seen before.

Dabo could care about people, he liked children, was an artist, smart, good with his hands. He also lied and cheated, took my Walkman, saying he would repair it, and never gave it back. He told the workers white people were bad. He would never be my friend. We were fighting for control of the station. If I won, he would hate me; and if I lost, I would have wasted two years and he would have no respect for white people. I would never be able to touch something inside Dabo, the way one-year-old Daoude could, no matter how hard I tried.

It was nine o'clock when we arrived at the station. I made a list of the things to be done and double-checked it against the list I had written in my date book, at the beginning of the week.

Linda was already working on the records. She had taken over my responsibilities, when I took over Dirk's. She had shoulder-length blond hair she wore in a ponytail, was attractive and petite. I hoped she never got parasites because she had no extra weight to lose to them.

We didn't speak much, we never did. I knew she was having a hard time adjusting. She didn't like the family she lived with, wasn't used to the hours or the work at the station, was working hard to learn Pulaar and French, and hated Dabo.

I understood her hatred. My own was just beginning to fade as he lost his power over me. I understood her hatred and yet felt loyal to Dabo. He and I had seined ponds together for a year, hated each other for a year. I knew Dabo and I didn't know Linda. I could no longer remember what it was like to be an American who had just come to this country: the shock, the fear, and the need to lean on someone. I knew I had gone through those emotions and that Linda was going through them now, but I could no longer feel them.

There was so much to do. I had no energy or sympathy left over to give to Linda. What energy I had, I used to run the station and the program, to love my village, and to fight my body. Most of the time I wished she was not there, and then felt guilty. I was the type of second-year volunteer I had sworn I would never become.

Sometimes I wanted to say, "Look, I know you must think me a monster who cares about nothing but the fish program. I am sorry, I was not always like this. I do know what you are going through, but I can't help you. Everyone has to go through it—alone. If I helped you now, it would only buy you time and you would face it when I left." Sometimes I wanted to say that, but I never did.

Today we sat in the broken-down Peace Corps chairs with our calculators, trying to determine feed ratios and conversion rates, kilograms per hectare produced, and profit made—or sometimes debt incurred. I kept making mistakes. My head felt thick. I couldn't think. It took me twenty minutes to figure out a feed ratio, and then slowly, like light through mist, it dawned on me I had done it wrong.

I changed into my pond clothes. At least I could do physical work. I had started toward the holding tank when Demba called to me. I was surprised to see him; he had to come to work in three hours. What was he doing here now?

I walked halfway back toward him and he greeted me. His child was very sick, he said. Could I take him, the child, and his wife, to the Moslem medicine man in Figo?

"Is your child very, very sick?" I asked. I didn't want to drive to Figo.

Demba said if the child was not taken to the *ceerno*—the Pulaar word for *marabout*—he would die.

"If your child is that sick, Demba, then I think he should be taken to a doctor."

"I have already taken him to the doctor in Podor and the doctor gave him three shots. The child is no better and the doctor said there was nothing he could do. It is not a disease for the doctor. It is a disease for the *ceerno*. It is a *jiin*," Demba said.

I had never heard the word *jiin* before. Dabo told me later it meant a devil.

Demba looked worried. Why did he think I could help? If I went to Figo I would not get home until after five o'clock. How sick was Demba's child, really?

"I don't know, Demba. There is a lot to do today," I said. "I cannot drive everyone to the doctor's or the *ceerno's*, even if they are very sick, especially when I am supposed to be working at the station."

Demba's face was blank. He nodded his head and said he understood. I was at work.

The fish had been in the holding tank for a day and a night and if they weren't moved they would die. How could I tell Demba I would not help, when he had said his child might die? The fish were my responsibility. His children were not.

"Did the doctor say what he thought your child had?"

"It is a *jiin*," he said. "He has only been sick for three days. The doctor can do nothing to help him." Demba seemed upset with me for not understanding.

I felt so tired.

"I will take your child, your wife, and you to the *ceerno's*, but I can't take you until after I have moved the fish at three o'clock." I said.

Demba looked relieved and thanked me. He would meet me at three.

I didn't know if I had made the right decision. I didn't want them taking advantage of me. When Abdoulaye's brother died he asked me to go to Figo and I ended up driving a truckload of old Pulaar men back through the desert to the funeral. They acted put out when I stopped at the station and said I had to work, that they could either walk to Guia or wait until I was finished. Finally, I had driven them to Guia and they had never thanked me, as though a ride in the project truck was their due. I wondered: what had Abdoulaye and Demba done before they had a white boss with a Toyota truck?

By three o'clock I was wet and cold and tired. The fish had been moved and Demba had not arrived. As I carried the last bucket of fish to the office to be weighed the canal broke through and water began to gush down the dike. For a moment I just stood there watching the water rip a growing hole in the side of the canal. I wanted to walk away from it, pretend I had never seen it, let someone else make the effort to fix it. Instead I went and got Dabo and we filled the wheelbarrow with shovels of dirt, pick-axed to loosen them from the earth, and dumped them into the hole. We did three wheelbarrow's full, stomping it down and hitting it with the flats of our shovels. My hands were badly blistered by the time we were through.

The canal was fixed and still Demba wasn't here. There was no reason he and his wife could not have walked from Kodite, carrying the baby. If Demba's child was really so sick, he would have carried him here to save time. I asked Dabo if Demba was expecting me to pick him up. He said Demba was waiting for me in Kodite.

It was three-thirty when I left. I was mad. I was sick myself and had worked all day, but Demba would never think of that. He wouldn't make the effort to walk to the station.

Demba was standing by the steps of the bridge that crossed the canal between his village and the road. I stopped the truck in front of him and he told me he would go get his child and be right back.

He came out of the house carryng a girl. She must have been eight or nine. I had thought it was the baby. Her arms and legs stuck out oddly from Demba's arms as though they were made of something stiff—wood, instead of flesh. An embroidered orange *pagne* was wrapped around her, but it kept falling off and trailing in the dust. Demba's wife ran behind him, frantically trying to pick the *pagne* up and tuck it in. Demba was hurrying, almost running, and he held the girl awkwardly as though she were a heavy sack of rice, not his daughter.

He started to lift her into the back of the truck the way he would if she really were rice instead of human, and I told him to bring her in the cab. Demba's daughter was sick, and he was going to set her in the back of a truck, to be bounced and whipped by the wind and to lie on the hard metal ridges of the truck bed floor. My Dad had taken me to the hospital once when I was five and stood holding my hand while they sewed up a cut on my leg. Afterwards, he had carried me gently to the car and taken me to the pastry shop to pick out my favorite doughnuts.

Demba opened the door and climbed in with his daughter.

At the same time his wife and two other women and two men began to scramble into the back of the truck. I said I thought I was taking him, his wife, and his child to Figo, not half the village. While Demba yelled, in a panic, for the others to get down I looked at the child's face.

Her eyes were strange, wide open, but not seeing. She smelled, a smell that filled the cab as though it were alive, clinging to Demba and me—sweet and rotten. That was why Demba had started to put her in back. He had not wanted me to have to smell her. It no longer mattered who rode in the back of the truck. I told Demba this and the people climbed back in.

Demba's daughter was dying. She wasn't sick, she was dying. Please God no. Before, I had made deals with God. This time I didn't. When I had first lived in Walli Jalla, one of our kittens became sick and I held it in my lap and asked God to take some of my strength to save it. I was so strong and it was so tiny and helpless. The kitten became well; I had been sick ever since. Later the cat died, but God did not release me. I looked at Demba's daughter and was scared. I did not offer my strength to her, to a little girl, because I needed it myself.

I began to drive, and tried not to think. The girl didn't seem conscious. I had never seen anyone in a coma. What could make her so sick in three days? I wished I had been right and it had been the baby. It would have been easier: a scrap of life going back to where it had come from, not a little girl of eight who laughed and hopped, wore flip-flops and a *pagne*.

The girl's bare feet stuck out from under the blanket at an odd angle. Her toenails were hennaed. The pattern had worn off from the flesh of her feet but the dye had remained on the nails. She must have hennaed them for *Tabaski*. I had seen the little girls in Walli Jalla making patterns with the tape, patting on the henna, covering it all with plastic bags and socks, while they were surrounded by the women of their compounds and much laughter. They loved to make themselves beautiful. They hennaed their feet and hands in celebration of holidays. They did not die that way.

Demba shifted her weight and her arm fell out from under

the cloth. She was wearing three plastic bangles. He took her arm and bent it at the elbow, bringing it back under the cover and then rearranged the fabric so it could also lie over her toes.

"Do you think she will live?" he asked me.

"I do not know, Demba," I said.

He said he did not think she would. He said it very quietly and without emotion. I drove on.

"She has died," Demba said.

It took me a moment to understand he had said she was dead, rather than she would die. I yelled at him to feel for a pulse, but could not explain in Pulaar how to feel for the heartbeat in her wrist. He didn't understand and felt her hands and her feet, pulling up her skirt to feel her naked stomach, a small, flat stomach. He looked at her eyes. They were rolled back into her head. His wife knocked on the window and I started to stop the truck. Demba screamed to keep driving. He had seen her eyes move.

He pointed to a group of three huts where I was to park the truck. We were engulfed by people. They greeted us, and then Demba climbed from the truck holding the girl and the women began to wail. I stayed behind the wheel. There was nothing I could do. A little boy in the crowd came up to me and said I should have brought Moussa Salif. I did not know who Moussa Salif was.

The women took the girl from Demba's arms and carried her inside one of the huts, leaving him in front of the doorway, empty-armed, and bewildered. He waited there for someone to tell him what to do. After a few minutes an old woman came out to him and said they needed Moussa Salif, Demba was to go with me, and I was to bring Moussa Salif to the hut.

We took the same path we had just come on—Demba and I in the cab and his mother and another old woman in back. I did not understand why they were returning. Demba told me Moussa Salif was the *ceerno;* he was at a meeting in the village by the fish station, and we must find him.

"Suzanne, you are good," Demba said. "Your heart is good.

You have helped me and I will have a charm made for you so that when you return to America, you will find work right away."

The sun still shone and Demba spoke excitedly about how he was planning on thanking me. He knew Dirk was still looking for work in America and he said that wouldn't happen to me. He would give me a charm with very strong magic. I was good, we were family. The cab still smelled of death.

I told Demba I was not so good. I had done nothing. I wanted him to listen to my words, they were important, but he didn't.

After we pulled into the station's driveway I didn't move. Demba went to find the *ceerno*. He was still trying, but I knew it was over. I leaned against the steering wheel, cradling my head in my arms. The old women climbed down from the back of the truck to pray—to turn to Mecca and bow their wrinkled foreheads to the earth for the fourth time that day. I wished I had their faith.

Dabo had waited until we returned and now he was ready to leave. He was dressed in his fancy Podor clothes, sitting on the doorstep to the workers' room. He walked to the cab after Demba left and asked if I thought Demba's child would live, and I said no. He told me he had stayed as late as he could; he had to leave now. Fine, I said without looking at him.

Demba returned with a piece of paper the *ceerno* had written on. He said he had to take it back to Figo. I asked him if I could take it for him. Someone had to stay at the station and it was his night to work. It was too late to do anything for his daughter, but I didn't say so. Demba said he needed to take the paper himself, so I told him Ouseman could work for him, but he would have to pay Ouseman's salary himself. In Senegal, you get one day off for deaths. Demba would have a day for the funeral.

The next morning, I got to the station early and sat at the pond's edge taking the water temperature. I was glad of an excuse to just stare at the water and hope the mother-of-pearl morning could color me inside. I kept hoping somehow Demba's child had lived, and thinking of how I had not offered my strength. Abdoulaye came to sit next to me and asked of Demba's daughter. As we sat there a little boy ran up to tell me the girl had died and to ask if I could take Demba and his family to Figo for the funeral. I said I would.

Linda arrived. She too, asked after Demba's child, and I started to tell in English what had happened the day before. My voice broke and I could feel tears in my throat. It was too painful to speak of in English, and so I stopped. In Pulaar it was not as bad.

For the second time, I drove a hearse. I drove the little girl's body, still wrapped in the orange *pagne* to the Figo graveyard. The cemetery was located in what was left of a forest, and there were small piles of dead wood I thought marked graves. I stopped the truck where Demba told me to, and said I would go away. I walked a ways and turned around to see if I had gone far enough. The men in their *boubous* yelled at me, "Go, go", and I turned and continued walking.

I walked until I could no longer see the men and then sat down and listened to the wind. I sat in the dust and hugged my knees and felt there was peace in the sound of the wind through the trees. My body was a hundred years old—so heavy. It felt good to sit, to sit without moving, here in this dead forest where the wind blew through the branches. I was glad women were not allowed at burial ceremonies. I sat there alone, a white woman hugging her knees, while the black men buried their dead—a little girl with hennaed toe-nails.

CHAPTER FIFTEEN

Mariyata Tookosel

Mbinté had a house to herself. It was white and the biggest house with the biggest thatched awning in the Diengs' compound. Inside, she had a wooden bed, a small glass-faced china cabinet, and a trunk. Her husband was Samba's oldest son, Baa Baa, who lived across the river in Mauritania. He was a *marabout* and came to visit once or twice a year. During Ramadan Mbinté crossed the river to stay for a month.

In December of the year before, I had hennaed my feet with "Merry Christmas", one word along the inside of each foot. Mbinté could read a little. She spelled out the letters on my feet, asking what they meant, and then, giggling, wanted to know if I could write "Welcome Baa Baa" on hers, the next time he came to visit. She liked the mural I had almost finished on the kitchen wall and was hoping I would paint one for her. She had two little girls: Maimoun, who was pretty and sweet, and Huley, who was vivacious and a little devil. They both had their mother's dimples and big eyes. Mbinté was pregnant with her third child, but she told me after this one she was going on the pill. She had gone to see a woman doctor in St. Louis who had said she was not well, and should not have children for a few years.

I looked at Mbinté when she told me that. We were sitting out on a mat under the stars waiting for dinner. She was wearing one of the three *boubous* she owned; her husband had forbidden her to ever dance in public; and she wanted to go on the pill. I asked her if Baa Baa would allow this, and she said he would have to because she wasn't well and it was medicine. I had a feeling Baa Baa would never be told.

Mbinté was like that, slender, pretty, and bright, wanting everything modern. She had spent part of her childhood in

163

Dakar, when her father worked as a guard, and been able to attend school. She spoke as much French as any of the men, could even read and write, although with difficulty. You could tell how quickly her mind worked and that she had a hunger both to use what she had learned and to learn more, but I felt she held herself back. A woman shouldn't be so smart; it makes the men feel dumb.

I knitted Ya Ya a white cap, and Mbinté wanted to know how I could work the thread. For Christmas, I gave her bright red and green yarn and needles and we spent night after night sitting in her room, touched by the warm glow of the kerosene lamp as I tried to teach her how to knit. Huley and Maimoun would tease me to play, climbing into my lap, occasionally pulling at the strands of their mother's yarn, or rolling a ball across the floor like playful kittens.

I cannot remember when Mbinté first told me she was pregnant. I think Fatiim teased her one day as we gossiped about Soya being pregnant. Fatiim said Soya was not the only pregnant woman in the village and looked at Mbinté with a grin. I asked Mbinté if it was true, was she going to have a baby, and she said it was. I had never had a pregnant friend. It was exciting. When I was in the States for my brother's wedding I went to a yard sale to look for baby clothes, digging through pile after pile until I found a yellow jump suit with sewn-in yellow feet, a zipper up the front, and a fish appliquéd on the left breast. I ended up with a whole small pile of baby clothes to bring back to Walli Jalla to give to Mbinté the day of the naming ceremony.

They sat inside my armoire, on the third shelf. Each time I looked at them I became more eager for the day to arrive. I watched Mbinté grow, not quite believing the woman I knew, my friend Mbinté, was growing a whole person inside herself. I asked her a lot of questions; how did she feel? would it be soon? could I help with anything? And she said yes, she wanted me to be there when she gave birth.

I did not know anything about giving birth, except what I had seen on TV, and learned in biology—something about breathing correctly, hot water, cutting and tying the umbilical cord, and slapping the baby on the rear end until it cried. I tried to imagine Mbinté on her neat wooden bed in labor and wondered if I would pass out, but I wanted to be there.

I told her I would be there when she had her child, but I wouldn't be much help, as I had never seen a child born. We had been sitting around the lunch bowl, and Mariam, who was eight, began to laugh. Mariam was one of Fatiim's children and looked like Oumar. She already knew something of life, was capable, practical, and loved to be amused. Now she was laughing hard. She could not believe a grown woman had never seen someone give birth. She teased me mercilessly and shook her head. White women knew the oddest things, how to drive a truck, raise fish in the desert, but not how to have a baby.

Still, Mbinté said she wanted me there, so if anything went wrong, I could take her in the truck to the Podor doctor. She had blind faith, as many of the villagers did, in white-people medicine, believing in it the way they believed in magic. I didn't have the same faith, but wanted to help her. It would be better than her hemorrhaging in bed, her life slowly seeping away in that white-washed room with her trunk and her glass-faced cabinet.

It was September when she asked me to be there and she didn't give birth until November. I spent the two months in between as though I was the father, always thinking of Mbinté and her child, when would it come, would it go all right, would I be there when she needed me? It annoyed me a little that she was so calm. Her belly grew bigger and bigger and I would ask, did she think it would be soon? and she would say yes, soon, soon, the same way she told Huley and Maimoun they could have new *complètes* for next year's *Tabaski*.

I was so afraid I would be in Dakar or St. Louis on business or on a tour of the village ponds, when the baby finally came. I didn't think she had room to grow much bigger. She was so slender, put together with such fine bones, and now there was this great huge thing growing in her; it seemed that it would rip her apart. Halfway through October I decided I would no longer leave the village. The coordinator work would have to be put off until after the baby. The last trip had been too nerve-racking. I had gone to Dakar to buy fish meal and then raced the whole way back, a voice telling me Mbinté was having her baby; it had come and I was gone.

Instead I worked the days at the fish station, thinking that if there was a problem they could send someone to find me and I would come with the truck. I tried not to, but I kept staring at Mbinté's stomach when we were around the lunch bowl. Sometimes I would lie awake at night feeling my own flat stomach, wondering what it would be like to hold another life inside my own, and thinking I couldn't wait to meet this little person.

One day there was a catastrophe. The truck wouldn't start. I cleaned the battery terminals, checked their connections, and the elements' water level. It still didn't work, and Dabo walked to the Cité to get a mechanic.

Two men came, raised the hood and looked very seriously at the battery, tasting its water. The mechanic said one of its elements had gone bad. I should replace it with a battery of 90 amps, nothing less. They jump-started the engine and he told me not to turn it off until I had bought a new battery.

I drove first to Podor to the new automotive store but they sold nothing but huge truck batteries, and anyway I had forgotten my money belt. I went back to Walli Jalla to get it and then drove to Richard Toll, wondering as the gas needle dropped closer and closer to empty if I had enough gas to get there. I didn't have enough to get back. Sometimes the Richard Toll station had gas and sometimes it didn't. I drove the familiar road past the mosque behind the sand dunes, Thilé Boubacar, where they had Thursday markets, cutting across the hopeless flat land covered only with a patch here and there of a few sparse strands of dried grass like an old man going bald.

I made it to the gas station to find they did have petrol, and prayed the ride had charged the battery enough that it would start after filling the tank. It did. I drove to the big *boutique* that had a Michelin sign in front, left the truck running, and went inside to ask if they had 90 amp batteries. They didn't. I tried all the mechanic shops along the Richard Toll strip. None of them had a battery of 90 amps, and everyone kept reminding me that my truck was running, as though I might not have noticed.

In the last *boutique* a young man said he knew someone who might have one, sending a child out to find him. A Wolof man dressed in fancy Western clothes returned with the child and we spoke in French. Yes, he said he had a battery that would fit, not a ninety but a seventy. He looked at my battery saying that a seventy would do, but all his batteries were at his house.

We drove down one dirt road after another to get there. We entered the front door and he said his batteries were in his bedroom. I wondered if I would be raped in search of 70 amps. We walked the long hallway single file, and entered his room. Up against the far wall was a huge stack of batteries. I let my breath escape, not realizing I had been holding it.

The man searched through all of the batteries for the right amperage but couldn't find it, finally saying he could get one from Mauritania by the next morning, I decided I would have to come back. He said he would meet me at the *boutique*.

The sun had sunk and I drove back to Walli Jalla dazed and in the darkness. I missed the turn for the short cut and had to drive to Torregi and around the long way. I almost missed Torregi, not realizing I had already passed the short cut. I wished I knew something about cars. My first year I spent wishing I'd been born French and my second, wishing I'd been brought up as a mechanic.

I was lucky, the next morning the truck started and I drove to the Cité to ask Kreuger, S.A.E.D.'s head mechanic, if he really thought 70 amps would do. He did. Linda came with me and I drove to the *boutique* where we found the battery man who said he had not been able to get one after all. He wrote a name and address on a piece of paper, saying he was certain this man would have one in St. Louis. We drove another two hours to the city, to a large shop, neat and clean with stacks and stacks of automotive parts and two men behind a counter. They didn't have my battery and did not know who would, unless I drove to Dakar.

I could not go to Dakar. Mbinté was going to have her

baby; but the project truck had to be fixed. Linda and I decided to go to lunch to think about it. We went to the *gare*, because they had good, cheap *ceebu jën*—rice and fish. We saw Ebu, the Cité's S.A.E.D. secretary, and asked him if he knew where I could buy a 70 amp battery. A taxi driver overheard my question and said he knew where to find one and that he would take us there in his car.

Linda and I sat in the back of the run-down taxi and I was wondering if this man would charge me for his help; even if he only charged for the taxi ride it would cost a fortune. We were going around a curve and the man pointed to an automotive *boutique* which he said might have the battery. We would try it later, if his place did not. I couldn't afford a taxi ride through the myriad streets of St. Louis, and yelled for the driver to stop. We would try this *boutique* while we were here.

Walking inside to greet the men behind the counter, I asked if they had a 70 amp battery. They did! It was the last one and I was sure it was the only one in all of St. Louis.

The taxi driver took us back to the *gare*, charging less than I had predicted the ride would cost. Linda left to catch a seven-seater to Thiès and I drove back to the station with my prize. At first I was filled with triumph, it had been a great thing to get the battery, but my triumph was leaky, slowly emptying to leave only exhaustion, shot through with nagging doubts. The battery had cost more than any one thing I had ever bought in Senegal. What if I had gotten the wrong one, or it didn't work? I could have taken the truck to the Toyota dealership in Dakar. How would I explain to C.R.S. that I was too stubborn to drive all the way to Dakar because I didn't want to miss Mbinté's baby?

I went to the Diengs' for lunch the next day, the way I always did on Saturdays. It was a good "bowl" with a lot of the crispy rice that fries in the oil up against the sides of the pot, the tangy *beesop* sauce I loved, and two of the big trucked-in *yaboy*, cleaned Senegalese-style with five slits along either side. I always wondered what the slits were for, to better cook the fish or to let out bad spirits?

Fatiim, Mbinté, old Maimoun, Aisata, Mariam, little Maimoun, Huley, Racine on Fatiim's lap, and I all sat around the bowl. We dipped our right hands in a bowl of water, said *"Bisimilla"* then dipped our hands into the rice, making little balls of it, bringing them to our mouths. I ate the slowest because my hand was still not quite accustomed to being used as a spoon and burned more easily than the others'. Little Maimoun and Mbinté always worried I was not getting my share and would pull pieces of meat from the fish, throwing them to my place.

I had come to enjoy eating at the women's bowl. I liked the feel of pushing the rice up against the metal surface, rolling it around in my palm until it was compacted and could be lifted to my lips without losing half of it to the mat; and I thought eating with one's hands made good sense because then you never burned your mouth. It took time, was shared movement, and I came to want the ritual of it, missing it when I ate Western style.

We did not speak much as we ate. Now and then someone would slap Huley's hand if she tried to take more than her share or to eat her sister's portion of crispy rice. Fatiim was trying to wean Racine and made tiny balls of rice to tempt him with, the oily white grains that didn't make it to his mouth sticking to his warm brown cheeks.

There was still fish left and lots of rice, when Mbinté pulled her hand back. She sat very still, far away, listening to what we could not hear, and then she came back, again making balls of rice with her right palm, and popping them into her mouth.

When Mbinté had stopped eating, we all had. Like a herd of deer when one smells danger and raises its head to sniff the air, the others sense the fear and also raise their heads. It was a false alarm, and like deer, we all returned to feeding.

After a few minutes Mbinté stopped again. I felt she was far away, somewhere down inside herself. For a moment she sat frozen, then washed her hand, stood with a little help from the awning post, and walked to her house without a word.

She must be having her baby! I could barely sit still and everyone else had gone back to eating, quietly making balls of rice, bringing them to their mouths with the same rhythm they had before. Why was everyone eating? I wanted to scream, "Isn't Mbinté having her baby? Shouldn't we be doing something?" I asked Fatiim if this meant Mbinté was having her baby and she said it might mean that. She finished her meal, washed her hand, and gave Racine to Mariam. Mbinté came to the door of her house and called to her and Fatiim went into Mbinté's house. When she came back, I watched her face for signs, but she was calmly cleaning up the lunch dishes.

"Is Mbinté having her baby?" I asked again. Fatiim looked at me with the patience she reserved for Racine and said they had just sent for the midwife. The life Mbinté had been growing was about to come into the world. I was filled with awe and anxiety while everyone else went about their afternoon chores.

The small children and I were the only people left idle on the mat.

I felt ridiculous sitting in the middle of the Diengs' compound, while everyone else was busy. I sat for half an hour as the horse ate his hay, the sun continued to glare, and Aisata pounded her millet. No one spoke to me and nothing happened. I watched the midwife arrive and enter Mbinté's house. The only sound was the thump of Aisata's pestle. It was an afternoon like any afternoon, except the white woman had come for lunch and hadn't left as she usually did. Finally, I decided to leave and go to the river to work on my painting of the curve by Guia that I wanted to send to Dirk for Christmas. That would be the easiest way to make the time pass. Then I could come back and see if anything had changed in the Diengs' compound.

I took my sketch pad and pencils and walked the path to the beach. There were not many people by the water's edge and I sat down in the sand facing toward where the blue water curved around the bend, in front of the little square brown houses of Guia and the solitary palm tree. I was having trouble drawing the acacia bush, where the kingfishers sat. It blocked part of my view and had to be in the picture. From where I sat I could clearly see every tiny delicate leaf of the bush, and I could not decide how realistic I had to be in its reproduction.

I leaned the pad against my knees and started to draw.

There was a quietness to the river—as though the passing water could swallow up the shrill, harsh noises of the village, and give them back softened around the edges. The color of its blue, the constant passing of its waters made people into small parts of something bigger. I wanted to catch a little of that quietness on paper, so Dirk could feel it in America when he was surrounded by concrete and skyscrapers and well-dressed, bustling crowds.

It took me a long time to draw one branch of the bush with the kingfisher perched on it. The kingfisher was very good, sitting as though turned to stone. As the minutes passed, small naked bodies lined up behind me to see the image the paper was becoming.

I decided one branch was enough for this day and noticed the children. They wanted to see what I was doing. They laughed and pointed to the drawing and then at the river, the branch, and the bird. They had never seen anyone draw, and wanted to know how I had put the river on my paper. I tried to explain, then gave up. I had been gone an hour and was anxious about Mbinté.

I walked back to my compound thinking surely Mbinté would be in labor by now and I would come and sit with her while she gave birth. I looked into the Diengs' compound. Everyone seemed to be going about their chores and I watched them for a moment before calling to Aisata.

She saw me before I said her name and came running up to the wall, excitement in her eyes.

"Have you seen Mbinté's baby?" she asked.

"What do you mean?"

She asked again as though I hadn't heard her the first time, "Have you seen the baby?"

"No. She hasn't had it yet," I said; and then, "She hasn't had it yet, has she?" She couldn't have. After all these months of waiting and worrying, she would not have her baby while I was trying to be patient and wait until she needed me, would she?

"Yes," Aisata said. "Mbinté just gave birth. She was asking for you, but no one knew where you were. She wants you to come see her baby."

I nodded my head silently. I could not believe Mbinté had

produced life in the time it had taken me to draw one branch and a bird. I had wanted to be with her; how did she have a baby so fast?

I walked to the Diengs' compound and into Mbinté's house. I didn't know what to expect. I thought right after someone had a baby the room must change somehow. What would have been done with the afterbirth, the umbilical cord, and the boiling water?

Mbinté's room looked exactly as it always did. Her wooden bed was neatly made up with a blanket and she sat on its edge. The only difference was that she was holding a tiny body wrapped in a green and yellow *pagne*, with only its arms sticking out.

Mbinté looked up and smiled at me. She had wide cheekbones and soft brown eyes. Her lips were very dark—I think they were tattooed—and her teeth looked brilliantly white against them. It seemed there was tiredness around the edges of her eyes, but that was all.

She handed me her baby and I held it in my arms. It was such a tiny human being. I had never seen someone so small. I put my finger by its hand and it took hold and I looked into its face as though it were a crystal ball, to see if I could find Mbinté's face. Its mouth was very small and round and it yawned as I watched. It was a miracle! I wanted to tell Mbinté that but didn't know the Pulaar word for miracle.

I wanted to ask if it was a boy or a girl, but no one was to know the child's sex until its naming ceremony. It was so perfect with ten tiny brown fingers and toes. The baby had been inside of Mbinté an hour before, and now it was in my arms.

The child coughed while I held it. It had coughed before, when I had first entered Mbinté's room. I hadn't known babies could be born with colds. If Mbinté's baby was born with one, I couldn't imagine how it would survive the cold season outside its mother's womb.

The worry must have shown on my face, because Mbinté explained to me that the baby still had a little fluid in its lungs; that was what made it cough. As she was speaking, the baby scrunched up its eyes and mouth and began to cry. I handed it back to Mbinté.

"What do you think?" Mbinté asked.

"It's a wonderful baby," I said, smiling. The baby's skin was very pale, the color of weak chocolate milk, and I could not help but tell Mbinté I thought it looked more like me than her. I laughed and asked Mbinté if she didn't want another *tubab* in the family? She smiled and told me all babies were born light and then darkened as the days passed.

She stood and walked to her *loonde* to fill a cup with cool water. She moved slowly and I thought she must be very tired and that the custom of having the mother and baby stay inside and rest for the next seven days was good. I told her I would go, so she could rest.

"Your baby is very beautiful," I said and turned to leave her room.

Six days passed and the night before the *innde*, the baby's naming ceremony, I lay in bed too excited to sleep. That afternoon I had seen Fatu at the river and she had asked me if I had a *binngel*, a baby. I was not sure what she meant, but I thought she might know whether Mbinté's baby was a girl or a boy. If it was a girl, Mbinté had said that they would name it Mariyata. It would be my *tokoram*, or namesake.

My head was filled with the thought of becoming a god-mother. I would buy her one of those baby *complètes* in Dakar, and a tiny set of the traditional silver bracelets women wore on each wrist. Maybe Mbinté would let me carry her one time, wrapped against my back like a Pulaar woman. She was the only person I had ever met the day she was born. She would keep hold of my heart, formally tying it to Senegal, and I would come back years later to visit.

It was odd to think that I would leave when she was only a year old. She would not really know me, and have to ask Mbinté and Fatiim and old Maimoun and Samba about who she was named after. They would tell her of the white Mariyata who had come to live in their village. I hoped they would explain to her that I loved her very much; and left only because I had to return to my own country. Maybe I would be able to help her when we both were older, pay for her to go to school, so she could learn the things her mother had always wanted to, but had never been given the chance. I

tried to tell myself Mbinté's baby was a boy, but couldn't stop
thinking of what it would be like if it was a girl.

Early the next morning I went to wash in the river. When I
returned to my house I could already hear the guests
gathered in the Diengs' compound. I dressed to join them. I
would wear my *malafa* to attend the naming ceremony. It was
from Mauritania, a length of very fine thin cotton that had
been tie-died blue and purple and was worn like a sari. It
took a little while to remember how to tie it and I fumbled at
the knots.

After I had dressed, I looked over the wall, to see how
many people really were at the Diengs'—just to know before
I went over there and was engulfed. The compound was
crowded and everyone seemed busy with talk, tea, or laughter. Mariam saw me watching and grinned at me. She said the
baby was a girl.

I went back inside the house to get my pile of baby clothes.
It seemed almost funny now to take them from their hiding
place where they had sat so long. I set the package of sugar
and the cone of tea I had bought for Baa Baa on top of them.
I had never met Mbinté's husband and wondered what he
would be like. I thought I might not like him because he had
forbidden her to dance. I started to walk outside and then
went back in to the little cardboard box where I kept my
earrings. I had a pair of small silver hearts I wanted the baby
to have.

I carried the things outside and locked my doors. I walked
slowly around the compound walls, feeling nervous. The
compound was overflowing with people, mats had been laid
out, the air was alive with conversation, and Aisata was making tea. I greeted the people and they called out, "Mariyata,
Mariyata," greeting me and smiling, asking if I had a *tokoram*.
I said I didn't know.

I was taken in to Mbinté's room to see her and the baby.
She sat surrounded by women, who were all talking, laughing, and taking turns holding the child. They greeted me and
I greeted them back. Mbinté told me I had a *tokoram*. She had
given the baby the name Mariyata and Baa Baa had given her
the name Kanza. I handed Mbinté the clothes and the earrings and said I was giving the baby my heart and would

come back in ten years to see if she still held it. The women said the gifts were good, holding up each piece of clothing and turning the silver earrings between their fingers. They teased me about having a *tokoram* but I was not sure. Did I really have a namesake if Baa Baa had named her Kanza?

"Who is Kanza?" I asked Mbinté, and she told me it was a white woman Baa Baa knew in Mauritania. I sat silent trying to think what white woman would be named Kanza, and why the child should carry the name of someone who didn't even live in Senegal. Mbinté's room was crowded with women, most of whom I didn't know. They spoke too fast about things I didn't understand, and I sat silently watching. It did not feel like Mbinté's room filled with all these women in fancy *boubous* and high pitched voices. I didn't stay long.

I went to pay my respects to Baa Baa. He sat inside another house, and he too was surrounded, only this time by men wearing fancy *boubous*. Someone was making tea. Baa Baa was very tall and handsome, very serious looking. I handed him the tea and sugar I had bought as his gift and then said maybe I should take it back and give it all to Mbinté, since she had given the baby my name, while Baa Baa had called her Kanza. Baa Baa looked concerned and said the baby would only be called Kanza in Mauritania, and everyone else laughed. He seemed so sincere, rather quiet, and traditional. He thought that was the right way to live his life and I understood why Mbinté had told me he was a good husband.

I stayed for awhile in the compound, greeting and speaking with people, but it was odd to be in my family's compound surrounded by so many people I did not know. They made me tired with their loud voices, and the foreign commotion.

I went back to my own compound and sat writing letters, listening to the sounds from next door, feeling guilty and a little let down. I couldn't decide if Kanza Mariyata Dieng was really my *tokoram*. Often villagers told a white person they had a *tokoram*, so the white person would give the child gifts and money, but the baby was not a true *tokoram*. It was just another way of trying to share in the white person's riches. I would rather not have a *tokoram* than feel betrayed by my family.

I went inside to work on my family's Christmas stockings. I

had decided to sew a red stocking, with each person's name embroidered across it in green. There were thirteen people in my family, and I had two weeks to finish them.

When the sun began to pale, and the afternoon had become quiet, I decided to return to the Diengs' to see how the *innde* had gone. There didn't seem to be so many people now, and I wanted to be with my family.

I went in to see Mbinté. This time she sat in her room alone with the baby. She put her in my arms and I felt all the things I had hoped to feel that morning. Mariyata *tookosel,* little Mariyata so small, perfectly made in miniature, just beginning life. She scrunched her face up, looking into mine, making baby fists. I thought she was probably the most beautiful baby ever born, my god-daughter, a tiny village god-daughter.

Fatiim came to tell me she had saved me a bowl of rice and meat. She sat with me while I ate and asked what I thought of the baby. She said it was good I had a *tokoram.* Now I was truly part of the family. I had become a Dieng.

CHAPTER SIXTEEN

Welcome to Walli Jalla

Every Saturday I swept my house. I would sweep out the kitchen, the living room, the two bedrooms, the library, and the little room in back where I sometimes hung my clothes to dry. By the next Saturday, everything would again be covered with an inch-thick layer of fine brown dust. I would sweep the floors and the tables, my clothes cabinet and the book-shelves, straighten everything in the kitchen and the few things sitting on my armoire.

I used a *baale*, a traditional broom, made of a clump of whisks tied at the top with a piece of rag. It was old, had come with the house, and was beginning to lose its straws, but I was used to the feel of it in my hand and didn't want to buy a new one. I would bend at the waist, swishing the broom almost horizontal with the floor, until I had a little pile of dust, insects, and debris which I would sweep onto a piece of cardboard to carry outside.

Sometimes the wind fought my sweeping and I would sweep the dust from my kitchen floor and stray gusts would blow it back, or I would carry my piece of cardboard with the little mound of brown dust outside, and before I could throw it in the yard the wind would throw it in my face. There were days when the wind deposited the dust as fast as I could sweep it up and we would end the day in a stand-off, but I wouldn't let it defeat me.

I liked to clean my house. I could think whatever thoughts I wanted and be responsible for no one and nothing but myself. Sometimes I would play music on my Walkman. I had bought two speakers that could be plugged into it to listen to the music without earphones. I would sing "Break Down" with Tom Petty at the top of my lungs and look around at the flippers and snorkel hanging on my bedroom wall, the mural of wild animals in the kitchen, the matching shelves and canisters I had covered with contact paper that looked like stained glass, and I would be happy with my home.

It was Sunday and I was still cleaning. On Sundays I tried never to do anything I didn't want to—usually I sat under the neem tree with my feet up against its trunk writing letters or listening to classical music and writing in my journal.

After I had swept the dust and dirt and bat droppings from each room, I began on the walls. They were covered with cobwebs and wasps' nests and strips of brown dust collected in their irregularities. Little chips of whitewash came away with the dust, leaving behind tan ticking, as though someone had shot the wall with a spray of pellets. The whitewash came off more easily than the dust, but I wouldn't give up.

I took the *pagne* covering off the piece of tin on cinder blocks that served as my coffee table, and changed it for another, arranging the year-old National Geographic and Smithsonian magazines on top of it. There were little brown lumps of honeycombed clay, wasps' nests, dotting the walls. They looked terrible; how could I have not noticed them? I tried to pry one from the wall with a screw driver. I finally got it off, but a large chunk of the wall came with it. I wasn't sure if there were any wasps in it or not, and imagined dive-bombers avenging their home.

I cleaned the gas stove until it was almost white and swept the walls again finding more cobwebs and spiders every-where I looked. I couldn't have my parents come to my house when it was full of insects, bats, and dirt. A spider tried to scurry away from my broom as I took down his silver-gray web, and I went after him. Mom would have a hard enough time with the flies. I hit the spider twice, then stopped sud-denly.

I never killed spiders. They killed the flies, and *Charlotte's Web* was one of my favorite books. My mother didn't kill spiders. When they were in the house in Virginia, she would pick them up and tell them they belonged outside in the sunshine, and put them out. What was happening to me that I swept and swept, tore chunks off my walls, then tried to kill a spider? I told the spider I was sorry, hoped he had gotten away unhurt, and went to sit on the doorstep.

Mom and Dad would be here in a week, and I was afraid it was all a horrible mistake. I had insisted they come to Senegal, told them they would no longer know me if they didn't. I wanted them to drink tea with my family, see how big the moon was, how bright the stars were, feel the power of the river, and the shade of my neem tree. It was important they hear the sound of Pulaar, and women beating millet in the mornings. How would they know me when I returned to the United States, if they never saw the fish station or met the men I worked so hard with? If they never saw the fish feeding, the ponds glassy in the dawn, how would they understand my reasons for giving body and soul to try to make the fish program work?

If they never saw my world, there would always be huge places inside of me they couldn't know. But I was afraid, afraid I had made them do this, take these risks—their voices had been nervous over the telephone. They had spent money and time I was not sure they could afford and it would all be for nothing. Once they got here, they still wouldn't see. They would have American eyes and everything would be dirty and smelly, the heat unbearable, Senegal so foreign. I had forgotten the power of American eyes. My home would become a crumbling hovel.

I worried about the flies. Mom hated them. If one got into the house, she would immediately get the swatter, and say how dirty they were. Here, there were millions of flies. They were like the heat, inescapable, a part of the land.

I decided to paint "Welcome to Walli Jalla" over my front doors, thinking it would be cheerful and upbeat. I went inside to drag out one of the Peace Corps armchairs. The seats had fallen through on all of them and this one showed springs and stuffing. I set it as far back on the step as could and climbed up on it, trying to get one foot on each arm, almost tipping over, as I clung desperately to the door frame. I had to throw my head back and stand on tiptoes to draw the letters, my muscles straining.

I drew them in pencil then got my tin of red paint and paint brush and climbed up again to fill them in.

Being up so high, I could see over the Diengs' wall, and they could see me. "Mariyata, what are you doing?" they asked. I said I was writing *"bisimilla"* in English for when my parents came. They knew my parents were coming as did everyone else.

Evening after evening one or two people from the village would trickle into my compound, to see the photo of my parents and to ask when they were coming to visit. They said my mother was small, just a child, and my father big. They wanted to know what my father did; was he a *ceerno* in America? How long would they be staying? Samba said he would buy them a chicken.

Mbinté, Fatiim, and Aisata walked into my compound to get a good look at what I had painted on the wall. Mbinté said I should write welcome in both English and Pulaar because I was a Pulaar now, part of the village. I agreed with her, but was too tired to get back up on the chair.

Well, it was finished. It hung there, the bright red letters arching over my faded green doors. "Welcome to Walli Jalla". It seemed corny, but it was too late to change it.

I hated the Dakar airport, all it had ever meant to me was trauma and upset. I sat in one of the orange plastic bucket seats and watched the people walk by, thinking the last time I had been here was to say good-bye to Dirk.

I couldn't imagine my parents here. Dad would look so odd surrounded by men in *boubous,* and Mom would be lost in the bright colors, noises, and myriads of people. I was very close to my parents and felt if they were really coming, I would know; some part of me would sense it. I felt nothing.

The flight they were supposed to have come in on had landed. A woman called the flight numbers out in French over the loud speaker. I was quite sure they were not in the room next door and wondered how I would stand the depression if I found out they had missed their flight, or canceled at the last minute. I went to speak to the guard who stood in front of the glass doors, keeping friends and family from entering the room where passengers picked up their luggage and went through customs. I was afraid if my parents were in the room, they might have problems understanding the French, or that someone would hassle them.

I stood at the rail watching the passengers arrive, peering into the crowd and seeing person after person get through the doors to meet friends and family. I went back to the guard, explaining to him it was my parents who were arriving from America and that they didn't speak French well. He didn't care. I was fantasizing about kicking him in the shins when my parents walked through the forbidden entranceway, holding their luggage, smiling and wearing new hiking boots, their eyes nervous behind their smiles.

These were my parents and they looked like Americans. Dad was tall, a big man. I had forgotten. He wore a straw hat and a red and white checkered shirt. Mom was wearing new khakis. They looked as though they ate well, were healthy and happy. They looked rich and that startled me. If they looked American to me, how did I look to them?

There was a confusion of greetings and hugs and smiles, while all of us talked too fast. They said I looked skinny and tired and I said they looked well. Mom thought the air smelled like urine. I yelled at the kids who were harassing us in French and Pulaar, and Dad said Ned had warned them against thieves, telling them never to set their luggage down. I helped them carry their bags to the truck. We put them in the open bed in back and Mom was worried they wouldn't be safe. I told her they would be. There was nowhere else to put them.

We spent that afternoon and night in Dakar, and the whole time I felt as though we were plump, clucking hens surrounded by a pack of dogs. I didn't like Dakar. There were too many high-rises, cars, noises, and people. It wasn't my life, and I was always amazed it existed in the same country as Walli Jalla. People made a living out of ripping off tourists. All white people were targets; Mom and Dad were prime candidates. I told them not to accept anything someone put in their hands "as a gift".

That was a traditional ploy. A man would come up to you with a fake silver barcelet on a bed of tissue paper, saying he wanted to give it to you as a gift. If you took it in your hands, you would never be able to give it back, and before the man left he would have extracted ten times the bracelet's worth. Other men would work in groups of two or three, one distracting you while another picked your wallet. They would say you dropped something, or pull on your pant leg, and the moment they had your attention their friend would have your money. I never felt safe in Dakar, and I had the protection of knowing a local language and wearing flip-flops— only poor people wore flip-flops in the city. With Mom and Dad I was too aware of how vulnerable we were.

My parents stayed in a fancy hotel while we were in Dakar. It must have had ten stories, and there was a balcony, a toilet and shower and clean ceramic-tile floors. There was a TV and two double beds made up with clean, pale yellow coverlets.

After lunch the first day, I left them in their room to rest, while I went to the Peace Corps office to finish typing a fisheries report. It was our plan for the future—goals set, specific plans to reach them, accomplishments of the past year, and a five-year plan by which the station could become independent of foreign advisors. I wanted it to be concise and professional, something to turn to when everything was a muddle.

I remember wondering if I was the only person who believed in the report; and if this was so, why was I typing it when Mom and Dad were two blocks away, having crossed an ocean to see me?

I was finished by evening and joined them in their hotel room. Mom told me about Ned's wedding—how they had been late, couldn't find the marriage license, and then got lost on their way to the justice of the peace. Grandma was becoming more confused and harder to live with. They didn't know what to do. Mom was thinking of quitting her library job. It felt good to lie on a double bed, to catch up on the family news, and odd because it seemed I had gone to visit my parents, rather than them having come to visit me.

The toilet seat was cracked, which Mom felt was an outrage in a hotel as expensive as this. She said it would collect germs,

and she wished she had brought her antiseptic spray. Someone had told her the best way to avoid parasites was not to eat
anything cold. They had a variety of pills for diarrhea.

I had asked the village *ceerno* to make them *gris-gris* to
protect them from runny tummy, parasites, and fever. The
charms were two little squares of leather hanging from a
thong meant to be worn around the top of the arm.

The road between Dakar and Thiès is three lanes, and the
middle lane alternates as a passing lane for west-going and
east-going traffic. Senegalese seem to drive in one of two
fashions: either as though they don't believe in traffic accidents, or as though they do believe in accidents but think
their charms from Allah will keep them safe. Our drive to
Thiès was an hour of playing chicken, but it was safer to drive
like a Senegalese than to hesitate. I tried not to notice how
tense Mom and Dad had become.

In Thiès we stopped at the Peace Corps regional house and
walked from there to the beer garden. The regional house
had a hammock and a toilet, although without a seat, a
refrigerator, and a stove. One of the doors hung by a single
hinge, and the floor of the front room was almost covered
with an army of empty, green beer bottles. The bookshelves
were falling down and covered with dust. A foam rubber
mattress lay half on and half off a broken cane bed. Mom
and Dad were disgusted. Just for a moment I saw it through
their eyes. I couldn't afford to see it that way.

The beer garden was a small restaurant with an open
courtyard, run by a Lebanese family. It was a place to sit and
look at trees, and drink beer that was a little colder than the
day. We went there for lunch and sat in dented metal chairs
with no backs at a sheet metal table. Next to us were five loud,
drunken men. Flies crawled on us and the smell of the toilet
was inescapable. I had always loved the beer garden.

If my parents didn't like Dakar and Thiès, where there
were trees and plumbing and fancy food, they would hate the
Fleuve. We drove the three hours to St. Louis mostly in
silence, Mom and Dad watching the country pass. There was
no scenery, nothing but flat brown land with a few tortured
trees. They thought it was ugly. Dad said they never would

have chosen Senegal for a vacation and wouldn't be here if it weren't for me. They'd spent all that money, taken a whole process of shots to come to Africa to visit, and I knew they were miserable. I thought of my own first weeks in Senegal. I had forgotten. How had I thought it would be different for them?

We passed two nights in St. Louis at the Hotel de la Poste. I was sure they wouldn't like it, thinking of the reaction to the cracked toilet seat. The walls in the rooms were covered with *pagne* material and in places it was peeling away or stained from leaky pipes. Sometimes there was no hot water, especially near dinner time, and only a trickle would come from the shower.

The hotel had been built in the mid-nineteenth century. It was across from the post office, thus the name, and had three stories and a balcony. The bar's walls were covered with hunting trophies from the time when the Fleuve had been savanna, before it became Sahel. There were antelopes' heads and boars' heads and one very old lion's head, that looked as though it had been about to die of old age when someone shot it. There were elephant tusks, water buffalo horns and old black and white photos of a Senegal that no longer existed.

Mom and Dad liked it. The Hotel de la Poste was the first place they had seen that actually touched my life. It was more the way they had imagined Africa. It was also in Pulaar land and I could laugh and joke with the people I knew in their language.

We ate dinner, a fancy meal in the dining room, that put us all in better moods. I introduced the waiters I knew, who welcomed Mom and Dad to their country with handshakes and bows and bright white smiles. We practiced Pulaar greetings over steak, Mom and Dad becoming upset when I said I had told some villagers my parents were learning their language.

We had freshly squeezed orange juice at breakfast. I hadn't known such a thing existed in Senegal. They bought postcards and cloth and Dad found a basic math book in

French, asking if he bought it, would it help anyone at the station. He knew I was trying to teach Dabo math.

The morning when we were to leave for Walli Jalla, Mom became sick. She was nauseous and her head ached horribly. I couldn't believe she was already sick in the world of clean sheets and comfortable beds. What would happen *en brousse?* She was not sure she could travel.

I had to get to Walli Jalla and the station. I had been gone for almost two weeks. There was so much work to be done, and I always worried about disaster when I was away. Abdoulaye and Demba had given me a puppy for Christmas, saying they thought I missed Sahné. I named her Henry and wanted to make sure she was being fed. More than anything I just needed to spend time in Walli Jalla and at the station. They were my center, like Samson's hair, a source of strength. Without them I was nothing and Senegal was nowhere. Walli Jalla was my home, and the station my obsession.

We drove and drove, Mom and Dad squished together in the one big seat to the right of the stick shift that was supposed to fit two. I knew they were uncomfortable. When we had driven up from Thiès, they finally had to ask me to stop because they were getting such bad muscle cramps. How could I have brought Mom and Dad to Senegal, to do this to them?

As we drove, we were enveloped by dust, lost in a brown blizzard. We couldn't see more than a foot or two in front of the truck's hood. It was the worst I had ever seen it. I couldn't believe the timing. Dust storms were miserable. All you could do was wait for them to end, dust in your eyes, up your nose, and in your mouth until your saliva seemed like mud. I imagined my parents and I weathering a week of dust storms closed up in the Walli Jalla house, and thought of crying.

The moment we were engulfed in dust Mom visibly brightened. She kept saying it looked just like the snow storms in New York, the way the dust swirled on the road, caught in the eddies of the wind. She thought it was an adventure and the two of us talked and laughed. Again Dad said he wouldn't have chosen Senegal for a vacation.

Along the short cut to Walli Jalla, we stopped at the deserted village and got out to walk among the walls. I showed them where Dirk's and my pumpkins had sat, the spot where I left sugar for the spirits, the two phantom trees that had scared us so. The wind blew softly as though it were very old and tired. Mom and Dad looked at the walls and off into the great flat distance. I wondered if they felt they had walked into one of my letters. For the first time they seemed to feel an echo of what I felt, and then all of a sudden they said how hot it was, how tired they were. Could we continue to Walli Jalla?

I had to stop by the station for a moment to check on things. I went to find Dabo. He told me Linda had been sick since I left. No one had been at the station that whole time? I thought first of the work which must not have been done, and then as a guilty afterthought of how often Linda had been sick. What if she needed me to drive her to Dakar? What would I do with my parents?

We left for Walli Jalla, drove inside the compound, and parked the truck next to the neem tree. I watched Mom and Dad's faces. Villagers came to greet us, but slowly in ones and twos, rather than in an overwhelming rush. One boy kept pointing to the words over my door and telling Mom and Dad it meant *bisimilla*. I explained that was their word for welcome. They had seen pictures of my compound and didn't seem too surprised.

I took out my skeleton key and unlocked the green doors, swinging them open to be held in place with the two cinder blocks. Mom and Dad walked inside the house, from room to room, at first not saying anything. Dad was shocked. His daughter lived in a hovel. He had thought somehow it would be different inside. It was falling apart, the rafters were rotting, and the door frames pulled away from their clay walls. I wondered how he could miss the important things: my curtains and fireplace, the papered shelves and matching canisters, my fish candle holder.

We moved the chairs out under the neem tree, and I brought out a mattress for the double bed. Samba walked through the compound's entrance leaning on his cane, holding a chicken upside down by its legs. He greeted Mom and

Dad and I said he was Samba, my village father. He handed me the chicken.

I had thought my family would keep the chicken and prepare it and we would all eat together. That was how they honored guests. I asked Samba if he would not rather do it that way, but he said he was giving me the live chicken because he knew American stomachs. He said he had seen how village food made me sick. This way, he said, I could prepare American chicken for Mom and Dad, and their stomachs would not be "afraid" of it. He wanted my parents to be well, to feel at home in the village. Then he said my parents must be very tired and that their daughter was good. He wanted me to translate this. He wished them peace for the night and walked back to his own compound on the other side of the wall.

I needed to go to Podor to buy bottled water, ice, soda, and eggs, but first I wanted to see Linda. She lived in a little house in a family's compound halfway between Walli Jalla and Kodite. No one was in the yard, so I walked directly to Linda's house and knocked on the red tin door.

It took a moment for her to open it. She walked as though she was on a tightrope, graceful with pain, the skin pulled tight around her eyes. She said she had been sick since I left and she was leaving for Dakar the next day. She asked if my parents were here, trying to smile.

Yes, I said. My parents were sitting under the neem tree when I left them. I told her I had to go to Podor to get things, did she want anything? I would come and get her after I went to Podor. She must come eat with us and spend the night. Could she stand public transport? She looked bad. Did she want me to drive her to Dakar? She said she would take a transport car, but would like to come for dinner. She had to pack.

When I returned to my compound Mom and Dad were relaxing in the neem tree's shade, as though they had been doing so all their lives. It hit me with a wave of emotion to see them there, warm and alive. I felt as though I should wipe my eyes in case they vanished, but it was true. They were mine to borrow from America for fourteen days.

I poured them glasses of cold Seven-up and Fatu came to greet them. She was very excited and kept chanting "*Haayoo* Mariyata", grabbing my hands and then theirs, laughing and rolling her eyes. She said Mom was very small and Dad was big. Ya Ya came to greet them as well, and sat on the plastic couch with my father. He could speak a little French, so he used the words he knew and they used their words, and everyone smiled because some of the words were the same.

Oumar walked inside the compound's walls, grinning shyly and carrying another chicken by its legs. I told him he didn't have to give us a chicken, Samba had given us one, but he insisted he wanted us to have one from himself.

Oumar spoke earnestly, a little soft with shyness. He told my parents their daughter's heart was good. I had helped them many times; I was part of their family. They looked blank and he told me to translate his words. I had yearned for words like Oumar's to soften the harshness of my days, but had not thought to hear them. I thought somehow words would validate my time and sickness and now they were said, but I didn't want to translate them.

I laughed, and felt both happy and uncomfortable. I hadn't expected my parents' visit to mean so much in the village. I had hoped someone would kill a chicken for them, because it was a sign of respect and if they did that for my parents, I would know it was not done for my white skin, or to get something in return. I had never thought we would get two chickens.

Linda came for dinner and we ate potato and onion omelets. You could see how she hurt. I hoped Mom could help her. Sickness made you so alone in the harshness of the Sahel. Linda needed to be hugged and my mother put her arms around her. I was glad Mom could give Linda a small piece of what she needed, and I no longer had to give.

That night we burned a scented candle in the latrine all through the night. Juliette, my new sister-in-law, had sent it. It was blue and my mother brought blue toilet paper to match. I always hated going to the bathroom after dark because I had to fumble around for a lantern or candle. I couldn't forget when we had first come to Walli Jalla and each night huge cockroaches crawled out of the hole in the darkness, then skittered to the corners when you touched their brittle insect shells with light.

We pulled out mattresses to set up the beds. Linda and I would sleep on the ground, and Mom and Dad could use the double mattress on the cane bed. Mom and Dad under the neem tree seemed like a trick photograph—as though someone had snipped a part of one picture and pasted it over another. I smiled because they really were in Walli Jalla, my Walli Jalla, with the rustling of the neem tree's branches, quiet dusk, and Pulaar greetings.

CHAPTER SEVENTEEN

Mom and Dad

My parents became a part of my world, stretching it just a little as they fit in. One afternoon the three of us sat in front of my house, Dad peeling potatoes, while Mom and I plucked chickens. Dad sat in the orange plastic armchair with the seat falling through, because he was too big to fit comfortably on the step with Mom and me. Mom was wearing her *gris gris* around the top of her arm. I could just see it under the edge of her sleeve as she dipped a scrawny chicken in boiling water, pulling at what was left of its feathers.

Dad was peeling potatoes with my Swiss army knife and his hands made my knife look small. As a little girl, I had always liked to slip my hand into his because it was so big and safe and warm. He had sharpened my knife for me the day before, something I had been meaning to do for months. Dad carefully peeled each potato, saying he did not think men worked like this in my village; maybe he should quit before someone saw him. Then he laughed, looking over at Mom and me.

I finished plucking another chicken and set it in the roaster with the potatoes. I told Mom and Dad I needed to speak with the workers, at the station and they said they would stay to finish preparing the meal. I sat in the truck waiting for it to warm up, watching Mom and Dad. They never looked up from their work.

I loved to sit on my front step. In the early morning I would watch the sun come up over the roof of Amadou's house, a huge orange ball resting for a moment on my compound wall. At night, I would sit watching the stars and look at the moon. Sometimes I would make silent wishes or thank yous, because the sky was so vast it seemed there might

190

be someone to listen. Now Mom and Dad sat on my step, fixing dinner, and I knew the next time I sat alone I would think of them—Dad peeling potatoes and Mom plucking a chicken.

It felt good to turn into the station driveway. Demba, Dabo, and I sat on the bank of pond number three talking of what had happened in the weeks past, of all the work to do in the next month, of Mom and Dad's visit. Henry came and jumped on me. I scratched behind her ears, and told her that I had missed her. We had just fed the fish and they made little round bull's eyes, where they came to the surface to eat the rice and fish bran. They were feeding well and the pond surface was completely dimpled, the bull's eyes expanding until they ran into one other.

Dabo stood up to go to the office and Demba told me he would give a *fête* for my parents. He would kill a goat. He told me so with words made slow by his seriousness, watching my face to see how I would react. I said he didn't have to kill a goat, that was too much. He said, "No Suzanne, you are wrong. To kill a goat is not too much for your parents." He wanted to know what I was going to kill for them. "You should kill a ram," he said.

He told me he wasn't going to invite Dabo, and I stared at the pond not speaking. There had been another fight with Dabo just before I went to Dakar to meet Mom and Dad. This time it was over a motorcycle. Dabo wanted a motorcycle more than anything. He felt I deliberately kept him from obtaining one. Other S.A.E.D. projects had them. He had heard there were extras and wanted me to help him get one, but I explained the project couldn't take that responsibility.

Next, he asked if he could take time from work to go speak to Kreuger, the head mechanic. I said no, he would have to wait until afternoon. His face became hard and he walked out of the office. He went to speak to Demba, telling him how unfair I was, trying to share some of his hatred.

It was as though the past six months had never happened. Again the station was filled with tension, the workers' faces sullen and mean. Dabo didn't surprise me, but that he could still influence Demba did. Demba and I had been working on his numbers—hours and hours of trying to get his threes and sevens going in the right direction. He had taken me to his *ceerno*, had me over for dinner, and I had helped him harvest his rice and move the huge log posts from his field to his compound.

Dabo was paid more than Demba and Abdoulaye, because he was the *chef d'equipe*. Since moving to Podor, he worked less than the other two. He had walked away when Demba's child was dying. He lied and cheated, drank and smoked. How could Demba not see who Dabo was? It hurt to know my white skin was still so blinding. This time I wouldn't let it go. I could speak a local language as well as Dabo. He spoke Wolof, but I spoke Pulaar. Dabo strutted and played the *grand patron*, living in a house with electricity and access to a refrigerator. Abdoulaye, Demba, and I lived in villages.

I called Demba to the office. I explained that I was trying to run the station and Dabo wasn't pulling his weight. I was not trying to be unfair. Demba listened, and when Dabo tried to break in, he told him to be quiet. He thought very hard, and then told me it was none of his business. It was between Dabo and me; he was sorry he had become involved.

Now Demba told me he would not invite Dabo to my parents' *fête*. He would do this to please me.

I watched the surface of the pond. Fewer and fewer fish were eating and the bull's eyes were farther apart. I told Demba no, I hoped he would invite Dabo. It would be better. Demba's thoughts always showed on his face. He was confused; Dabo wouldn't have done that. Power was to be jealously guarded. He didn't realize, but I did. I could have him invite Dabo because Dabo was no longer a threat. Dabo had lost. I sat watching the water, the sun glinting off the ripples, feeling unbearably sad.

Two days later we went to Demba's *fête*. We sat in his compound on a millet stalk mat, watching the paleness of late afternoon and talking about Demba's two wives. He had taken the ugly one as his second wife and no one could understand why. She was pushy and outspoken. There was a story that Demba had paid the bride price for a third wife,

but the woman's father had taken the money and the day
after the marriage ceremony the woman had run off. Everyone said Demba should have known better.

Dad was worried about eating goat. His stomach and
Mom's had been taking turns feeling sick, and he'd been
queasy all day. The thought of goat was unappealing. He
didn't want to insult Demba. You could see how much it
meant to him: host worries pulled the skin of his face tight
over the bridge of his nose and filled his eyes. It was especially important that my father eat a lot, because he was
large. He looked like a *grand patron*—something I had never
thought of before—which made the men happy. He was a
suitable father for their boss.

Dad said he would eat what he could, but he looked ap-
prehensive. We sat in the late afternoon sun. They had
wanted us to sit inside, but it was so much nicer outside that I
had broken protocol and asked if we could sit in the compound instead of the house. Dad looked even more American in his red and white checkered shirt and straw hat
against the background of a Pulaar compound. Mom had
asked to borrow my rooster *boubou,* because sitting on the mat
was uncomfortable in pants. It was huge and green, open at
the sides and batiqued all over with strutting cocks. She
looked wonderful in it and I smiled. Mbinté had tied my
pagne for her, after I had tied it incorrectly, Mom telling me I
should learn the right way to tie them because Mbinté's was
so much more comfortable. I preferred my method, because
then I knew it wouldn't fall off.

The sun began to set, bleeding its colors of red and pink
and orange into the flat dusty land. A little boy herded his
family's goats along the dirt road running in front of the
compound. He was very thin and black against the brightness
of the setting sun and carried a stick across his shoulders.
Now and then he used it to bring a wanderer back to the
herd, the dust kicking up behind them, catching the redness
of the light.

Aisata and Bana worked over the cooking fire while Demba's children played in the dirt of the compound. His young-
est child climbed into his lap, to sit and stare with huge,
round eyes at his father's white guests. Mom spoke, her

words hushed, as though to match the fading light. "No one will ever believe I have been here," she said.

She would never be able to explain. It was stepping into the pages of National Geographic and yet not at all like that, because she was having dinner with a good friend of her daughter's. She could tell the women at the Smithsonian she had sat in a Pulaar compound waiting to eat goat and listening to the quiet blur of African languages, while watching a boy and his herd silhouetted against the sunset. What she would not be able to tell them was how comfortable she felt. That was what she found the most bizarre.

Every five minutes Demba asked if my parents were all right. Each time I told him we were fine, but he didn't relax until the goat and macaroni were served.

Aisata set the platter down in our circle, the steam and a good hot smell rising from the meat. We rinsed our right hands in a bowl of water, said, *"Bisimilla"*, and began to eat, scooping the goat and noodles with our right hands and dabbing up the juice with pieces of bread. The goat tasted wonderful, surprising Mom and Dad. I told Demba they liked it, and he smiled.

After we could eat no more, a bowl of water was again passed for rinsing our hands. By now it was dusk and Bana lit the kerosene lamp while Aisata brought out the *feurnot* and began to make tea.

Demba announced he had been taping our conversation, so he would have our voices forever—a remembrance of this night. When we were gone and he missed us, he would listen to the tape.

The soft light of the lamp shone on our faces—Demba and Dabo's so warm, as though their skin could hold the light, and Mom and Dad's very white against the night like two small moons. It was odd to hear Pulaar, French, Wolof, and English all intermingled. We spoke about the station and the program and Mom and Dad thanked Demba for his hospitality and friendship, which I translated, while the coals glowed like red-orange eggs under the teapot and we drank round after round of tea.

It became late. I had told Dabo I would drive him home to Podor, and Demba asked if I could take him as well, to buy something at the *boutique*. We were drinking our last glass of tea when Demba's first wife got up to go inside the house. She came back, standing shyly in front of Mom, holding a gourd ladle, its bowl intricately burned to make black patterns against the yellow. She held it out toward Mom, smiling a little uncertainly. It is a gift for the mother of Suzanne, she said.

Mom smiled in surprise and held the ladle in her hands. There was a word burned in Arabic at the base of the handle and she asked me what it said. I didn't know and asked someone to translate it for us. Dabo said it spelled Bana, the name of Demba's wife.

I looked at Demba. A long time ago, when there had been gourds growing at the station, I had said when they were dry maybe someone could show me how to make the traditional ladles, so I could decorate one for my mother. Both Abdoulaye and Demba had heard me and now both of them had presented my mother with ladles.

Abdoulaye had come two days before riding his bicycle to the house. He had waited for us at the station since seven that morning. When we finally didn't arrive he decided to find us. It was now twelve.

He was very excited, holding my parents' hands as he greeted them. He grinned and handed my mother a ladle. It was like Bana's but smaller and the design was finer. He had been as animated as a child at Christmas. My mother had been touched and tried to say thank you. Abdoulaye said it was nothing and rode off.

I had not known Abdoulaye and Demba would take my words so seriously. Mom held Bana's ladle in her hands and looked at it in the light of the kerosene lamp. Now she had two, the Diengs had given them two chickens, and Demba had killed a goat. She said the people should not give so much. The ladle might mean something to Bana. Maybe it had been a wedding gift. I tried to tell Demba and his wife what Mom said. It would be terrible if Demba had made Bana give the ladle to Mom because of my casual words.

Both Bana and Demba shook their heads. The ladle was a gift for the mother of Suzanne. I told Mom they would be

hurt if she didn't keep it. She told me to tell them she was
going to hang the ladles in a special place on her kitchen wall
in America and she would take a photo of it to send here for
everyone to see.

We all smiled, and said our good-byes. I told Aisata and
Bana what good cooks they were, how delicious the goat had
been. My parents had liked it very much and were honored.
I said we would come back another day when there was more
light and take pictures of everyone with my parents' Polaroid—photographs of themselves they could watch come
alive. Everyone shook hands and smiled. They told us to
spend the night in peace, and I wished them the same, as my
parents, Demba, Dabo, and I all climbed into the truck.

I dropped my parents at the house and took Demba and
Dabo to Podor. We didn't say much, the three of us sitting
close together in the cab. It felt good, to have no need to
speak. Demba, Dabo, and I had worked together—sweaty,
dusty, and tired—through so many days. There were things
these Senegalese men knew about me and my life that my
mother and father never could. I wondered if Dabo felt
guilty he had done nothing for my parents. I hoped so.

We stopped in front of Dabo's compound and he climbed
out of the truck and wished us peace. Demba and I continued on to the *boutique*. On the way back to Kodite, Demba
told me my heart was good. I took care of them and was a
good *patronne*. Now the station worked and we were all family. I didn't want to hear it any more. It was he who had just
killed a goat, he, whose wife had given my mother a ladle. I
had wanted to hear these words, fought to hear them. I had
meant to bask in them. Now they were mine, and they made
me ache.

"Demba," I said, "Your heart is as good as mine. I'm not
better than you. We are friends, that is good."

He said I spoke the truth. I parked the truck in front of his
house. He shook my hand, telling me to pass the night in
peace and smiled at me—a child's smile, full of trust and
loyalty. I wanted to say, "Demba, I am just a child myself, who
knew nothing before I came to your country. Don't think I
am more than that."

I said good night and drove back to Walli Jalla. I wanted to sit by myself somewhere quiet with the sound of the wind making the silence deeper. I had not known everyone would give so much.

Samba and Oumar had each given a chicken; Fatu sent her daughter over with *niiri;* and Amadou's brother came with cherry tomatoes. Mbinté, Fatiim, and Aisata sent over lunch bowls every day, the rice heavy with oil—richer than they ate themselves. Even Jeuldé, the miser, drove his *charrette* from the station to my compound, to greet my parents, saying he had a chicken for them.

I had taken my parents to meet the village chief. thinking it might be disrespectful if I didn't bring them by. Racine Jack was very tall, leaning just a little on a walking stick, for he was old. He wore a huge, traditional *tingaadi*—a conical straw hat rimmed with leather, a leather point sticking up at the top, and spent his words as sparingly as Jeuldé spent money. His presence had the feel of greatness, as though in another country and time he would have been a Lincoln or a Churchill. When we entered his compound it was already full with a delegation of village elders, and there was no way to leave unnoticed.

I introduced them to my parents, then wasn't sure what to do. We had our Polaroid with us, so I suggested we take a picture of the chief with his delegation, as a gift. They stood in a line—the elders on either side of the chief and after the photo, Racine made a speech. He said I had been here a very short time but everyone knew me as though I had lived in the village ten years. I had tried to help them, he said, and they would miss me when I returned to my own country. He asked me to tell my parents they thanked them for sharing me; they knew it was hard to have a child so far away.

The chief would say a sentence and then wait for me to translate it. I didn't want to translate any more compliments. They were not all true, and I didn't know how to convey to my parents that part of it was just Pulaar etiquette.

Still, it was a great honor to be spoken of by the chief. His words had touched me—spoken in his clear, wise voice, while the wind had blown, catching at the men's *boubous,* and softly rustling the thatch.

We gave the photo to the chief. It was a wonderful one:

strong faces of traditional old men standing before their clay and thatch houses. Mom wondered if she could take one for herself. I asked the men and they stood once again in a line, but it was wrong. These were important powerful men, not exotic creatures to photograph and carry back to the States. We said our good-byes and left. I hoped the chief would forgive me.

As I drove back to Walli Jalla, I thought of the chief's words, the ladles of Abdoulaye and Bana, Demba's smile. It was too much. I wished I could sit somewhere and cry.

Instead, I would go back to the house to set up my bed: light my kerosene lamp to see by and drag a mattress out under the neem tree. The sheets would have to be tucked in and my net tied to four branches and then tucked under the mattress to keep the insects out. After I set up my bed, I would take a little time brushing my teeth because it was so wonderful to know my bed was ready. I could stand almost anything during the day, but to set up my bed at each day's end had become an unbearable hardship.

I drove along thinking about Mom and Dad. Sharing dinner with Demba's family and my American parents made me feel our worlds had finally met. I thought of us drinking rounds of tea, slurping at the foam, Mom and Dad saying, "*Ene welli*—it is sweet," having learned the words that afternoon. I wanted to know if drinking sweet, brown tea in the desert had felt to them as it had to me. I was rich; in five minutes I would be able to ask them.

I pulled the truck into the compound and its headlights shone on the neem tree. Mom and Dad's bed was set up under it on the cane platform, and next to it was my bed—set up and waiting for me, mosquito net and all.

The whole two weeks was like that, and I began to wonder how it would end; I thought we would sit together in the orange plastic chairs at the Dakar airport and each know what the other was thinking. Someone would talk about the evening we ate Doritos and drank Seven-up under the neem tree as though they were caviar and champagne; or the night we were awakened by the sing-a-long and found out later it was Mada's brother-in-law whose voice rang through the village night.

We would talk about these things and laugh, and underneath would be the deeper memories—to be taken out and looked at later. I thought of Dad at the Torregi gas station when the owner came to greet my parents.

He was a big man, his *boubou* making him look even bigger. He went to stand by the open window, to speak with my father. He and Dad were men of the world, *grand patrons,* but Dad had to shake his head and say he didn't understand Pulaar. The owner looked disappointed then suddenly became excited. He held up his hand in front of Dad, counting to five in English, bending one finger down at each new number. After he finished, he chuckled with pride. Then Dad held up his fingers and counted to ten in Pulaar. I had never seen him look so proud. I laughed, thinking of his Ph.D. in mathematics.

Amadou had taught Dad his numbers the day before. Amadou was six, very dark with an upturned nose and big eyes which often became bigger with wonder. He was a good friend of mine. Sometimes he would come and spend my afternoons with me, but for a long time he couldn't sit in my house without looking as though he was ready to run away at the first sound of demons. Many times he explained things to me.

Amadou entered the compound that afternoon while Dad sat out under the neem tree reading a book. Amadou was shy and Dad so big and white. He greeted my father very softly and then sat down on the cane bed next to him. Dad searched for something to say. They sat in silence looking at one another and then Dad held up his index finger and said, "onnnnnnnnnnne?" He was hoping Amadou would tell him the Pulaar word for it, but instead Amadou looked sad, hanging his head as he stood to leave. He had looked forward to meeting my parents. He had told me so.

Dad called me, telling me to come quickly. His face was lined with concern, while little Amadou was walking away very slowly, his head low. I called to Amadou and told him to come back; my father didn't want him to leave. I asked Dad

what had happened. He said he tried to ask how to say one in
Pulaar, and I smiled. In Pulaar you say you want to be one,
when you would like people to leave you alone. I told
Amadou my father wanted to learn how to count in his
language, not for him to leave.

I sat on the front step and watched them. They were very
serious, both leaning forward a little with their index fingers
held before them—one white and strong and one uncertain,
small, and black. Dad made each English number into a
sentence and then Amadou tried them on his tongue, carefully, softly, as though they were flower petals and he didn't
want to crush them. They sat for a long time like that, under
the neem tree—Dad teaching Amadou English numbers and
Amadou teaching Dad how to count in Pulaar.

The day before we left the village for St. Louis, we went to
Abdoulaye's. Abdoulaye had made me promise we would
visit his compound. By then I should have known there
would be a *fête*, but I thought maybe we would just drink tea
and he would introduce his family.

He served chicken and macaroni and we sat in his house on
a foam mattress he reserved for special guests. Abdoulaye
wanted to tell my parents how things had changed at the
station, the things he had learned. He spoke while I translated, my parents nodding their heads, having become accustomed to this pattern. As we spoke his five-year-old
daughter came in to stand between Abdoulaye's bent knees.
He held her there, putting little pieces of meat into her small
round mouth. She swayed back and forth on horribly emaci-
ated legs—two thin brown sticks. She had a bright, perky
face, with Abdoulaye's smile, and laughed as he fed her.
Abdoulaye saw the look on Mom's face, and said his daughter
was better now, the month before she had almost died.

After the feast, he brought out the things to make tea,
holding the fat-bellied pot high over each glass to make
foam. There was a peace at Abdoulaye's, something comforting that wrapped around you, given by a family well-cared
for, content with their lives. My parents and I felt it pulling
us in, making us want to stay. But it was Mom and Dad's last

night. We had to pick up clothes at the tailor's, and Jeuldé's chicken had to be killed, cleaned, and plucked before it could be baked. I tried to tell Abdoulaye we could not stay for three rounds of tea and he said we must have at least one. After drinking our tea we said our good-byes and thank-yous and walked to the truck. Abdoulaye held my parents' hands telling them to travel in peace. All of a sudden he grinned, told us to wait one moment and ran back into the house. We could hear him tearing things apart, looking for something. After a few minutes he came back to the truck smiling at Mom. He handed her two small black and white passport photos: one of himself and the other of his wife, Bana. He said they were for Mom to keep, to remember them by.

The next day Mom and Dad packed their things, loading them back into the bed of the truck, where they had been only a week and a half before. Except for saying good-bye to the Diengs, they were ready to leave. I closed my green doors and the three of us walked the dirt path to my village family's compound. Only Samba, Maimoun, and the little children were there, everyone else having left after lunch to finish their afternoon chores.

Samba and Maimoun sat on a mat under the awning of their house, coming to their feet as we entered their compound's walls. We greeted them and I said my parents must leave. That is wrong, Samba said. They should stay with their daughter in her village. He and Maimoun had thought my parents were moving here. I explained that my father and mother lived in the U.S., as did my brothers and sisters-in-law. They owned a house, and my father had a job there.

My father told me he wanted to say something to my Senegalese father; I must translate for him. I told Samba this and he nodded his head, my American and Senegalese parents standing facing each other, waiting for my father's words and their daughter's translations. Dad spoke slowly, his voice ringing in the empty compound. He said the parents of Susan Lowerre now knew the parents of Mariyata Dieng. There was a small silence while I thought of the translation. Samba wanted to know who Susan Lowerre was. I said my

American parents now knew my Senegalese parents. Dad said they were very happy to have been able to meet them.

"We have seen what good people you are and we will no longer worry about our daughter because she has family here. Now, we have family here too."

I translated the English words into Pulaar, looking first at my American father in his red and white checkered shirt and then to Samba in his *boubou*. The wind blew, catching the thatch of the awning, little gusts of dust playing around our legs, making Samba's *boubou* whip a tattoo against his calves. They seemed very much alike to me—my American parents and my Senegalese.

We left after that, my compound seeming very empty as we pulled away. I had to stop at the station to go over the work to be done with Dabo while I was away.

I gave him a list and told him how important it was that the work be completed because of the upcoming S.A.E.D. training. He nodded his head, saying it would be done.

I waited for him to say something about the drawings he had promised my mother. She had found some of his doodles and asked to see more of his work, saying she might like to buy something. He had said he would bring drawings from home for her to look at before we left. We stood in silence; I thought he had forgotten. Finally, I asked him if he had brought them and he became nervous and shy. He glanced at Mom, walked out of the office and returned with a manila envelope which he put into her hands without a word.

There were three drawings and Mom slipped them out to look. Two were cartoons. One was of two men wearing *chias* doing acrobatics and the other of a man holding a fish. The third drawing was a serious one. It was of a Pulaar woman holding a broken *lall*, a traditional wooden bowl, looking off into nowhere. She wore a ripped shirt with a *pagne* and a look of suffering—not dramatic suffering, but rather daily suffering, slowly wearing sad lines into her face and soul.

Mom looked at each of the drawings and then said she would like to buy the woman, could I ask Dabo if he would sell it and if so, for how much?

Dabo was in debt to everyone. The month before, the S.A.E.D. cashier had told me he was holding half of Dabo's salary because he owed it to one of the Podor merchants. I wondered how bad his debts were that people had begun to come to S.A.E.D. I contemplated what price he might tell my mother. It would be ridiculous, but I would ask.

There was a strange look on Dabo's face as he listened to my words. He looked trapped, as though he wanted to run away. He stood shifting his weight from one foot to the other, looking from my mother to me. Then he flicked his hand toward the envelope, saying the drawings were a gift and walked out of the door before he could see anyone's reaction—the tears on Mom's cheeks.

He said good-bye to us, as we stood next to the truck. He shook Dad's hand, grinning a little foolishly, telling me he would see me soon and that the work would be done. When he said good-bye to Mom his face became very soft, the way it had been when he held Ya Ya's little son in his lap. I hadn't known he could show that side of himself to an adult. Dabo's face was beautiful.

We climbed into the truck, and I backed it up, out of the station's driveway. Dabo continued to stand where we left him, in front of the station, looking very small in the flat wasteland. He stood there alone, waving, and Mom and Dad waved back until he had turned into a stick figure and then dissolved into the dust.

I became sick in St. Louis and we had to spend a day at the Poste where I stayed in my room with a fever. Mom and Dad said they would change their flight to stay with me, until I was better, but I wouldn't let them. I had been afraid I might be too sick to drive them to Dakar, but managed to take them and had even started to feel better.

We went to the Auberge Rouge for our last dinner together. It was my favorite restaurant in Dakar. The food was wonderful and they played soft American music. You sat out in a courtyard open to the stars with a tree growing between the tables. We all relaxed a little, eating the rich food, talking and laughing, and it felt very good.

Dad and I ordered *profiteroles* for dessert—pastry filled with ice cream covered with fudge sauce. When they were set before me I knew I couldn't eat them. I stood abruptly, and went to the bathroom to be sick.

Mom and Dad didn't want me to drive them to the airport, but I was determined. That was not going to be taken from me. I just couldn't do it right now. I needed to sleep for a little; then I would take them.

It was my last two hours with my American parents and I slept them away.

I didn't say anything profound at the airport. They wouldn't even allow me to go inside to wait with them. I let them convince me, because I knew I was going to be sick again and didn't want them to see. We climbed from the truck to give each other quick hugs. They looked so worried and I told them I would be fine. No one would hug me for seven months. When I returned to Walli Jalla their footprints would be in the yard and they would be an ocean away.

I helped them get their luggage from the back of the truck, watching them walk inside the glass doors. Mom kept motioning for me to leave. I didn't want the doors to ever shut. I got in the truck and drove away.

I had to run to make it to the Peace Corps bathroom. I knelt on the tiles throwing up food I couldn't afford, thinking of how many times I had been here before. It smelled of sewage. Often the toilet would not flush. Always the flies would buzz around you and your vomit because you woke them with the light. When the toilet didn't flush, there would also be no water to wash my mouth. I was alone in the night. My parents were on a plane for America. I lived in Senegal.

CHAPTER EIGHTEEN

A Flock of Pelicans

I had amoebas again. My body was a prison. It was as though everything was underwater, taking so much energy to move, to walk, to think. The whole world changed. Everything was an effort. I didn't want to climb out of bed. I didn't want to work. I didn't want to have to speak Pulaar or French. I just wanted to sit and do nothing. I hated this person with no excitement for life. Every day I felt hung over, as though I had drunk a bottle of whiskey the night before, the heat baking my headache into my head, making my eyes burn. I felt a hundred years old, and tried to remind myself I was twenty-five.

Mariam's *beignets* were the only things that got me out of bed. It was Monday and I had to go to the station. There was so much work to do, and I wanted no part of it. I lay still in the early morning, staring up at the branches of the neem tree, not sure there was anything in the world worth moving for. I hated knowing ten *beignets* were the best that would happen to me between getting out of bed and when I could finally climb back in.

The day had a bad feel to it. The wind had come up and brought the dust. You couldn't tell where the flat desert land ended and the brown desert sky began. It beat against you, the browness. The dust particles stung your skin working their way into your eyes and nose and mouth. There was no escape. I was so tired I didn't think I could stand a day at the station.

I sat at my desk in the cinder-block office, trying to write up a history of the project and reading old reports. We were having a fisheries training session for government workers in a month. Over and over again the same projects failed, for the same reasons. The people had changed and the new people had no memory of their predecessors' work, hopes and failures. I thought anyone who read the six-year history would see why we couldn't afford to build big ponds, or to expand before we got a core of ponds working profitably.

Report after report I read of volunteers before us, their efforts and expectations, their abandoned ponds. The Fleuve was dotted with them. There was even an abandoned station in Bakel. It was a bleak history of a poorly thought-out and poorly executed program. There were ponds built that would never drain, ponds built of sand that sucked the water and the profits dry. It was easy to see the futility of the ideas in retrospect, and it made me wonder if in a year or two there wouldn't be someone sitting reading my reports about an abandoned station in Nianga.

The door to the office was open, but it might as well have been closed. It was an opaque rectangle of brown. I couldn't even see to the edge of the ponds. I wondered where Linda was. She had made the right decision. She had decided to leave.

I thought of our last trip together, when I had brought her back up to the Fleuve to collect her things. We had spent the night in St. Louis both too tired and sick to travel any further. We had checked into the hotel, immediately going to bed to sleep straight through to the next morning when we had to drive to Walli Jalla.

That first day back in the village, I wondered what Linda was doing. I looked at my parents' footprints in the yard, at the material my mother had bought me as a present, at the cooler and the empty Seven-up bottles, and burst into tears. I sat on the broken floor in my kitchen, holding the cloth in my hands, wondering how my parents could have left me here. They went back to the U.S. with souvenirs and photos, but I had to stay. I set up my bed and went to sleep. I slept for the next two days and my family was very worried about me.

Samba kept popping his head over the wall, asking if I was o.k. How was I feeling now? Was I better? His eyes and face looked worried. They sent me bowls of food for lunch and dinner. I was too tired to eat with them in the compound. They told me to rest, I would be better in a little while.

I had gone to Linda's house the night before I was to take her to Richard Toll, where she would catch a public transport car to Dakar. We sat inside her white-washed house, two white sacks of bones, held up by the walls, and talked. We talked the way we had not before—as people, scared, sick women, and I thought how much I would miss her, of all the things I had never done to help her.

She said maybe she shouldn't leave; she wasn't sure. We spoke of the station and our hopes, of how far it had already come, of how much she hated Dabo. I hadn't known, but I knew she wouldn't stay. We both knew, although it was easier not to say so.

I asked her to come back to Walli Jalla for a dinner of potato and onion omelets, thinking of all the times she had asked to come visit. I had resented her so, wishing she would leave me alone to finally have a year to myself, and hating her because she was not Dirk. Now the times we had shared at my house seemed like such good times.

The next day we drove to Richard Toll. Dabo came with us because we needed to get the threads on a pipe ground at the sugar factory there. Linda and I went first to the bank, to close her account, and then to the *gare*, to catch a van to St. Louis.

On the way she asked if I wouldn't like to come to St. Louis for lunch, she'd buy. She knew I would say no, the way I had known she wouldn't change her mind about leaving. I said I couldn't leave Dabo. We found a car going to St. Louis and I drove her to it, helping her with the bags. She had so little. There were people all around us, people bargaining and laughing, splashes of brightly-colored clothes, in between cheerful blue and red and yellow vans, children selling hard-boiled eggs and bananas to passengers already seated.

Linda was so skinny. It seemed she was nothing but skin and bones, huge eyes and a little ponytail. She needed some-one to take care of her, someone who could worry and put her to bed and hug her. I wished she knew I would have done those things if I could have. I wanted so much to give her something. In her three months here it seemed all she had was pain. She never got to the point where she could see the magic.

Linda had been in Senegal a month when a flock of pelicans flew over the station. They were beautiful, a hundred fantasy birds—majestic and huge with black trimming on the undersides of their outspread wings. That day the sky had been blue and they had circled over the station, high up in the air—graceful, free—a pelican ballet. They were performing for us. It was something to touch the day, making it different from all other days.

I had been washing my hands in one of the ponds after lunch and looked up to see them. I called to Dabo and Linda and we watched them circle. I wondered what they were doing so far inland. Pelicans had never flown over the station before, and I knew we wouldn't see them again. I watched them until they were swallowed by the sky. Linda hadn't lived in the desert long enough to know she had seen a miracle; all she had seen was a flock of pelicans.

You had to learn to see the magic, to let it touch you, to hold onto its brightness against the brown of every day. If you did not, this world would suck you dry. I was sorry Linda had never found it. I could have helped her, but it was too late now. All I could do was try to tell her she had made the right decision.

"Linda you deserve to be healthy. You should never feel guilty. You were too sick. It's not worth ruining your health," I said.

"What about you?" she asked.

That was what I wanted to tell her; I didn't have the kind of courage it took to admit I was wrong, to admit I was sick, had met my limit. That was a different kind of strength than I had. She had it. She had nothing to feel guilty about.

We hugged, and walked away from each other, before our tears had a chance to escape our eyes and touch our cheeks.

That was the week before. I hoped by now Linda was lying somewhere on clean sheets, smelling of America, eating pizza and peanut M&Ms. I tried to work on the project history, but couldn't make myself care about it. Haawa came by to tell me she could no longer cook my lunch; I did not pay her enough, and then Ouseman's older sister came to ask if I could take him to the Podor *dispensaire*. He was very sick. One moment the door would be a rectangle of brown, the next, a person would stand framed between its walls, wanting something, always wanting something.

I told Haawa I wouldn't pay her more. I was tired of her whining, tired of her always begging for rides and food and money. If she didn't want to cook my lunch that was fine, but she would no longer eat with us. I would not drive her to Podor, or include her in station *fêtes*. More than anything I wanted to slap her. She left.

I told Ouseman's sister I would take him to Podor at three, when I got off from work, but I couldn't take him before then. Ouseman was the new guardian. He worked very hard.

He had been at the station for a little over a month. At first he had withheld judgment—both on his white boss and on the project. He would listen to what Demba and Abdoulaye told him, but he would wait to make up his own mind. The week before he had told me I spoke Pulaar well. He asked me to help him transport bags of cement from S.A.E.D. to his house, and I drove them in the truck. I had said the men at the station were my family. How could I not take someone in my family to the doctor?

The red bucket, we filled with blood at the butcher's, sat in the corner of the office. It was empty, and Dabo had not come to work. He had been sick off and on for two weeks. If I went to Podor I could check on him. Also, I couldn't stand another minute at the station, and if I didn't buy food in Podor, there would be nothing to eat for lunch.

I drove to Ouseman's house. His sister had to help him walk to the truck. He seemed very, very sick. You could see the pain on his face, the way he held himself way down inside and tried not to feel or think. He greeted me with lips unwilling to move and sat silently as we drove. I had never seen Ouseman when he was not grinning or working or talking. He had a habit of talking with his whole body, and when he was excited he quivered.

There was a line of sick people standing outside the *dispensaire*, waiting to see the doctor. I asked Ouseman if he was going to be all right. He said his sister would help him and thanked me for the ride. I said I would come back in half an hour or so, to take them home.

I dropped the blood bucket off at the butcher's, bought a loaf of bread, then drove to Dabo's. I had visited him two days before, on Saturday. He had a genital cyst, but had just tried some new medicine and seemed to be better. He had said he would come to work on Monday, and I wanted to know what had happened.

I parked in front of the compound, where he lived with a Wolof family. The doors were open to his building and I walked into his room. Dabo was sitting on the floor in a corner. His foam rubber mattress had been moved there from his bed. Three men sat in the room with him. Dabo's eyes were sunk back into his skull, his face looking like dry leather, the bones showing through. His knees stuck up in the air, just brown bones. His legs looked like the legs of Abdoulaye's daughter, two thin sticks that would never hold him. But the worst was his eyes, recessed in his skull, so that you had to look at him directly to see them, and then you saw the fear. He had wasted away. Dabo had wasted away in two days.

"*Bonjour,* Suzanne," he said, his voice cracking. He tried to smile at me, but it turned into a grimace. I gave him my hand to shake. His was the hand of a very old person—a claw with no flesh. He said he was sick; he had gotten worse.

"What do you want to do Dabo? You have to see a doctor. We had better take you to one right away," I said.

Yes, he wanted to go to the *dispensaire.* He had been waiting for me. The men in his room were his "brothers" from the family, whose compound he lived in. He couldn't move so they carried him to the truck. He lay there on the little metal ridges looking up at me and he laughed, as though to apologize for how weak he was.

"You see I cannot walk," he said.

I drove to the *dispensaire* for the second time. Dabo was a brown skeleton in the back of the truck, and I tried not to think of the two corpses I had driven to graveyards. One of his brothers sat in back with him, and the other two sat in the

cab with me. It seemed as though some demon had come to
suck away Dabo's flesh, leaving only skin and bones. I
couldn't imagine anything else taking such a toll in two days.
It made no sense to me. In America you are sick for a long
time before you begin to die.

Dabo could not die, not Dabo. I would not let him. He was
strong. When we fought, he often won. I thought of the
kitten, and my asking God to take my strength. I thought of
Demba's daughter. I would make a deal with God, to save
Dabo. I would do whatever it took to save his life, but I would
only talk to God if I was sure I needed him. God had seemed
much more understanding in the U.S. In Senegal God took
what you offered.

I stopped the truck in front of the *dispensaire,* and told his
brother to go in and tell the doctor we had an emergency. I
saw Ouseman, who had been given medicine and was better.
He came to the truck to greet Dabo. I hoped a Pulaar would
see Dabo differently than I did, and watched Ouseman's face
closely. They knew sickness and death. For a second, there
was fear on Ouseman's face, and I knew things were bad.

The men lifted Dabo, locking hands to make a rough chair
for him to sit in, his arms around their necks, his legs dangling useless in the air. They walked very slowly, but Dabo
couldn't stand the pain; his face twisted horribly with each
step.

We all walked into the doctor's office, the men laying Dabo
on an examination table. The doctor ushered everyone back
out of the room except for one of the men, Dabo, and me.
The doctor was Wolof, small with glasses and fancy Western
clothes. He walked over to the table, said a few words to
Dabo, and then looked over his shoulder at me.

I didn't know if I should stay. Dabo had tried to show me
his cyst the other week, but I had not really seen anything,
and hadn't thought he should be showing me his genitals. At
the time, I had wondered if he did it just to see how I would
react. It was obvious the doctor wanted me to leave, but I
wouldn't if Dabo wanted me to stay. I wanted to find out what
was wrong and what I could do.

The doctor started undressing Dabo, so I asked Dabo if he

wanted me there. "Yes," he said. I sat in a wooden chair
facing the table. Dabo was naked and the doctor had put on a
rubber glove. The doctor put a finger up Dabo's anus, the
one brother and he having to hold Dabo down. Dabo
writhed, Dabo, who was so strong, moaned for the doctor to
stop, to please stop; he couldn't stand it. Dabo, who had
pulled a bloody leech from his skin and laughed. The doctor
snapped at him to be quiet, as though Dabo's pain was
nothing but the brush burn of a whining child. I hated the
doctor. He didn't know how Dabo loved to strut, that he was
young and strong, more than flesh squirming like a snake on
his shiny examination table. I willed myself not to pass out.

It was over. The doctor threw away his glove in a trash can
and the man from Dabo's compound helped him on with his
pants and carried him to the truck. Dabo should go to the
hospital in Ndioum, the doctor said. He had a urogenital
infection and it was getting worse.

I said I would do whatever was necessary to help, including
taking Dabo to St. Louis or Dakar. I wanted to get Dabo to a
city doctor, to a real hospital. The doctor's attitude completely changed. Before, Dabo had been a cringing dog this
man must look at but would rather kick. Now Dabo was
someone a white woman cared about; that seemed to make
him a human being. The doctor said I should take Dabo
immediately to St. Louis, and that I should pay him something to cover his services. He said five hundred francs and
the money was in his hand before I thought.

The *dispensaire* was free. It was a free health service. I told
him I hadn't realized they charged patients here. He said
they didn't for the *"population"*.

"Isn't Dabo part of the *population*?" I asked.

The man had already put my money in his pocket.

"Yes, but he works for you," he said and tried to smile. His
face was oily.

"He works for S.A.E.D." I said, and the man handed back
my bill.

It seemed the drive to St. Louis would never end. Time
took on its own dimensions, heedless of measurement. Before we left I had to stop in Walli Jalla to get my money belt,

my soap and shampoo, my pink shirt, and a pair of jeans. I reminded myself five times on the way to the house to bring my amoeba medicine, and then forgot it. I gave Dabo a foam rubber mattress and my sheets and pillow. I grabbed my Walkman and some tapes as I meant to listen to them myself, thinking they might take me away from this nightmare, but I couldn't listen to them with the men from Dabo's compound sitting in the cab and Dabo lying in back. So I walked to the bed of the truck and handed my Walkman and tapes to Dabo.

I dropped Ouseman and his sister at their house and we went to the station. I told Abdoulaye we were going to St. Louis; I wasn't sure when we would be back; he must take care of the station. He nodded his head, and we left. The road would not end. I had traveled it so many times, knew it by heart and now it tricked me. The flat land could not go by fast enough. The huts seemed to stand still. I wondered if we would ever arrive.

I wanted to take a shower, to lie in one of the hotel's clean beds. I was happy to have an excuse to leave Walli Jalla and the station behind. Maybe this would all work out for the best. I could go by S.A.E.D.'s headquarters the next day and talk to the cashier about the workers' *primes du transport.* Dabo would have to change his ways, if he thought I had saved his life. None of his fancy friends had helped him.

I tried not to think these things. Dabo might be dying in the back of the truck. What type of person would think of anything but him? But I did. I wouldn't put the thoughts into words, but I felt them underneath the things I allowed myself to think.

Before we could go to the hospital, we had to get some forms at S.A.E.D. saying they would pay. There were two forms. One I had to take to the hospital, admitting Dabo for a consultation. The hospital had to fill it out, and then I was to return it to S.A.E.D., at which point they would give me the second form covering the hospital costs.

I explained to the S.A.E.D. official in his air-conditioned office that Dabo was very, very sick. Was there some way we could forgo the first form? No. What would someone do without a vehicle and friends? Would S.A.E.D. let them die? What the hell did a printed piece of paper mean next to a person's life?

We drove to the hospital and I went to stand in line. There were two huge oak doors opening on to the street. A rectangle at eye level was cut into one of them, with a sliding window so the guardian could look out and see who to let in. People begged and pleaded with him, claimed to know the people he knew, tried to bribe him. Some he let in; most he did not. All I could picture was the guard in *The Wizard of Oz*. I was the only white person in line. For once the color of my skin helped and the guardian spoke to us almost immediately. I explained the situation and he said to get Dabo; he would let us in. A man standing behind me started to curse in Pulaar. White people, they got everything. This was their country. White people did not belong in Senegal, in their jobs, their hospitals. I turned around to glare at him with real hatred.

Dabo was admitted to the hospital after another quick examination. They put him on a stretcher to carry him, through the building into a courtyard past a dry fountain, and into another building and up a flight of stairs. Four people, each held an end of the stretcher, and they had to tip Dabo at an angle to get him up the stairs. I looked at him lying there on the stretcher—his head was huge, his eyes sunk deep into their sockets. He looked funny. He looked into my eyes and smirked. We began to laugh and couldn't stop. The stretcher bearers looked at us as though we were crazy, and I thought of the books by white people on Africa telling how shocked they were by Africans laughing when someone was hurt, even near death.

I left Dabo, took the form back to S.A.E.D. and checked into my hotel. I have always hated the stale antiseptic smell of hospitals and needed to escape. It was not until I had bought a cold can of pineapple and two oranges and was sitting comfortably on the bed inside my hotel room that I realized how tired I was. I hadn't eaten all day, had forgotten my medicine, and the place where I had cut my thumb the day before was infected and throbbing.

I felt like such a white person, to have left Dabo and the others in the hospital with the smell of too many sick people and medicine and dirty sheets and noise, while I came to a hotel to eat pineapple chunks and take a hot shower. But wasn't that my right as an American? Indoor plumbing, and canned food? It felt so good to be away from the pain and the dirt.

I ate the pineapple and took a shower. I decided to buy some bread and cheese and oranges for Dabo as well, carrying them to the hospital in the same dirty pillowcase Dabo had laid his head on.

I was halfway there when a young Senegalese man dressed in Western clothes started following me. His clothes were perfectly clean; there were creases ironed into his pants, and he was wearing expensive sunglasses. I knew who he was. I had seen dozens of men like him in St. Louis and Dakar. He thought I was a tourist and he would offer to show me around St. Louis then charge me for the tour, or show me a trinket he wanted to sell.

I didn't look at him. I continued to walk with the pillow case slung over my shoulder, bulging a little with the bread and cheese and oranges. He came up to me, speaking perfect French, saying he lived here, was Senegalese, and knew his way around. He would like to help show me his country. If I needed any help with directions. . . .

I looked at him, looked at his fancy clothes and his well-fed, healthy body.

"I live here too," I said. "I do not need directions. I live in Senegal too, please leave me alone."

CHAPTER NINETEEN

White Man's Medicine

There were three single beds in the room, made up with dirty green sheets and no coverlets. A young Pulaar man sat on the middle one, with a bandaged right wrist, while two men hunched down on the dusty floor. Dabo lay in the bed closest to the door. He was still covered with the filthy pink sheet he had lain on in the back of the truck. I think the walls were meant to be white, but they were dirty. Everything was dirty. The room smelled of human waste, sweet sick sweat, and bitter astringent.

Dabo had set my Walkman up on the little table by his bed. Piano notes splashed clear and pure from the black rectangle, out into the room, out and over the sick Senegalese men and the dust and the smell and the dirty green sheets. Dabo was playing my George Winston tape. It was what I listened to when I sat out at night, alone in my plastic, broken-down armchair staring up at the desert stars. I knew all the melodies and could hear the next note before it came. These were the songs I listened to when I came home from the station, empty from muddy day after muddy day, aching from having found nothing beautiful between sunrise and sunset. This music cascading out into the dirty hospital room was what I listened to when I was the most scared and felt very small, very tired, a hundred years old with no desire to laugh, and sure I would never feel young again. I had listened to the tape so many times that the music became a part of me, and now it was in this room, and it was not I who had called it. It was Dabo.

I walked into the room, greeting Dabo and the men from his compound. Dabo introduced me to the Pulaar man and we spoke a little in my village language. I sat in a chair by

216

Dabo's bed and held out the pink pillow case that matched his sheet. It bulged with the oranges, the loaf of bread, and a wheel of Camembert cheese. I grinned and Dabo grinned back at me.

He looked better. His head was still huge, a huge round black ball dangling on a skinny neck, but there was no longer the same fear pulling his skin tight against his skull and filling his eyes. He told me it was good he was here; a *tubab* doctor had already come by to see him. We could relax a little now. *Tubab* had become a magic word with great power. We had been able to get Dabo to one and they would take care of him.

He pulled an orange from the pillow case and started to peel it. I watched his fingers as he ate. I knew well the ring with the flat pewter diamond he wore on his right hand and the twisted copper, pewter, and brass band he wore on his left. So many times I had watched them catch the light as Dabo's fingers wrapped around the handle of a hammer, fixed the plumbing to a holding tank, held a pickax, or counted fish. His hands were always deft and often I had envied them. Now they worked very hard to peel an orange.

"Suzanne," he said, "it is good to be here. Last night I was very frightened. I was so afraid all through the night and the night was very long. I knew I would die. I cried. Suzanne, I cried all night long because I knew I would die and I was afraid."

I could never imagine Dabo crying. He had made me cry once when I was still new, when he hated me and made fun of my French, mocking my instructions and ideas, my right to be manager. I had sworn I would never let him make me cry again. He looked at me after he finished speaking, looked to see if I understood what his words meant, and then he laughed quietly, relieved at being alive.

"Dabo, why didn't you send for me?" I asked. "It was only by chance that I came to your compound."

Dabo had thought he would die; there had been no one to take some of his fear. He had cried alone in the night.

"I did send someone, didn't they come?" he asked.

"No. No, Dabo, no one came to tell me you were sick. I came to Podor because I had to take Ouseman to the *dispensaire*."

He didn't say anything. I wondered who he had sent, who could have known Dabo was dying and still hadn't made the effort to tell me, which of his fancy new friends? Dabo hated me, resented everything I stood for, everything I did, and I had taken him to the hospital. He had spent all that money on fancy clothes and beer and soda for parties he couldn't afford. He had played the part of the *grand patron,* for what? to spend the night alone in his room when he thought he was dying? No one had cared enough to sit with him, to lessen his fear, to tell him he would be fine. I hoped his body still hurt too much for him to feel anything else.

Dabo told me the doctors here were very good. The *tubab* doctor had said he would be operated on early the next morning.

I would come after the operation. In the morning I had to go to Centre N'Diaye to ask about the workers' salaries which were almost a month behind. I said I would come around noon the next day, to see how he was doing.

Dabo said by then he should be fine and could drive back to Podor with me, but I didn't think so.

"I know nothing about medicine," I said. "These people can take care of you. You are very, very sick. It is as important that you rest and are taken care of after the operation as it is that you are operated on. You must get well. You must take care of yourself."

Throughout the night I woke up to the pulsing of my thumb. It was bright red where I had cut it the day before, surrounded by a ring of pus, and the redness was spreading. It was slowly moving out further, encompassing all of my thumb, like ripples on smooth water. I lay on clean sheets in a bed with a white coverlet, listening to the air conditioner and my own heartbeat. I needed to sleep very badly, but kept thinking over and over that Dabo would be operated on in the morning.

I didn't stay long at S.A.E.D. the next morning. They had no money. The cashier told me now even the important people in S.A.E.D. were not getting their salaries on time. He didn't know when my workers would get their *primes du transport.* Suleyman Fall, the director, was in his office which was great luck. I told him about the program, our salary problems, how far the station had come and the words came faster and faster. I knew I sounded like a true believer. I couldn't help it. I did believe. Suleyman wrote a nasty note to the assistant to the director of S.A.E.D. to try to hurry up the salaries.

I had an hour to spend before noon. I lay in bed reading *Zorba the Greek,* but kept thinking of Dabo. When I awoke I had wondered if he was awake. When I went to S.A.E.D. I wondered if he was in the operating room. Now I wondered if he lay in dirty sheets, maybe stained with his own blood, while I lay reading in bed. Just before noon, I closed my book, packed my things, and drove the truck to the hospital.

I have always hated hospitals. I hate the smell and the whiteness and the pain. My mother had been in the hospital four years before. She had done something to her back, and she had lain looking very small in her white bed, wearing a white hospital gown and crying for her painkiller. I had tried to read to her, tried to force her to listen to every word, every syllable, and she had still cried.

My words seemed to fill up the room and all she felt was the pain. I left, and leaned up against the wall outside to put my head between my knees, watching nurses walk by in white dresses, stockings, and shoes. I felt as though I could not breathe because there was no air—nothing but the smell of medicines and sickness.

I walked up the stairs to the third floor, and down the hall to Dabo's room. The door was open, but he wasn't there. The only person in the room was the Pulaar man with the bandage where his right hand should have been. Before I could ask him about Dabo, he began to yell at me. He said Dabo was being operated on and that Dabo had told me to come to the hospital at seven that morning. He hated me for having let Dabo down.

"Where were you?" he asked.

I stared at the room, Dabo's empty bed, the places on the floor where the other men had slept, the ugly green sheets. I had not understood. I had told Dabo I was going to Centre N'Diaye. Had he asked me to be here? He would have been frightened before the operation. I could have helped, if I had known.

Maybe the Pulaar man read my thoughts. He stopped yelling and his face became a little less cold. He led me to the waiting room, as though I were a small child. We said nothing.

There were two brown swinging doors on one side of the hall and across from them wooden benches overflowing with people sitting, staring at the doors. One of the men from Dabo's compound sat on a bench and the Pulaar man led me to him. The people on the bench somehow made room for me and I sat squeezed in between them smelling the unwashed bodies and waiting for the doors to open and bring back Dabo. I thought of nothing. All I remember is there was a baby crying and everyone's clothes seemed filthy and torn, and I wasn't sure if they were waiting for patients to return or if they were patients themselves, waiting to enter the operating room.

The doors opened and two men appeared carrying a stretcher. Dabo lay on the stretcher. His eyes were rolled back into his head, and his bones seemed to jiggle around in his skin with each step of the stretcher-bearers. He was still covered with the same dirty, pink sheet and a corner of it hung off the stretcher to drag along the floor. There was no life in his face or his limbs. He was a discarded doll, like the kind the street merchants try to sell to tourists.

I would make a deal with God now. He could have anything he wanted, anything I had, if he would let Dabo live. It seemed as though it took a very long time for the stretcher-bearers to come through the doors. I thought of a Star Trek episode where a woman had the ability to take the hurt of others onto herself, and then heal the wounds. But if the wounds were too great, she could not overcome them, and she would die herself. She was afraid; she didn't want to save someone at such a price to herself. She had to learn to care enough to risk her own life to save another.

Finally the stretcher was carried down the hall and the man from Dabo's compound and I stood and followed it. Once, on the way upstairs, it knocked into the wall and the stretcher-bearers laughed at their clumsiness. I walked behind them and little drops of blood and pus dripped out from between Dabo's legs and onto the steps. I stared at the cloudy red drops on the white tile steps unable to turn my eyes away.

In Dabo's room, they lifted him onto his bed while I stood in the hallway motionless. My blood was cold inside me but the air was hot, and drops of sweat trickled down my back. I felt as though a headache was starting at the very top of my head and it was a voracious parasite taking my blood, my strength and my consciousness.

The stretcher-bearers left the room and I quickly sat on the chair by the wall. If I sat, I was safe. There was a beautiful breeze coming in from the balcony; it was soft against my face and somewhere far away it made me think of spring. The Pulaar man was there and he was trying to tell me I had to buy Dabo his medicine but I couldn't move. I said I was a little sick.

The Pulaar man told me to lie down on his bed, and I said no, I would be all right, and then walked to his bed and lay down. I lay on the green sheets feeling the breeze. Dabo lay to my right and another man was on my left. I felt ridiculous, a silly, weak, white woman who had begun to faint. How could I lie on these green sheets? The men who lay on them had been through so much, surviving things I would never imagine. I had no right to lie there, and yet I had no choice. The breeze still blew across our three bodies. Dabo was lying with his eyes rolled back into his head, and suddenly it struck me as funny. I lay there in the Pulaar man's bed, and began to laugh.

"Suzanne," Dabo said, and I got up and crouched by the side of his bed. I would have done anything for him then. He wanted to know if I had gotten their salaries, only his words were garbled like someone talking in their sleep. I told him

S.A.E.D. had no money, but he didn't understand. The Pulaar man came and gently pulled me away. He took me outside, onto the balcony. He said it was only the anesthetic that made people look as though they had died, that it would take awhile before Dabo came to. I stood listening to his words, feeling my thumb throb where it circled the metal railing for support, and decided I would drive to Dakar. I had to get my medicine; the doctor needed to see my thumb. I could get back that night. There was time because Dabo was asleep.

The next morning, I drove the road from Thiès to St. Louis quite slowly. I had a loaf of bread from Dakar and an apple and I ate them both as the truck passed by villages and baobab trees and once, a herd of camels. I looked at the hazelnut chocolate bar that cost 800 francs sitting on the dashboard melting in the sun. The candy bar I knew would be molded into little squares you could break apart, thirty-two of them. A hazelnut candy bar was what I bought myself whenever I was in Dakar and very, very sick.

I had thought I could drive to Dakar and back in an afternoon. I would just show the doctor my thumb and maybe he would put some salve on it, give me more medicine, and then I would get back to St. Louis by evening. I would not stay in the *tubab* hotel. I was going to spend the night in the hospital with Dabo where I should have spent the night before.

The previous afternoon had become a personal war between myself, the truck, and the road from St. Louis to Thiès. The road was pock-marked with holes, and the pavement had buckled repeatedly from the heat, making wave after wave of asphalt, catapulting the truck from their crests. I wouldn't slow my pace and the truck bounced from the waves to land wrenchingly in the booby-trap holes, too numerous to be avoided.

The truck could not go fast enough. I held the wheel with my right hand, so I could watch my thumb, and swore at the top of my lungs. The sweat made my body stick to the seat. It ran down my sides from my armpits and the dust collected in it on my face, hands, and forearms. I watched my thumb to see if I had been a fool. Was it worse? Was I a fool to have left Dabo? I had to get to Dakar by three o'clock in order to get back to St. Louis by eight. I was pulled over twice for speeding.

The Peace Corps doctor looked at my thumb, lanced it, and said I must soak it overnight, he would look at it the next morning. I said I had to leave that night, and he said he wouldn't let me go until he saw if the infection was better the next day. I told him about Dabo, why I had to get back to St. Louis, and he said he would try to get to Peace Corps as early as possible the next morning.

I spent another night in a hotel, refusing to stay in the health hut, because Peace Corps had no water again. I was supposed to soak my thumb. I smelled. I was filthy. I bought bread and cheese, a Napoleon, a bottle of Sprite, two apples, the hazelnut chocolate bar and then checked into the L'Atlantique hotel. I took a hot shower and ate the food in bed, thinking of what the A.P.C.D. for fisheries had told me, and of what I had almost told him.

The refunding proposal for the fisheries program still was not submitted by C.R.S. Peace Corps had done nothing to find out why, to try to quicken the pace, or even to get C.R.S. to acknowledge whether they still meant to submit it.

The A.P.C.D. had no idea who would end up doing Linda's work at the station. He wasn't sure if Peace Corps could get me a gas refrigerator, even though there was a rule saying all volunteers were entitled to them, and they now had Linda's living allowance of 80,000 francs a month. It didn't matter that I would do her work.

Finally, I slept between my clean hotel sheets. Dabo would wake up to find I was not there.

I drove to the St. Louis hospital and parked the truck. The chocolate bar had almost completely melted and I still hadn't eaten it. My thumb was much better. I had a magic bottle of Iodoquinol and another of Tetracycline. Again I knocked on the huge wooden doors and the hospital guardian slid open his panel to look at my face and let me enter. I climbed the tile steps to Dabo's floor. Someone had cleaned up the spots.

I walked through the doors to the third floor and looked down the hallway. Dabo was hobbling from the doctor's office back to his room. He had a dirty towel wrapped around his waist and wore a ripped blue shirt. One of the men from his compound had been wearing it the day before. He tottered unsteadily. His legs moved in unpracticed jerks as though someone were pulling strings you felt might snap at any moment, but at least, Dabo was walking! He was alive. Thank you God.

He looked at me and grinned, his old, cocky Dabo grin, on that scarecrow body. I was moved by his courage.

He made it back inside the room and I followed. He went to a closet to the left of his bed. He wanted to change his sheets. They smelled. The Pulaar man was still there and he said something to Dabo in Wolof. I didn't understand the words, but Dabo turned slowly away from the closet door to look at the *Puloo*. His face looked frightened, like a dog expecting a beating. I didn't understand why. This was not a Dabo I knew.

He lay back down on the dirty sheets and told me about the operation. The doctors said he would have died if they had not operated when they did. I wondered if there was anything left inside Dabo, except his bones and pulse. He had been eaten away and was afraid of this overbearing *Puloo*.

The Pulaar man mentioned that I had almost passed out. Dabo watched me. He said I had been brave. I wanted to scream "Why? why do you think that Dabo? Because I was brave enough to drive you to St. Louis, to stay in a nice hotel, to leave you here because of my thumb?"

"No Dabo, I was not brave. You were the one who was brave," I said. "You have real courage."

He thanked me for saving his life.

I went to talk to Dabo's doctors, two overweight men in white lab coats. They laughed when I asked about Dabo, saying yes, he would be fine. Between giggles they told me he had lost control that morning and gone to the bathroom all over everything. They thought it was very funny and couldn't stop laughing.

I went back to Dabo and left him money for food and for public transport, if by some chance he had to take it, but I told him I would try to find someone to give him a ride. I couldn't stay in St. Louis any longer. Two brood ponds had to be harvested. I had to tour the old pond sites and write a report, before Duncan came to inspect the program. I had to set up meetings and have Abdoulaye build an awning over the holding tank. There was so much to get done. I couldn't see that it would ever be finished in time, but it had to be.

I explained to Dabo about the professor from Auburn coming to evaluate the program, and how he could make the difference between the fish program continuing or being canceled.

"Dabo, if you really want me to stay, I will," I said.

No, he said, I must do my work. I looked at him lying in bed. He so obviously wanted me to stay, but I couldn't.

I touched his hands, his arm.

"You know you can't stay here too long," I said, grinning down at him. "There's too much work to be done at the station, man's work. We're going to save it for you. You must get well and return to do it. It will wait for you." Dabo seemed so broken. I wanted to give him some of my fierceness. It was so hard to leave him.

I unlocked the truck's doors and climbed inside. I was about to turn the engine over when I saw the melted candy bar. All of a sudden it was very important that I give it to Dabo.

I carried the soggy bar as though it were some precious, fragile treasure as I ran back to Dabo.

I climbed the stairs and returned to Dabo's room, handing him my offering. I tried to explain that I had bought it in Dakar; that was why it was melted, but it would still taste good. "Chocolate is good for your health," I said and then added, "My Mom used to give me chocolate when I was sick." It wasn't really true but I thought maybe it would make him feel better.

The Pulaar man said I should stay and talk with them, but I had to go. I had to leave quickly before I changed my mind.

CHAPTER TWENTY

La Projet Du Pisciculture

It didn't feel like a month. It felt like one of those dreams: the kind where you close your eyes and dream a million different things, and none of them are connected, and you cannot imagine once you wake up how they all could have been packed into one night's sleep. You wake up in the morning exhausted with these little spots of memories— speaking to some woman who you barely knew in high school, driving along a road you have never seen, reading a book, ripping your pants, something about graduate school—and all day you wonder how so many things could have happened to you in eight hours the night before. That is exactly how it felt, like an eight-hour dream.

I spent a day at the station. Demba, Abdoulaye, and I sat at the edge of pond number six while Abdoulaye took the temperature with a thermometer tied to a piece of string. They asked me about Dabo, and I told them he had been operated on, was better, and resting in the hospital in St. Louis. They nodded and said I had been right to take Dabo to St. Louis. We were all family.

The three of us sat on the bank and the pink from the sky was reflected on the surface of the pond; the world seemed pale and cool—soft. I loved this time of day before the sun and the wind had completely awakened and regained their power over the land. I would spend it walking the ponds, seeing which needed fertilizer, or the weeds cut, or the inlet screen cleaned. Their surfaces were so smooth in the morning, like opals half-hidden in the dirt, now and then flashing with the fire of the sun. We sat silently while the water moved the mercury and we thought our own thoughts—thoughts touched by the quiet warmth we shared.

I had changed the schedule so that both Demba and Abdoulaye could help me work during the days Dabo was still in St. Louis, and the three of us sat hunched over the thermometer as though it were our morning coffee. Demba wore the red shorts Dabo usually wore. He sat back on his heels, his round face so serious, his skin made more brown against the red. Abdoulaye had not yet changed into his work clothes. He was wearing his green pants with a broken zipper and his old green raincoat. It seemed these were the clothes Abdoulaye had always worn, always would wear: his overcoat, the pants, and the *tingaadi* hat from my kitchen wall. I wondered how many hundred times I had seen Abdoulaye pedaling his dilapidated bicycle, as though his very life depended on it, the tails of his coat flapping behind him and the pointed straw hat bobbing up and down on his head, making me hum the wicked witch song under my breath.

Abdoulaye had come to me the month before because he had rubbed himself raw from pedaling too fast. He was frightened because it hurt to have sex and he wanted me to look at the inflamed spot. White people had such strange knowledge and he was never sure what I would know and what I would not. I explained that it would do no good to show it to me because I was not a doctor and couldn't help, but I would take him to the S.A.E.D. doctor and we had driven there together.

This morning, after telling Demba and Abdoulaye about Dabo, I looked first at one and then at the other, unable to keep the laughter from my eyes. I said quietly that I thought there had been a lot of penis problems lately, and I was not sure it was so great to have one of those things. They saw the teasing in my eyes, spreading to my lips and then their faces until the three of us could no longer hold the laughter back, and broke the morning's quietness with it. We laughed for a long time and they slapped their knees with the palms of their hands. A gentle morning wind came and carried our laughter off over the pond, and then away into the *waalo*— the land that was desert now, but would flood with the rains.

Abdoulaye smiled and said his wife was pregnant. He said that was good, and Demba and I nodded our heads in agreement—that was good.

Abdoulaye pulled the thermometer from the water. He read the mercury and marked the sheet where we recorded each pond's morning and afternoon temperature. He knew all of his numbers and was just beginning to learn how to read and write Pulaar. He had asked me to teach him to read the day of my birthday, and we had stayed at the station late that afternoon while I tried to explain letters to him and how they worked. Abdoulaye was on fire with learning. I could see it burning in his eyes, feel it in his questions, making me wonder how long I would be able to feed the blaze, before it outdistanced me.

I told the men there was a lot of work to do this day. We needed to fish one of the brood ponds—for stock to be transported to Matam, make up another batch of blood meal, fertilize the ponds, and set up the holding tank—as well as taking temperatures, feeding the fish, and unclogging the screens over the ponds' inlet pipes. I said I did not care how the work was done, but it must get done this day, and that we would have to stay until it was finished. Abdoulaye looked into my face.

"Suzanne," he said, "we will stay until nine o'clock tonight if we have to."

I smiled at him, and wished I thought they were doing it for fish culture, instead of for me. In six months I would leave. I had to give them something which would keep them working after that, something besides Suzanne.

We seined number four together. Sometimes I thought no one would ever know me again as well as these two men. We took the seine from its hooks in the storeroom, tied the lead and float lines to the brails, took turns passing the brails over our shoulders, leaning our chests up against the wooden bars, pulling the weight of the net. First Abdoulaye would be the one to sit in the muck at the edge of the pond, pulling in the lead line, and we would joke and tease him and say he sounded just like the old motorcycle that always backfired. Next would be Demba, and then me.

We had worked together so many times, knew the work

and each other so well, that we would fall into a rhythm—three parts of something bigger. There was no need for words between us and I liked the feel of it: the quiet underlying rhythm, like the movement of silent dancers, or the wings of a flock of geese flying north. When words did come, they brought laughter, joined laughter, which deepened the rhythm, and made it warmer.

When it was my turn to pull the lead line, Demba watched me. He was thinking of something. I could tell. Suddenly his face became happy, and he smiled.

"There are no pregnant women here, no *debbo reedus* at the station," he said. "Everyone here works like a man."

I grinned up at him, and continued pulling in the net.

The work was finished at five. I was somewhere past exhaustion. I wondered if Demba would ever learn the numbers eighteen and nineteen. Would he ever be able to count the little lines on the scales between pounds? Still, the men were learning. They made a batch of the blood meal by themselves, weighing out the rice bran and the fish meal, and mixing it with the cow's blood. Before, Dabo or I had always helped them with the proportions.

I dropped Demba at Kodite on my way home. Abdoulaye hadn't brought his bicycle, and so I dropped him at the pumping station. I started to turn into Walli Jalla. Guia was only a kilometer or two down the dirt road, but I didn't have the energy to drive Abdoulaye there. All I wanted in the world was to wash before the sun had sunk behind the river. I wanted to sit, needed to have twelve hours between this ten-hour day and the next. Abdoulaye would not have far to walk. He should have ridden his bike. He would have had to walk the whole way home if I had not brought him from the station.

I turned the truck around and went back to where Abdoulaye was walking along the road. He grinned at me, climbed back into the cab, and I drove him to his compound.

It was five days before I returned to Walli Jalla and the station. I couldn't decide if those days had passed quickly or slowly. The amount of work accomplished seemed impossible, as though each day had been a month, and yet it seemed I had blinked my eyes once, while I drove away from the station to take the fish to Matam, and then blinked them once more and I was back at the station harvesting the big pond with Abdoulaye, Demba, Cindi, and Kevin.

We did a *tourné* of the old sites, all the places between Matam and Bakel where records said ponds had been built, but were not being used: Navelle, Woundé, Barkevey, Gababé, Gaol, Yafera, Khounghani, Diaware, and Gandé. We were having a training for S.A.E.D. counterparts in a month. If they could read the history of the project, see that thirty-two village ponds had been built, five of which were workable, then maybe they would understand why we wanted to keep the project small and manageable, to get a few ponds working before we started building more. Five new fisheries volunteers would arrive in June. Someone would have to be posted in a new village. I wanted to see if any of the old ponds were redeemable, if there were sites where fish culture had been started and then stopped before it was given a chance. Professor Duncan was coming from Auburn to evalute the program in two weeks. I wanted to be able to point out to him how far the program had come.

Woundé did not have any ponds. Cindy, Ken, and I drove out to the village. It took us awhile to find it and then we couldn't find anyone who knew about a white person having come there to grow fish. Finally, a young boy in ripped Western clothes said we must be talking about Mamadou, and that he would take us to the compound where he had lived.

It was a big village with two mosques, and I wondered what it had felt like to Mamadou to live there for two years. He had finished his tour and returned to the U.S. before I ever came to Senegal. Now, we were walking into his memories.

The young boy led us inside a compound's walls and we went to greet three old men who sat on a millet stalk mat. We greeted them in Pulaar and they asked us to sit, so we took off our flip-flops and joined them. We explained why we had come, and they told us a white man, Mamadou, had lived there, but there were no ponds. We couldn't understand that.

What had Mamadou done for two years? The oldest man kept talking about some other way of raising fish, but we didn't understand his words.

He went inside one of the buildings and came back out carrying two pieces of P.V.C. pipe which had been joined at right angles. He said Mamadou had told them there was nowhere near their village suitable to build a pond and these pipes had been the floats to a cage. They had put fish in it and tried to grow them, but the cage was left in the river when the rains came and the fish had all escaped. He said no white people ever came back after Mamadou left.

He said Mamadou was good, his heart had been good. I wondered why he had saved the broken pipes, and then what Samba would show white people if they came to Walli Jalla asking of me, two years after I had left.

Barkevey was only a few kilometers from Woundé. There was a pond there. One of the men who had worked with the volunteer who built it, led us over dry fields he said they no longer irrigated, to an indented rectangle of dark brown clay. It was a fairly good pond. The soil would hold water. It had been built on an incline so it would drain, but the man said they no longer used the canal which supplied water to it; the canal had been used to irrigate the abandoned fields. We asked if he thought there would be a chance of reopening it, if people in the village wanted to grow fish in their pond, and he said it was possible.

He told us Mamadou had come to their village and found the site. Then a woman came, lived in their village, built the pond, and explained how they were going to grow fish. She left after the pond was completed, but before it was ever filled with water, before any fish were ever brought. The man said she had never returned; no one had, and the pond had been left empty and dry. He was not sure if the village would want to try fish culture again. He would have to talk to the village council.

The man was talking about Patty. She left Senegal after three months, because she didn't think the program would work.

The next morning Cindi, Marsha, a young American tourist who wanted to see Pulaar villages, and I drove out to Gababé, Gaol, and Oudourou. Marsha, who was posted in Gababé, had arrived with Linda. She had taken water tests in the feeder canal, knew its hardness, wrote her quarterly reports on a computer in the city of Kaedi (across the river in Mauritania) and had done market research on the price of fish in her village and where it came from.

The ponds in Gababé had been built two years before and had no inlet canals. Marsha needed bulldozers from S.A.E.D. They had been promised for months. Even if they came, there was a fifty-fifty chance it would be possible to get water to the ponds because they were higher than the surrounding land.

Cindi, Marsha, the American woman, and I left Gababé for Gaol. There were no ponds in Gaol, never had been, but someone from the village had heard of the ponds in Oudourou and written to Cindi saying they were interested in having ponds too. We drove over the sand track, jarred by the bouncing of the truck, squinting against the sun, and sweating in the heat.

At Gaol, we stopped in front of the mosque to ask the men where we could find the village chief. Someone led us to his compound, and the chief invited us to sit upon a millet mat under the shade of a thatched awning with two other men. He explained how his son had gone to France to be educated and then returned to help his village. The village already had some irrigated fields, but they wanted to expand and were hoping to grow fish as well. We sat in the heat, watching the dust devils dance across the flat land and the old man rolled out his French-educated son's dreams for the village's future, painting the flatness and the dust into green fields, ponds, and livestock projects. It was the first time I had heard development dreams from a man speaking Pulaar, who wore traditional clothes, and did not need to speak over the background noise of an air conditioner.

They had found a spot which they thought would be good for a pond, and the old man climbed into the cab of the truck to direct us to it. The soil seemed good—hard-baked clay with deep fissures, but we had to explain that we couldn't build any new ponds for a long time. The old man nodded his head at our words. He didn't seem disappointed, or even surprised. Change took time, he said.

I explained how we were making records of all the old sites: where ponds had been built, what shape they were in, if they had the physical requirements needed to grow fish and if the villagers seemed interested. I said we would also make records of possible new sites, that I would write about his beautiful village and their plans. Maybe the people after us would read about it and be able to help him and his son. I hoped someone would.

On the road from Gaol to Oudourou the sun beat against us, unsoftened by any form of shade. There was no escape from it. The sweat poured from our bodies, and we drank hot water from our canteens to replenish it. Caught in the power of the afternoon sun, the paleness of morning was forgotten, and the paleness of dusk unimaginable.

A layer of red-tan sand covered everything. We could hear the grains of sand caught between our teeth, and could feel them in our eyes fighting with the sun to blind us. It seemed like the road would never end. It was four o'clock by the time we stopped at Oudourou. This was Cindi's village and she took us to the compound where she ate her meals. The Bas took us into the shade of their house, and gave us cool water from their *loondes,* and hot peanut sauce and rice to fill our stomachs. We sat around the bowl which they cooked especially for us and they said we should pass the night in their village. The shade and the words felt soft and cool, but we couldn't stay. We had to go to Bakel that night.

I knew the road from Oudourou to Matam. It was as bad as the roads from Gababé and Gaol, but at least I knew when we were getting close. We had to go up an incline, take a few more turns and then down and through the dry riverbed and back up the other side. Then we would be on the road which came out at the Matam dump.

When we came to the incline, there was a huge irrigation pipe across the road at the very top. It was leaking and the road below it was pure mud. The truck stuck, slid, and then stuck again. I put it in reverse; it slid backwards and forwards and then we were at the top of the little hill with the front wheels a foot from the irrigation pipe.

The road forked at the top, and it took us a moment to realize that the pipe crossed both tracks. We had thought we would be able to go around it. They couldn't have completely blocked the only way to get to Matam!

There was a crowd of children by the pipe, and we asked them where the road was. They said there was no road and laughed at our confusion, chattering in high-pitched, sing-song voices. They said the road would be cut off until eight o'clock that night, when they finished irrigating their fields. They were obviously enjoying this. Four thwarted *tubabs* had become their entertainment for the day. Adults joined them saying the same thing, their laughter mingling with the children's.

"What do you mean there's no road?" we asked. How could they just cut it off? Public transport cars used this road. It was a regularly traveled road. Now it was five o'clock. We were filthy and would have been in Matam in half an hour, where there was a refrigerator, and a cold shower. We still had three hours to drive to get to Bakel, after we got to Matam.

We said they would have to move their pipe, and they said they would not. It was incomprehensible they could just choose to close off the road between Matam and Oudourou for four hours.

Cindi and I were both yelling in Pulaar, saying we had as much right to the road as their village did and that we knew S.A.E.D. had not given them permission to do this and we personally would speak to the director. The people laughed at us, thinking it was funny that we were at their mercy, a carload of *tubabs*, who could go nowhere unless they chose to let us go.

I said if there was no road, then we would make one—over their fields. We turned down a little dirt path to the right and followed it to the end. Unfortunately, it was bordered on one side by a canal and on the other by a ravine. I wanted to beat these taunting Senegalese at their own game, show them we were not helpless. I itched to drive the truck through their ordered rows of young, green millet plants just coming up from the irrigated earth.

There was no way to win and we had to turn around. It would be worse to face these people a second time, to see their grins deepen as they threw our empty threats back at us. Our anger grew.

We drove back to the main road. Someone had gotten the pumpist and his assistant. He came up to the truck and said he could move the pipe for us for a *cadeau*—a gift. The bastards! We had just spent ten hours bouncing from village to village, covered in sweat and dust, fighting the heat to try to determine where fish culture would work and where it would not, trying to make sure no more empty promises were made by white people to Senegalese villagers.

I wanted to backhand the pumpist. We said we had come here to try to help his country and he said we had come here for the money. White people came here to make money and live in fancy houses and drive fancy cars.

Everyone was screaming. There was so much frustration and hatred and misunderstanding. I stopped yelling and listened for a moment. Suddenly the anger leaked out of me, was swallowed up by the dust of the road. I thought of our American tourist, wondered how she saw us—Cindi and I yelling in Pulaar at the top of our lungs. I thought of Keith in the bar telling us there were assholes in Senegal. For a second I stood apart and watched, seeing a wall between us and these Senegalese. We were white people, not real people at all and would never win. Why should they do anything for the white people, who had everything, while they were so poor?

I spoke to the pumpist, telling him that we had been on the road all day looking at villages, trying to determine if they were good places to grow fish. We were here to try to run a fish program. We lived in villages ourselves, just like their village—that was why we spoke Pulaar. We ate millet and leaf sauce and *gosi* each night and slept out under the stars, just like they did. We talked for a long time and finally he agreed to move the pipe. We handed him the ears of roasted corn which the Bas had given us, and then drove on to Matam.

We did drive to Bakel that night. It was dark and cool and we saw two jackals, their coats caught in the glow of our headlights as they ran across the road. The next two days we looked at the old fish sites in the Bakel region. Bakel was Kevin's post, and now it was he, Cindi, and I who drove from abandoned site to abandoned site. They were more of the same: a white person had come, lived there for awhile, built ponds and left. In Diawara and Gandé the people did not even seem to realize the identations in the clay had been made in order to grow fish.

Cindi and Kevin drove back to the station with me, after we finished our *tourné*. They came to help me with the work. It would not have gotten done without them. I had left a lot of tasks for Abdoulaye and Demba to do, more than I had ever left before. I had been worried it was too much, but Demba had said, "Go Suzanne, we will do the work. You will see."

My first year, each time we returned to the station, it seemed a catastrophe was there to meet us. I hadn't yet learned to forget that feeling of dread, and I wanted to know the worst right away. In the back of my mind a part of me truly believed in Abdoulaye and Demba and wanted to hear all had gone well, see their shining faces, and be filled with pride. But I couldn't afford to think that, because things didn't happen that way, not at the station, not in Senegal.

When we stopped at the station, the only person we could find was Ouseman's Dad, and he knew nothing of what had been done or left undone.

The next morning we drove back. Abdoulaye and Demba were there. In the five days I had been gone, they had harvested a pond, sold some of the fish and kept the rest in the holding tank, kept records of their weights and numbers—numbers that Abdoulaye explained to me with great seriousness—fed the fish and fixed the dikes and even cleaned the debris from the screens over the inlet pipes.

Their faces shone as they told me all this and I looked first at one and then the other. They looked a little silly, as though they cared too much to completely cover it up. I could feel the lines of my own face and knew they were reflections of theirs.

In the second five days we stocked a brood pond, harvested one of the thirty-three are ponds—over two thousand fish—sold the fish in Podor, did a growth sample of the *marigot* in Guia, and bought wood from the village in the dead forest to make an awning over the holding tank. Normally it took three or four days to harvest one of the big ponds. We worked straight through the weekend, ten to twelve-hour days.

Those days were nightmares of work. The big pond did not drain well, and when the water was almost gone it looked as though there were about fifty fish left to scoop from the muddy puddles with dip nets, but there were almost a thousand. The five of us: Cindi, Kevin, Abdoulaye, Demba, and I were covered with the thick wet clay from head to toe. It dried on our skin, pulling it tight, and then cracked and fell away, only to be replaced by another layer. Thick drops of it were flicked into our eyes as fish tried to escape, skittering their tails in the shallow brown water. We had already been working for eight hours, but couldn't stop. The fish were gasping for air, and we had to get them out of the mud, or they would die.

After all the fish were caught they had to be sold. Friday and Saturday we worked twelve-hour days. Saturday night, when no one could stand to work another minute, Cindi and I went to the village in the dead forest to collect the wood we had cut for the awning to be built over the holding tank. It was after dark when we got there, and the old man who had cut the wood, and was supposedly guiding us to it, became lost, leading us this way and that over the thorns and stumps of the dead forest.

Finally we found it, parking as close as we could, but still the logs were a ten minute's walk into the bush. The boy the old man had brought with him refused to help carry the posts, sitting in the cab in his fancy Western clothes. Angrily, I walked into the forest, only to bruise my shoulder with the great weight of a log slung over it. I had carried posts like this once before with Demba and sworn I would never do it again.

There were nine posts altogether, the old man carrying two at a time, staggering under their weight as though it might kill him. We made three trips back and forth to collect the posts while the young man in red polyester never moved from his seat.

Back in Walli Jalla, we drank beer with Kevin Nelson and Kevin Turner, who had come from his village, talking about being fisheries volunteers, all the same things we always talked about: the mud and the spines and our fisheries training in Oklahoma. We would say the program had its problems, was more messed up than any other Peace Corps program, but we would say it with pride, and I would point out how much better it was doing now than it had been when we first arrived in the country.

The moonlight was so bright, prettier even than dusk or dawn, because you knew you would never have to fight it. It illuminated our faces and brought us closer together. Cindi made potato soup, and we ate it out of tin cups and pulled on our beers. I thought if the night could just be a little longer and leave me a little more time to spend sitting and talking with Cindi, and the two Kevins, I would have enough peace inside me to finish the month.

The next day, Calel, a S.A.E.D. extension agent, and I went to look at the old fish sites in the Podor region. Not one of them was good. Either they did not drain, or they were built of sand which drank the water and profits, or they were located too far from the river. All of them had been abandoned at least two years before and none of them were worth trying to reclaim.

I liked Calel. He was down-to-earth, no fancy airs, and we spoke about the program, and Professor Duncan's visit to evaluate its progress.

Professor Duncan was a fish person. He would understand all that had been accomplished in the past year, see the progress, validate all the hard work and our hopes with his official praise. Maybe the funding proposal would finally get sent in and then the Peace Corps administration would take our program seriously. I realized as I spoke to Calel that I thought Duncan would see the progress I saw, that he would be able to understand it where others could not because he was a fisheries expert. If Professor Duncan saw it, it would be real.

I was wrong.

We went to Dakar, to finish writing the program's history and have it translated into proper French. I spent one day back at the station, and saw Dabo for long enough to see he was still very thin but healthy. He wanted to show me his scar. I said, "No thank you." I had already seen it too many times. He thanked me again for saving his life, and I wondered why he had stayed in St. Louis for so long.

The next day I went to St. Louis to meet with Professor Duncan, and Sarah from C.R.S. There was another week of meetings and conferences. Sarah said it would be nice if everything worked out the way it should, and the results matched the energy and work put into things, while Duncan said maybe we should look for other funding. I repeated what Peace Corps administration had told me: they wanted a fisheries program, even if the funding fell through, and they would look for funding elsewhere if necessary. I don't remember Duncan's words, but I remember thinking he was letting me know Peace Corps had told him just the opposite.

We had a meeting, all the fisheries volunteers and Duncan, the day before he left for Dakar. The six of us sat around a long narrow table, talking about the program's past and future. We had come so far, so much had been done. The station was running better than it ever had.

It was physically impossible to build a good pond along most of the Fleuve. The pumped water was so expensive that tilapia would never make a profit until there was no longer the trucked-in *yaboy*. There was a great need for fish and it would increase now that the salt-water intrusion dam had been built in St. Louis and they were completing the head-water dam in Mali. It was important to have a means of producing those fish before the need became a disaster. Tilapia aquaculture in man-made ponds with irrigated water would not become profitable until there was a disaster. They had been growing rice with the same irrigated water for thirty years and it still was not profitable.

It was odd, just like a dream again: a feeling in the back of your mind that something happened which could not have possibly happened. You tell yourself it was something you dreamt the night before, but you aren't sure because it seems so real.

I listened to everyone's words and tried not to panic. I couldn't understand why I had the feeling that we were all looking at the same thing—only we called it success and Duncan seemed to think it was failure. It didn't make any sense. Everyone agreed the program was doing the best it ever had, and everyone could feel it was going to die.

Duncan never said the program would be canceled, but we knew. After he left, everything changed. No, not everything. There was still as much work to be done, only before, we had been working toward something. Before, it had been worth giving up a piece of myself for, and now somewhere inside I had to admit it was not, but it still demanded the price.

CHAPTER TWENTY-ONE

Gile ene Moussi

The mourning doves were as regular as the dawn and I sometimes wondered, what would happen if they no longer came. Every day they came and sat on the top of my roof, cooing softly into the light. I would listen to their calls and think to myself I would never forget them, never listen to the sound again without thinking of Walli Jalla mornings: the neem tree's leaves rustling in the wind, Aisata pounding millet on the other side of the compound wall and Fatu's voice off somewhere in the distance scolding a child.

This morning the doves sat on the roof and cooed while I sat in my broken-down orange armchair under the neem tree, my feet propped up against its trunk. I had meant to write in my journal, but it sat open in my lap, dust collecting on the lined white pages. It was horribly hot—over one hundred degrees; and it was Ramadan—the Moslems' holy month of fasting.

My family and the people of Walli Jalla did not eat or drink while the sun was in the sky and the heat sparkled off the dust, and as the month wore on many people became weakened and fell sick. It seemed everyone's eyes became bigger, rounder in their faces, and the skin over the bridge of their noses and across their cheeks became tighter. Last year I had eaten while they fasted. This year I would not. I said Walli Jalla was my village, the Diengs were my family, how could I fill my stomach while they went hungry? Because I was sick, I let myself drink water with the sun still in the sky, but I would not eat food.

The hot wind blew pinpoints of dust against my skin and made the leaves of my neem tree dance. Samba was speaking with someone next door and I sat very still, listening to his

241

voice. I couldn't catch the words, but it didn't matter. They were unimportant. It was Samba's voice: warm and alive, mellowed around the edges with time, Samba's voice, rising and falling with the cadence of Pulaar, that I wanted to hear. His voice meant I was home, maybe even more than the neem tree and the doves and the dust. His voice meant it was true; I had returned to Walli Jalla.

I had gone to Paris, and for two weeks I had yearned for Walli Jalla—yearned as though my heart would break. Dirk and I had planned to meet in Paris for a two-week vacation, even before he had left Senegal, and for seven months I had saved my money.

When I arrived, I had no idea why I had come. Dirk and I were from different worlds. The modern city was part of his world, not mine. Paris could have been any first-world city. It didn't seem so different to me from Washington. I didn't care too much about museums and cathedrals. All I wanted was to eat good food, take hot shower after hot shower, wear a pink dress, and rest. I didn't understand the things Dirk told me about America—the people in blue suits, the metro, the loneliness and the crowds. I didn't understand when he tried to tell me he could find nothing to believe in. America sounded horrible, and Dirk said he had not realized before how sheltered we were in the Peace Corps.

Dirk needed something. I knew that, but I couldn't give it to him. He was mad at me because I hadn't written in two months, and I pointed out he had written almost no one during his two years in Senegal. I felt badly. Dirk didn't understand how little of me was left: the pieces given and sometimes taken by the death of Demba's daughter, Dabo's illness, the program's failure.

He wanted me to feel what it was like to return to married friends and bank accounts, taxes, medical bills, and car insurance. He needed me to feel those things but I couldn't. I had gone somewhere past them and couldn't imagine ever returning. Dirk tried to explain feeling like a grown-up, and I tried to explain feeling old. Neither of us really understood.

I had been afraid to go to Paris. Some part of me had known I would become sick. It started on the plane out of

Dakar, got worse the night I passed in Tunis, and raged in Paris. My body was ruled by fevers that would take it over, turning the world to nothing but pain, and suddenly leave me wondering if I really was better or had just been given a reprieve. The fevers would go higher and higher and I would lie in bed shaking, some part of my mind wishing they would go just a little higher, so I could at least become delirious. Then the fever would break and quickly Dirk and I would try to squeeze in a cathedral or a nice dinner before another fever came.

One day we went to the Musée d'Orsay. It was very beautiful and we walked quietly from one impressionist painting to another. I liked them, many of them I knew, and thought were lovely. It was nice to see something beautiful, but they did not touch me. They were not of my world.

Two seemed different and I stared at them for a long time. One was of a young woman in a bright red jacket, happy and young and full of herself. She seemed so excited, without a care in the world. It felt good just to look at her. The other was of soldiers, two or three of them leaving a little town. The landscape was flat, gray, and white with snow and I felt as though it pulled me inside it. I could hear the dog bark, the noise far away and muffled by the snow. I felt the happiness of the soldiers, happiness tinged with sadness and fear because it was only one free afternoon. It would end, and they would go back to the war.

We walked from room to room, looking at the clothes, the food, and the expressions of nineteenth-century France, then we walked through a doorway into a small room and were in the desert. There were camels, *kaalas*, the red-tan dust, and Moslem heads bowed to the earth, turned toward Mecca. Each of the four walls was hung with pictures of the desert and I turned round slowly looking at them all, smiling. I wanted to laugh out loud, to tell someone how wonderful it was to see camels and dust, and how odd it was to find my world here in this little room in the Musée d'Orsay.

I watched the faces of the people looking at the paintings and thought they must see these scenes as something from a book, someplace exotic and far away; and I wanted to say it was not like that at all. I wanted to tell them I had a family who came from scenes like these, and that Mbinté had just had a beautiful baby girl, and how Samba's eyes danced when I asked him what he was always doing at the *beignet* woman's compound so early in the morning. The desert room felt comfortable, the only place in all of Paris that did.

Paris was horribly cold and I wore jeans, two sweaters and a jacket and was still cold, cold from the inside out. I had special clothes made for Paris by the tailor in Thiès, but none of them were warm enough, leaving me to wear the jeans and the sweaters day after day.

We took the train to Blois for the weekend and I realized I was getting worse. We went to a grocer's to buy food for lunch and I had to sit down while Dirk paid the cashier. I sat very still, trying to pull myself way down inside like a turtle, somewhere the pain could not reach, wishing I had stayed in our room. The grocer saw me and told Dirk to take me to a doctor.

I didn't want to go to a doctor. I knew how to be sick. I had been sick for two years. What did a white doctor know of really being sick?

That night it was worse. A line from a song went round and round in my head, "L.A. streets ain't paved with gold. I know I'm young, but I feel just like I'm dying." The world turned into a grey-brown land with silly-putty mushrooms and vague grey shapes that kept moving in on me.

I vomited over and over, and there was nothing left inside me, but I had to try anyway. I would hear someone moaning, and be surprised it was me. Each time I got up, Dirk would come stand by me and try to help. One time, I lay down by the toilet and told him to leave me alone. I just wanted to lie there. He pleaded with me to get up. Finally, his words penetrated my gray world and I remember hearing fear in his voice. I got up and walked to the bed, but it did not seem to be me moving.

By early morning I was soaking wet, the sheets drenched with sweat. My sweat had a horrible sweet smell that scared me a little, but it took my fever with it. I fell asleep at five o'clock, then Dirk woke me up. He said he came out of the bathroom to find me lying there so quiet and peaceful, he thought I was dead.

That last day in Paris, Dirk left early in the morning and I had all afternoon to myself to wonder if I would get another fever on the plane to Tunisia. I didn't think I could stand being that sick on a plane. I was so afraid. I went to the post office to mail a pile of postcards, putting three stamps on each card, one green, one brown, one red. I kept saying to myself one green, one brown, one red, one green, one brown, one red, and some voice inside me whispered I didn't know one person in this city, not one person in this country. I felt weak and flushed; the floor was starting to move. I grabbed my cards, half-stamped, half-unstamped to run outside into the rain. It was cold. My body could not pass out in cold rain.

I had not eaten anything for two days and bought two croissants, taking them back to my hotel room. Sitting on the edge of the bed, I didn't think I could eat them. I told myself I would have to: small bite, chew, swallow, small bite, chew, swallow. Outside the raindrops were coming down in straight lines, over and over again, gray against the windowpane.

How would I get to the airport? My flight had an overnight in Tunis before going on to Dakar. What if I got a fever in Tunis? I was not sure I could survive by myself. I finished the croissants and curled up into a ball, pulling the covers over me. Nothing would happen to me as long as I stayed in bed. This was where I had spent most of the past two weeks. I had one more hour before check-out time and looked at my watch every fifteen minutes, watching it slip away, until the maid came in to clean, telling me I must leave.

I took my bags downstairs to the *concierge*. He tried to call a cab for me, but the line was busy. I was afraid I would pass out at the airport. I told the man I was very sick, and needed somewhere to lie down for the afternoon. He must have seen my panic and rented me a room for fifty francs.

I found the room but didn't want to enter. It was as though someone had been able to see inside my mind and had taken all the grayness and the fear and put it into this room. It was tiny, no bigger than a closet, with a rumpled single bed on sagging springs, cringing up against the far corner. It smelled damp and dusty. There were no windows, no escape, only an opening to an airshaft, a concrete square of gray air. Everything was old, dirty, broken. I felt as though some horror lived here, and I could already sense it touching me. This room was a place where things died, where they were left to die alone.

I didn't know what to do. I lay down on the bed and kept telling myself "It's all right Sue, everything is all right, you are all right," but I didn't believe it.

I couldn't take care of myself and decided to call the Peace Corps doctor. He would have to fly with me to the United States. I would not see Senegal again. I would never say good-bye to my family, Abdoulaye, Demba, or Mada.

I carefully walked the three blocks to the post office, to use their phone, but it turned out to be the director's home phone number on my I.D. card and his houseboy said he wouldn't be back for another two hours.

I returned to the room, climbing under the covers of the bed as the walls began to close in on me. I told myself if I could walk to the post office, then I could get on a plane. I tried not to give in, but I was drowning in waves of fear.

What if I had to spend a night here? I had almost no money left. The room would grow stronger with darkness. If I stayed too long, the room would win; sooner or later I would give in to it. It was too gray, too ugly, too close to death. I would wither away into nothingness. This room would kill me, bleeding away what I still held onto of life.

Taking my bags, I returned to the desk of the *concierge*, who finally managed to get me a cab. A woman with her dog came in a silver car to drive me to the airport. I entered the terminal and walked down a hallway. I would not die here or on the plane. I would make it back to Senegal, that was all that mattered. My bags felt heavy and I decided if they became too heavy, I would leave them, but keep my camera. I had to go to the bathroom, but it didn't matter. It didn't matter even if I fouled my pants, vomited, or passed out. I would get to Senegal. That was the one bright single light inside me and the brightness of that desire burned away everything else. I had never felt so light before; everything gone that was a part of me, everything but my need to return to Senegal.

I arrived in Senegal on a Wednesday afternoon and Kevin Turner was there to meet me with the truck. I didn't have a fever, had not been sick on the plane or in Tunisia. I thought maybe I was getting well. Everything was familiar and yet shiny as though it were new: the beggars, the huge mosque across from Peace Corps, Wolof and Pulaar and French, the smell of sewage and outdoor coffee stands, men peddling straw prayer mats, the streets of Dakar. Paris had been a horrible, cold, foreign place, but I had lived through it, and I was home.

By the next day I had made up a list of the project's receipts, so the floating fund could be reimbursed, attended a meeting with C.R.S. and Peace Corps about the fisheries program, bought a scale for the station that was in kilograms and visited a string of auto stores until I finally found a battery cap for the truck to replace the one that had been lost the month before. I was beginning to feel as though I had never left Senegal, except that I was tired, unbearably tired.

By Friday I knew I was getting another fever.

This time the doctor came to get me. It was Saturday and Jon, the Peace Corps guard, called him after he saw me trying to walk from the health hut to the first floor bathroom in the Peace Corps office building. I suppose I ruined the doctor's weekend. He didn't seem at all happy when he finally arrived at the health hut to find me lying curled up in a ball on one of the beds.

In the car on the way to his house, the doctor asked me if I was ready to get on a plane to the States. No, I said, bracing myself for the turns, each curve adding waves of pain. I wanted to moan. Somehow, it seemed putting the pain into sound might make it hurt less.

I had to go back to Walli Jalla. The things I loved most in the world were there. The river, my house, the sound of Pulaar, pale dawn and dusk, my family, my work—these things were who I had become. I wasn't sure if I could ever leave them, but I would not leave without saying good-bye. I couldn't explain all this to the doctor. He wouldn't understand it was worth it to me to return to Walli Jalla even if there was a chance I would die.

I watched the leaves of my neem tree dance in the wind. The fever had passed, and although he had not understood, the doctor had let me come home. I thought of the lizard named Jim, who had lived in my neem tree. He had a yellow head, a gray body and always seemed to be doing push-ups, which was why I named him Jim—after my oldest brother. I hadn't seen him for a long time and hoped nothing had happened to him.

It was good just to sit in my compound and think of all the days I had sat here under the neem tree, writing letters and writing in my journal. Maybe I would study a little Pulaar later in the afternoon, maybe take my book next door to sit with Mbinté and Fatiim and we would laugh together as the sun glared and we were safe under the thatched awning. I wanted to take my dishes to the river in my red plastic bucket, to wash them in the water, scraping them with the sand, in slow, deft movements, as I had so many times before.

I was disappointed when Cindi walked in. I had wanted my day in Walli Jalla to myself. Then I was glad because it was always good to talk to her. She had come to see me because she got my note from Dakar, telling her about how bad Paris had been.

We pulled out another chair and sat together under the neem tree, talking all through the afternoon. I told her how cold Paris had been, how one day I had decided to buy myself a lipstick and the women in the store had thought I was strange because I had no idea what shade to choose. I tried to explain that I lived in a small village in Africa, and they looked at me as though I should have a ring through my nose or tattooed lips. I wished that the women from my family were there because they would be excited and laugh and say, "Mariyata, she wants to be a woman," and try to help me to look beautiful. I never wanted to go back to Paris, for as long as I lived.

We went down to the river to wash, returning afterwards to

the house and to talk through the evening. Cindi told me about Ramadan in her village, how hard it was to go hungry and thirsty. We talked about our plans to travel overland to Kenya. We had decided to travel together across Africa after we were finished with our two years in Senegal, having gotten the idea months before when we read about a woman in National Geographic who had made the trip to study different types of jewelry.

We talked about the big Fourth of July party the embassy gave and how we were actually going to make it this year. I had told her I felt a little sick. Maybe that was why we talked, the words splashing out all in a rush, as though if we talked fast enough the words would come true, somehow covering up what we both felt underneath and refused to believe.

Samba called "Mariyata," into the night and I went to greet him, to shake his hand, as he passed me a bowl of *lacciri* for dinner for my guest and myself.

The next morning my fever came, and words could no longer cover it. I do not remember how many days I fought it. During the day, I would lie on my foam rubber mattress, and the flies would buzz and land in my sweat, their tiny bodies prickling my feverish skin—a thousand needle points piercing my nerves, while I prayed for the day to end.

My family was very worried, my family and Cindi. The Diengs' heads kept popping over my compound wall to see if I was any better, to greet me, to tell me to get well, and to send food for Cindi and me to eat.

At nighttime, the fever would let go a little and I would think I was getting better, and Cindi and I would start to giggle about something and then not be able to stop, my family looking over the wall to see what was happening. Each night we tried to cover it up again, pretend it wasn't so.

I would say how I had missed the Fourth of July party for two years and I refused to miss it this year. There were five new volunteers coming in for the fisheries program and I was supposed to be a trainer. I had to give them a little of my love for the program. I had to meet the person who would work at the station, tell them Demba had a hard time making threes and sevens, and that Abdoulaye wanted to learn everything, had started on his letters, but also wanted to know mathematics, how the scale worked, how to stock a pond. I needed to know them, so part of me could stay in Senegal, and then I could send things to them to give to my family and maybe they would be able to translate my letters.

Each day the fever came back. It did not get better; it became worse.

The afternoon of the second day, Diop drove his moped into my compound. He supposedly worked with us at the station and I detested him. He was a dandy who wore fancy clothes and could not pull a fish net. He once suggested I cook lunches for the men at the station.

He walked inside the doors of my house to talk to me, saying that Dabo was very sick. I must drive him to the hospital in Ndioum. I said I was also very sick. He said Dabo was spitting up blood and I told him to ask someone at S.A.E.D. to help him. I was too sick to drive, I said, and he looked at me as though he thought I was lying. He turned and walked away. The kitchen felt very empty after he left, as though he had taken more away than just himself.

I would not be able to stay. The fevers had won. I had to see the river one last time. Cindi helped me walk there.

I loved the river. It had such power. It had always been able to wash away the bad things. The water was blue in a brown world, blue and alive, never ending. I had liked swimming across it, and sometimes I would swim to the point of land on the opposite bank to sit in my wet *pagne* with the sun warming my back and my feet and legs resting in the cool water. Everyone seemed more alive at the river and I would come to wash my dishes, to laugh with the children and joke with the women as they washed themselves or their laundry, telling me I was truly a Pulaar now because I carried my dishes on my head. Maybe I loved the river most just at dusk, when no one else sat at the water's edge but me, the colors becoming quiet while the birds swooped down to drink, and the fishermen set their nets.

I sat in the water, just at the bank. The river hurt, the cool water making me shake. I could not bear the feel of the river against my skin. It was the last time I would feel the water of the Senegal river; I knew that now.

That night Cindi and I talked of how she would drive me to St. Louis in the morning, stopping at Podor first to make sure Dabo was all right.

The next day I went to the Diengs' compound. It seemed as though they became very quiet when I walked inside. Mbinté and Fatiim were preparing *haako*. I sat down next to Mbinté, and Racine climbed into my lap. He called me Ha Ha, because he was only two and couldn't pronounce Mariyata.

He had such spirit, and I thought he would grow into a man like Samba. Christmas Day, the year before, I had been bored and stood on a cinder block in my compound singing the theme from Hawai Five-O and pretending to surf. Aisata had caught me in the act, when she brought me my water, and asked what in the world I was doing. That night Aisata and Mariam started humming the Hawai Five-O song and I held onto Racine's chubby hands and we pretended to surf together. He loved it.

I held him now. I wanted to hold him tightly, but it was too hot, he would be uncomfortable. I said to the open compound that I was very sick. The white doctor had told me if I became sick again I must go back to America. I would not come back to Walli Jalla.

I spoke the words slowly. Sometimes I had to stop, and there would be a silence with no one making a sound, and then I would continue. Huley, Mbinté's daughter, sat next to me and she started to pull at my shirt, teasing me to hold her as well. Someone yelled at her, told her to leave me alone, and she began to cry. I said it was all right and picked her up to sit next to Racine.

She turned to look at my face.

"*O woyi*," she said. "Mariyata cries," and pointed to my tears, laughing. It was very strange. Grown-ups didn't cry unless someone died, and then they did not cry like this— silently with tears escaping sunglasses to roll down their cheeks.

I wiped my face. I had tried hard not to cry in front of these people, who reserved their tears for death, but Racine and Huley had sat in my lap so many times before and now I would miss the day Racine made his first sentence and Huley learned to pound the millet. I tried to say it was an American custom to cry when you said good-bye, but I had to stop. Mbinté filled the silence, saying it was a Pulaar custom as well, to cry if you had to leave people who you loved very much.

I had to get out of the Diengs' compound. I would break into a million pieces if I stayed any longer. It was haunted with my memories. I had sat there Thanksgiving day, worrying that my kettle of stew would fall from the wall before I could give it to my family. On Christmas Day we had sat out under the awning in front of Samba's and Maimoun's house, while everyone brought out their stockings, digging for peanuts down in the toes, asking me questions about their gifts, and Fatiim made the popcorn I had given her over her cooking fire.

I stood to return to my compound and Samba asked how long it would be before Cindi and I left. I said we would go as soon as we had packed the truck. I walked back to my house. Something inside me was being lost forever. How would I live, when so much of me would stay behind in Walli Jalla?

A land that had died—that was how I had described Walli Jalla, and now leaving it, I felt the same desolation I had once seen, down inside myself.

When the truck was packed, the Diengs filed into my compound one by one to come stand under the neem tree, to say good-bye. Samba wore an old white *boubou*, the edge of which he kept pulling to his face, and everyone seemed so solemn, their eyes very big. Fatiim handed me a woven trivet and Mbinté gave me an enameled bowl with a lid, a design of roses painted around its edge. I said good-bye to each of them, trying to tell them how much I loved them. I hugged Mbinté and Fatiim and they tried not to pull away from me. Mbinté had wanted to learn how to knit and to have her white friend there when she had her baby. Fatiim one night had seen how tired I was, how I watched with envy as Mariam rested her head in her mother's lap. She had looked at my weariness and told me to lay my head in her lap as well, that she would be my mother, and I lay my head down while she stroked my hair.

The children were easier. They let me hug them, and

didn't understand this was good-bye. I wanted to hug the men. Tiijon went stiff at my attempt. I could feel I had done something wrong so didn't hug Oumar or Samba. I said good-bye to Samba last. I might never again see this man, who had become my father, and I could not hug him good-bye. He had taken such good care of me, always been there, always worried over me. I couldn't imagine a lifetime without Samba's voice calling, "Mariyata, Mariyata," each day, to greet me, or to tell me to rest, or to give me a bowl of food.

I didn't pretend not to cry. The tears streamed down my face and I was so sorry there was no Pulaar custom for me to tell Samba how much I loved him.

"Samba," I said, "you are my father, truly, and I will miss you very much."

Samba looked old and a little scared as he pulled the edge of his *boubou* to his face nodding his head. I turned to look at my family, as though I could burn them into my eyes to hold them there with me, for however long it took before I could come back and see them again. Mbinté was crying.

She had sung a song for me once, one night when I was sitting in their compound and I had missed my parents very much. I had asked her if there was a Pulaar word for love, and she had sat straight-backed with little Mariyata in her lap and Maimoun and Huley at her sides and begun to sing with a sweet, lonely voice, "*Gile ene moussi, gile ene moussi, gile ene moussi, ko ngummi kodit* Allah." Love, it hurts. It comes from God. Her voice was small, and very beautiful against the huge desert night.

There was a second verse. Aisata and Fatiim had been sitting on the mat with us, and they sang the second verse with Mbinté, "If you leave I will cry, if you leave I will cry, if you leave I will cry, but when you return I will be happy." Mbinté and Fatiim were on either side of me, and they sang the Pulaar words with my name, Mariyata, if you leave we will cry, but when you return we will be happy. They sang; the words hanging in the air after the song had ended, as Mbinté and Fatiim each lay their heads on my shoulders.

I watched Mbinté's tears. If you leave, Mariyata, I will cry, she had sung. Her song had been so fragile, offered up to all that blackness, unafraid. Cindi and I climbed into the truck.

Mbinté's song would haunt me. We drove away from Walli
Jalla. I had driven away a million times, only this time I was
not driving, and I would not come back.

Gile ene moussi, ko ngummi kodit Allah. The words still haunt
me, and I wonder, "Mariyata, when will you return?"